INDEPENDENT
MONTHLY
LITERARY
MAGAZINE

Adelaide

REVISTA
LITERÁRIA
INDEPENDENTE
MENSAL

ADELAIDE

Independent Monthly Literary Magazine
Revista Literária Independente Mensal
Year IV, Number 19, December 2018
Ano IV, Número 19, dezembro de 2018

ISBN-13: 978-1-949180-67-1
ISBN-10: 1-949180-67-0

Adelaide Literary Magazine is an independent international monthly publication, based in New York and Lisbon. Founded by Stevan V. Nikolic and Adelaide Franco Nikolic in 2015, the magazine's aim is to publish quality poetry, fiction, nonfiction, artwork, and photography, as well as interviews, articles, and book reviews, written in English and Portuguese. We seek to publish outstanding literary fiction, nonfiction, and poetry, and to promote the writers we publish, helping both new, emerging, and established authors reach a wider literary audience.

A Revista Literária Adelaide é uma publicação mensal internacional e independente, localizada em Nova Iorque e Lisboa. Fundada por Stevan V. Nikolic e Adelaide Franco Nikolic em 2015, o objectivo da revista é publicar poesia, ficção, não-ficção, arte e fotografia de qualidade assim como entrevistas, artigos e críticas literárias, escritas em inglês e português. Pretendemos publicar ficção, não-ficção e poesia excepcionais assim como promover os escritores que publicamos, ajudando os autores novos e emergentes a atingir uma audiência literária mais vasta.

(http://adelaidemagazine.org)

Published by: Adelaide Books LLC, New York
244 Fifth Avenue, Suite D27
New York NY, 10001
e-mail: info@adelaidebooks.org
phone: (917) 477 8984
http://adelaidebooks.org

FOUNDERS / FUNDADORES
Stevan V. Nikolic & Adelaide Franco Nikolic

EDITOR IN CHIEF / EDITOR-CHEFE
Stevan V. Nikolic
editor@adelaidemagazine.org

MANAGING DIRECTOR / DIRECTORA EXECUTIVA
Adelaide Franco Nikolic

GRAPHIC & WEB DESIGN
Adelaide Books LLC, New York

CONTRIBUTING AUTHORS IN THIS ISSUE

Jessica Simpkiss, Diego Lorenzo Leyva, Bari Hein, June Kino-Cullen, Barbara Bottner, Alexis David, Helen Goode, Deirdre Barragry, Katrina Johnston, Mimi Karabulut, Andrew Mitin, Halle Carter, Thomas Genevieve, Mark Kaye, James Christon, Mariana Sabino, Brian Stumbaugh, Mike Walker, Joe De Quattro, Larry Hamilton, Neal Storrs, Whitney Judd, Janet Barrow, Joram Piatigorsky, Michele Sprague, Claudia Geagan, Myla Grier Aidou, Gabrielle Rivard, Michael Milburn, Dimitra Tsourou, Brianne Bannon, Derek Nast, Joseph Fleckenstein, Pete Warzel, Leslie Bohem, James Deahl, Norma Linder, Dr. Raymond Fenech, Tomas Sanchez Hidalgo, Nate Tulay, Hannah Paige, Margarita Serafimova, A.R. Francis, Roger Singer, Dr. Nathanael O'Reilly, Laura Solomon, Dayna Lellis, Heide Arbitter, Ayanna Lopez, Linda Barrett, Martina Reisz Newberry, Caitlin Muse, Dominique Williams, Gail Willems, Philip Wexler, Keith Hoerner, Cynthia Pitman, Dorsía J. Smith

CONTENTS / CONTEÚDOS

POETRY

Cover image and illustrations:
Serra da Estrela by A. F. Nikolic

EDITOR'S NOTES

Stevan V. Nikolic

THE FOURTH YEAR

This, the nineteenth issue of the Adelaide Literary Magazine marks a very important anniversary in the magazine's history. We are now in the fourth year of our existence. In the past three years, in nineteen issues, we published over one thousand submissions by the same number of authors. On average, it was sixty submissions per issue. Of course, this made all our issues pretty large, with around three hundred pages each in it's printed edition, and in many ways, each of our issues was more of an anthology of literary works than a literary magazine.

Some people value the literary magazine by the number of submissions published in each issue. A smaller number would signal the highest editorial criteria and better magazine rating. However, over past three years, we received nothing but praises for the works published and we are really proud of it.

Our mission of "promoting the writers we publish, helping both new, emerging, and established authors reach a wider literary audience" is more important to us than sticking to some artificial numbers of published works, just in order to have the appearance of strict editorial standards. In all truth, our publishing standards are pretty high, but the number of quality submissions is even higher. Most of the submissions published in this issue were submitted at least six months ago, and the waiting period to get a reply is between three to six months.

Besides publishing nineteen issues of the literary magazine, we managed to organize three literary competitions, each in three categories, and publish seven volumes of Anthologies of the winning works. And on the top of all that, we published over sixty books of novels, short stories, poetry, memoirs, and essays by our contributing authors.

At the end of January 2019, we will launch the first issue of yet another publication by Adelaide Books – Adelaide Book Review. Adelaide Book Review will be completely dedicated to reviews of the new titles published by independent US publishers, interviews with the authors, articles on writing and publishing, and news from the publishing industry.

I hope that our work will contribute to the general advancement of the independent publishing in the USA and to the promotion of both new and established authors, we thank all our contributing authors and readers for their support and wish to all a Joyful Holiday Season and a Happy New Year.

NO BOYS ALLOWED
by Jessica Simpkiss

Clint was fifteen when an accident killed our father. I can still remember the look on my mother's face as she tried to tell us that he wouldn't be coming home for dinner. The fried chicken and mashed potatoes she'd already made sat on the table for nearly two days before she let us clear it to the trash. It had been my father's favorite. She never made it after that, even though it had been my favorite too.

I tried to remember back to the summers before, when we'd still been kids, but it felt like it hadn't been real. It was something I dreamt. When I was alone at night, lying in bed staring at the peeling paint on the ceiling, I would find snippets of our childhood memories in the rapid eye movements I made trying to fight sleep. I could vaguely remember the way the rope felt in my hands, just before I'd let go and fall into the dark water below. There was a split-second to make the decision to let it go and you knew if you didn't the bank would erupt in laughter and taunting screams. When the angle was just right, I'd let go but the fibers of the rope would leave a lingering sensation on my skin, as if to say it wasn't too late to grab hold again. No one ever grabbed hold again.

The first time, it didn't even feel like water. It was more like falling through glass. The water would sting against my feet, slicing through skin, leaving a bloody mess to deal with on the mile and a half pedal home. But we would always come back, hungry for the feeling of freedom that only falling from forty feet above the earth could give young boys. It was the only time we'd ever tasted it.

I'd always wake up in the morning, wondering if the things I dreamed had really happened or if they were just wishful thinking. I'd ask Clint, sometimes, about my dreams and he would laugh as a thick film of nostalgia appeared at the bottom of his eyes. I'd lose him for a minute, sometimes a few. I knew better than to say anything in those moments, ruining for him what must have felt like even more distant memories. It didn't really matter, if they were real or imagined. There was no getting them back either way.

The summer had become a death sentence. Each day took with it a little more of his innocence, a little more of the childhood we thought was promised. When we should have been ghosts in our mother's eyes, at least while the sun was out, we had become homebodies, zombies, lurking around the house, tiptoeing around the elephant in the room. We were naive to assume that things always worked out. Things rarely ever went according to plan. Just ask my father.

Sonny, he whispered from above me one morning. I have something to show you.

I opened one eye and when there wasn't any light sneaking in under the plaid curtain dressing the window I groaned assuming he'd woken me up far earlier than any twelve-year-old boy had ever woken up on a Saturday, even if our Saturday's were numbered. But I'd had it all wrong.

We sped past the turn for the lake and kept going straight. Layers of heat still clung in the air above the pavement and we sliced through it like a knife in summer butter. Even in the dead of night, the heat was unforgiving. There was rarely a breeze enough to make any difference. The downhills were the only time we felt any kind of relief, both from the heat and the strain of pedaling halfway across Worth county.

At the end of the 409, we stopped at the faint remains of an old dirt road. The weeds and underbrush had almost claimed it as its own, but not completely. I could see a thin lane of tire marks worked into the remaining dirt and footprints that had trampled some of the grass. Clint told me to follow him with a hushed voice but said nothing else.

We ditched our bikes behind a sweet-smelling bush at the side of the road, and in the light of day I might have recognized it to be blackberry, but I couldn't be sure in the darkness. I couldn't be sure of anything. We dove further into the wood line and as we did, the only light we'd had to guide us trickled through the heavy treetops and was almost nothing by the time it reached us on the ground. I followed closely behind the sound Clint made in front of me, entirely sure I'd never make it out if I lost him.

Clint, I whispered hoarsely, where the hell are we going?

Shhh, he hissed back, you'll thank me once we get there.

We moved like moss through the woods. Our steps over broken branches echoed through the silence. Small night time creatures scurried about, unseen but not unheard. Crickets sang to one another, letting those of them ahead of us know something was coming.

We came to a clearing and Clint stopped as if he wasn't sure which way we were going.

Do you hear that? Clint asked, turning his face upward toward the night sky, it's this way. He turned to the south and continued into the darkness. There was a faint hum drifting through the trees, and we followed it like bloodhounds until we came to a hindrance in our path.

When the trees shifted, bits of moonlight filtered down, enough to see the metal cattle gate and the signs that hung brashly on its face. I didn't need the light to know what they said. They were the same on every gate you came to. *Stay out, private property, no trespassing.*

Clint sat, straddled on the top metal rung of the gate, looking back at me with a Cheshire smile I could barely see. A gentle wind blew through the trees, rustling the leaves and waking a hoot owl in the distance. The gray moon dribbled down through the branches and glinted off his white tee-shirt and the metallic finish of the gate, making it look like he was almost swimming in its light and I finally knew where he was taking me.

I jumped the gate like a thoroughbred instead of the common field horse I knew I was. The hum I'd heard before morphed into radio music and laughter the further from the gate we moved. I looked back in the direction we'd come and the moon was still shining down on the gate. Somehow, the empty backing of the signs that had tried their best to forbid us from moving past them felt more threatening than when I'd been able to read their warnings. The empty white space gleamed out at me in the hazy light. They were the only thing I could see clearly.

Listen, Clint whispered, you're too young to be here, but …

He didn't need to finish his sentence. I knew what he was doing and why.

I'd heard rumors about it. We all had. He'd make me swear not to tell any of my friends that he'd brought me there, or else they'd all be begging their older brothers to bring them too and it would ruin the everything.

The structure itself was dilapidated, leaning in more than one place. The tin roof was rusted in places and missing in others with falling down walls, none of which were matches for containing the sound coming from inside.

A boy older than Clint stumbled through what they used for a door as we stood outside while he told me the rules. I was only allowed one beer and if anyone asked I was fourteen and not twelve.

Inside, stringed Christmas lights replaced the wispy light from the moon and the stars we'd used to get there, but it was still dark enough that everyone was hidden in some level of shadow. An old radio in the corner blared the latest hits. Couples in the middle of the room danced too close to each other, their lips and tongues exploring their partners deeply. Other couples closer to the walls danced to music only they could hear as their bodies twisted and heaved in singular movements. Clint smacked me on the back of the head, telling me to stop staring with his eyes.

Here, he said, shoving a warm beer into my chest.

What am I supposed to do? I asked, feeling very much a kid out of place.

Clint smiled. Enjoy yourself, find a girl.

He winked and disappeared, becoming another face brushed with greens and reds and yellows as they danced wildly and without fear of parent's eyes or ears learning their secrets. Our parents had been here or somewhere just like it when they'd been their age. It was a rite of passage in Worth. Boys become men and girls becoming women overnight. They all knew where their kids because they'd been their once too.

I stood in the corner and sipped my sour beer trying to be inconspicuous, which wasn't hard to do. I became a fly on the wall inhaling the smoke from their cigarettes and listening to the music that would later define all their lives. I thought about the summers before our father had died, when we were still kids. Our biggest worry was the condition of our thrift store bikes and who was coming swimming. I watched the kids in front of me, desperate to become anyone other than the children they'd been or still were. They were stuck in the middle, too old for swimming all summer but not old enough to be adults in public. Except for Clint. Clint would be an adult in the morning when he showed up at the Feed and Seed for his first day of work. Even I wouldn't be a kid anymore by then, at least not the same kid I was the day prior. It felt like we'd grown up overnight, but we were just too foolish to notice that it had been happening all along.

By the time the sun woke up, the air reeked of stale cigarettes and sex. The music had quieted and the dancers moved slower, like sleepwalkers moving in the night. We leaned on the wall, savoring the idea of being us one last time before the ride home when we'd become different people. But at that moment, we were just us, without a father who'd died and a mother who'd never recovered. We were just boys in the woods learning to be men before we knew what that meant.

About the Author:

Jessica Simpkiss lives and works in Virginia Beach, Virginia with her husband and daughter. She studied Art History at George Mason University. Her work has most recently been published or is forthcoming in the Hartskill Review, Zimbell House Anthologies, The Write Launch, The West Trade Review, The Dead Mule for Southern Literature, The Bookends Review, amongst others. Her debut novel, The Spaewife's Secret, was published in November, 2018 by Solstice Publishing. She is currently working on her second novel tentatively entitled, Bone in the Blood.
Find more of her work by visiting
jessicamsimpkiss.com

THE DECAYING AND BLOOMING MIND

by Diego Lorenzo Leyva

Psychotic Break

Bring on the psychotic break! We're strong enough for it! We shall let this heavy burden ride our backs until we, proud horses, perish.

Welcome to the End

Goblins and demons move about you—welcome to the end. Reality becomes an illusion, a delusion, "What is real?" you question—welcome to the end. They are after you, surveying you, planning to take you, planning to kill you—welcome to the end. You died as ashes and awoke not as a phoenix but as a caged bird—welcome to the end. Heavily medicated but the world's still dark—welcome to the end. Welcome to your end, welcome to your imprisonment, welcome to your death. Ready or not your world shall now implode. Can you survive all this? Are you strong enough? Brave enough? Warlike enough?

You Shall Perish

You shall survive your insanity. You, on the other hand, shall perish. You are too weak, too effeminate, too unwarlike to survive all this. You shall cry for help and the help shall come, but in the end only you can pull yourself out of this terrible world. Oh my weak friend, you sacrifice, allow me to cry over you. What a sad life, what a tragedy.

New World

Like a phoenix I arose this dark morning. Last night my life changed forever. The war of my mind began. My world is now overcast. Lightning echoes repeatedly, the grim reaper can be heard if you listen attentively enough. I became ashes, but I naturally grew wings in the process. I am now stronger than ever and weaker than ever. A doomed phoenix flying toward the sun. When will he stop? Until he becomes ashes once again. But what happens to ashes? They are stored in golden urns and remembered, smiled upon, and cherished.

You Are Not a Tragedy

It is dusk and a young woman sits at the halfway point of a bridge with her head on her knees. Her mind is quickly deteriorating and turning on her causing confusion and fear. She feels terrible. Life is terrible. You sit by her in the same posture under the same mental conditions. You feel terrible. "Life could be terrible," you say, "but it isn't." "Now this?" the young woman says regarding her new unexpected plight. "Oh, why this?" "Wow, this?" you say in awe regarding your first plight. "Finally something!" You get up and leave the girl and the bridge feeling unique and necessary as only those about to go to war can feel. "My life is not tragic," you say, "my life is beautiful." You walk the rest of the bridge enjoying the fading sun that you know you will soon see again.

The Relief of Exhaustion

After you tell me your symptoms, after you share with me your world, I reply, "That sounds exhausting." You immediately disagree. "No it isn't," you say, "though it sounds like it is it's actually not that at all. All my life I wanted some adversity, some real adversity; I now have it. None of this is exhausting. It's actually a relief."

War, Bliss, and a Glow

My life is a constant battle with my mind, a constant struggle for control. Will it work for me today or will it cause my undoing? In the past I was hopeful that this war might have an end, but now I see that it won't. Perpetual war is my life, temporary bliss is my goal, an everlasting glow is my destiny.

Inferno

An inferno is our lives. Indeed, we have been burned many times. But after each burning we grow deeper, happier, more determined. We are the masters of the flames. We know how to live engulfed in them and not die.

Slavery

My mind is a defiant and resilient slave. It is on fire and perpetually whipped by a master that wants death—what else could this treatment lead to if left unanswered? But my mind answers, "Damn you! I shall do what I want,

think what I want, you are not my master," it roars, "I am free!" The master then dies like he's supposed to. As he dies he lovingly grants my mind freedom like he's supposed to.

The Ass

While your mind is collapsing you manage to ask yourself this: "Will I always be like this?" Does the ass ever ask itself if its terrible, terrible lot will ever have an end? But you're a horse. "I shall perish of this load," you first say, "but don't think I'm unhappy because of that," you then later add. "My words have become fatalistic," you then later say. "I feel stronger now than I have ever felt in my whole life," you then later say. "I am thankful for this load!" you then say. "I don't feel a load!" you then say. "I am no donkey. I'm a horse!" you then finish.

Every Cloud Has a Silver Lining

Psychiatric illnesses don't lead one to discover silver linings among the clouds but bright rays of gold. In addition, the clouds that emit these golden rays are of a golden hue and really aren't clouds at all but suns.

This is Good

"Know this now: this is never detrimental," said a peer to another. "Your plight might hurt, but in time you'll realize you were never in pain. This is painless and good. 'This is good!' you'll say to yourself while in a state that would've frightened you before. 'I'm glad this is happening!' you'll also say. You will mean all of these things wholeheartedly." The young peer walked away still doubting the mentor, but nonetheless saying to himself, "This is good. I'm glad this is happening." He was short of breath and scared, but he nonetheless put faith in himself once more and said, "This is good. This is good." He walked home feeling very frightened and not meaning the things that he said, but nonetheless continuing to say them.
Idiots Dancing in the Rain

A rain dancer wrote the following, "Life isn't about waiting for the storm to pass it's about learning to dance in the rain." Only idiots dance in the rain. Imagine actually seeing someone do this. Wouldn't they look silly? But some would smile and proceed to dance alongside him or her wouldn't they? I would walk by them, umbrella in hand, and say, "Why are you guys dancing? It's raining horribly." One of them would turn to me all the while still dancing and say, "When it's raining this much one should learn to love it. Be happy in it and smile while you're soaked!

You're drenched more than us. Join us!" "Actually," I'd respond, "I'm not drenched and it's actually not raining." "Yes, it is," he'd respond. "No, it's not," I'd say. "Yes it is," he'd respond and point up at the grey raining clouds. "What rain?" I'd say and look up at the sun and blue cloudless sky, "What rain?"

Smiling at Beautiful Things

Oh, how weak this illness is! How I love the intrusive thoughts that are attempting to darken a mind covered in sunlight! "More golden rays," I think to myself when the dark rays that don't know they're golden enter my mind. Because of these golden rays I proceed to smile even wider as I walk with a much beloved beautiful little niece through our beautiful little village that is protected by a bright and warm sun. She noticed my smile and asked me why I was smiling. "Because of you, because of this little town, because of that sun," I don't say. I smile when I'm around beautiful things. I proceed to smile even wider when the dark rays intrude and say, "How could you smile if I am here?" "You heard me think it," I respond. "Because of my niece, because of this walk we are having, because of this little town, because of that green valley and that sun and its warmth, and because of you. All these things that I have listed are beautiful and I smile at beautiful things."

Perpetual Din

How is one to live, let alone write, under a perpetual din? Undoubtedly you have come to view yourself as a bit of a sacrifice and so who cares that your ears are bleeding a little or a lot? And so with this philosophy you proceed amid the prolonged, loud, painful sounds which you can't control to create the sounds that you can control: your music.

The Flipping of a Switch

An apt expression to describe the sudden intensifying of paranoia, psychosis, and derangement, would be to call it the "flipping of a switch" like I heard a young man once put it. Hopefully what was switched on in this young mind were strong lights powered by powerful electricity. Hopefully torches were lit in this young mind as well. Flip all the switches! Bring in ugly florescent lighting and pretend it is sunlight. Let the inferno in his mind spread aimlessly before finally developing a beautiful pattern, a beautiful stride. Before his mind was absent of color and dim in light and now its colorfulness is a bit blinding, its light vast and warm just like the sun's.

Blinding Light Next to Dimness

As is inescapable for many of us, I ended up working at a residential treatment facility for people with mental illnesses. I remember an occasion when one of my co- workers said to me, "Isn't this a pleasant and cheerful place to work despite the darkness that walks through the doors?" She was right. This was a pleasant and cheerful place to work, but what walked through those doors was not darkness but blinding light. When they're gone and it's just my co-workers and I I'm engulfed in dimness. But then a scorching sun pierces through and is mistaken for a rainy cloud.

My colleagues attempt to brighten the dark grey cloud that they see while I squint my eyes at the blinding sun that I see. They continue to attempt to somehow stop the cloud from raining, but what they should do is figure out a way for the sun to use its fire and light to its advantage. So much can be done with the fire and light of these suns; however, not nearly as much can be done with dimness.

The Sun and its Light

You are a sun and what you give us is light. The sun blinds sure, but one feels great under the sun. One feels so great that one stares at it—at you. But the sun shouldn't be stared at for it hurts. I'm not going to stare at you for it hurts. But the light that you give me, for that I am grateful.

War Forces Specialness

This forces specialness. This forces triumph. All wars are special and all wars have a triumph. You and I and many others are the victors of war. Therefore we triumphed and therefore— as is immodest and uncomfortable to say but needs to be said—we are special. I feel like all wars are special.

From the Foreground to the Background

Seeds of ugly black trees were scattered in the front of your mind. These trees grew and they became nearly all you could think about. Bringing this forest from the foreground to the background became the goal. Over time these trees retreated to the background—and you joyfully missed them as you watched them leave your life! Come back beautiful green trees!

Phoenixes and Ashes

The details of my chaos, of my illness, of my rain and hail and fire, don't matter, I say to myself. Many people have these elements, but do little with it. Our brains are on fire, but few phoenixes rise from the ashes. Look at the phoenixes not the ashes!

Blooming All This Time

You were blooming all this time, I say to myself. Behold, here in my arms is all that you have sprouted, all of these words! Your mind was never in decay for rotting and dying soil sprouts nothing. Yes, you were blooming all this time, man who was afraid, man who thought he was insane and done for.

Beautiful Minds

Let's not embrace the "Beautiful Minds." Honestly when you act out, Mr. Mania, I look at you in amusement. I stare and laugh. I laugh at myself. None of that is you. That thought you wrote the other day while feeling calm, clear, and happy was you. Not your screams and rampages. The colorful false reality another man dwells in from time to time also isn't him. For that man his writings are him. That's his mind. This is my mind. Beautiful Minds: laugh at it all now that you're better, but only once you're better.

Smile at Yourself

Actually no, don't laugh at yourself once you're better! That feels like something a person who dances in the rain would say. "Someday, everything will make perfect sense. So for now, laugh at the confusion, smile through the tears, be strong and keep reminding yourself that everything happens for a reason." A person who dances in the rain wrote that! Don't laugh at yourself or cry at yourself, rather, smile at yourself always. Laugh at Mr. Mania, but smile at yourself as he also smiles at himself because he too loves being his own person. We are all smiling at ourselves. The writers, the artists, and whatever else people call themselves, are all smiling at themselves.

Smiling Because of My Luck

At times I am envious of those who have gone through more. At times I wish my plight had been as heavy as theirs. But then I listen to their war stories and lose much of that envy because they weren't joyful during their wars like I was. In retrospect they now have gratitude for their battles, but in the moment they lacked joy. Most of these soldiers marched into war depressed with feelings of supreme ill-fate; few marched into it smiling with feelings of great luck. Even though I was scared when I saw that dark figure I was also immediately happy that I got to experience the fright that I felt. I smiled because of my luck. I was joyful every time my heart sunk in fear, I smiled at every wound. I was smiling through it all. They never smiled and perhaps it would have been hard to smile when witnessing what they witnessed, but I think they would have smiled had they realized how lucky they were.

Veteran's New War

You are the veteran of a won war. Those who know you suspect you possess many invisible scars. But the war wasn't traumatic for you won it thoroughly. Zero casualties, zero mistakes, nothing but triumph and glory. But that war is gone and celebrating past glories has run its course. You hope for a new war—actually no you don't for you're already in a new one. Few of those in the middle of war wish for a new one to add on top of their current one. We all know the war you're in, the war of the veteran, the war of all veterans: life.

Statements That Save

"I am now stronger than ever," I remember saying to myself when I was the weakest I have ever been. During those days I also said to myself, "I am now weaker than ever," but I repeated the first statement much more often because I said it with hope. Statements like those saved me and I needed to be saved.

You Exist

This man and I wrote together. Though he was much older than me I was the one with more writing experience. His stories were graceful at times, even a bit beautiful at times, but what was always present was a strong will for only this trait he could consciously add to his works. Eventually this man submitted a story to a literary journal and was accepted. This brought great joy. "I now exist," he said when he learned that his work was accepted. The day that his story was published he was hospitalized for the eighth time in his long life. Once he regained coherency I visited him in the hospital and brought with me his published work. He didn't care to look at it. "This is no way to live," he said as he laid in his bed wearing a white hospital robe. "All this," I said and surveyed the room, "is unavoidable. But so is this," I said and pointed a finger at the page in the journal that bared his art. "I would tell you to be happy," I continued, "to be optimistic, but at least take solace in the fact that you now exist." "I exist," he said. "Damn right," I responded.

EVERYTHING TASTES LIKE TIN

by Bari Hein

Wherever Joe's youngest son goes, trouble follows.

His older two, Jacob and Luke, managed to grow up without breaking a single bone between them. Matthew, on the other hand, broke both legs, one arm, and his collarbone. Oh yes, and a toe. Not all at the same time.

Another example: The only phone call Joe and Shirley ever received from a school principal on Jake or Luke's account was to commend Luke's perfect attendance during his sophomore year. Matthew, on the other hand; well with Matthew, there'd been too many phone calls to count, and always over stupid things. Things that showed no common sense. Like refusing to dissect a pig in science class. Or telling a teacher her presentation of U.S. History was skewed, whatever that meant.

Since his arrival to New York a week and a half ago, Matthew has programmed two left-wing news stations onto his parents' television set to make them more easily accessible (as if they would ever want to access such reporting), clogged their shower drain with his long, unkempt hair, and purchased caffeinated tea instead of decaf and the wrong brand of toothpaste, despite having been issued a very specific shopping list. Joe will have to make a return trip to the market to exchange those

items; while he's at it, he'll pick up a bottle of heavy duty drain cleaner.

Most perplexing, on Tuesday, Matthew forgot to bring Shirley's blanket to her third round of chemo and left her alone for nearly two hours while searching the hospital for croissants and coffee, instead of offering his mother one of the perfectly palatable snacks from the little kitchen area of the infusion therapy unit. As if all that weren't enough, he got lost coming back and ended up on the wrong floor of the hospital. He returned to find poor Shirley hooked up to her drugs, shivering and quivering and on the verge of tears.

How, for the love of God, does that constitute taking good care of one's mother?

Well, it's almost over now, this so-called "help." Today's the last day, and tomorrow cannot come soon enough. When Joseph walks into his kitchen on Saturday morning, he decides that for his wife's sake he will keep the peace through this last day and a half. For reasons that make no sense whatsoever, Matthew has always been Shirley's favorite, although she will never admit it. When Matt joins his father about five minutes later, Joe does not greet him with the usual, "What's the matter? Forgot to pack your razor?" Instead, he says, "Good morning. How'd you sleep?"

Matthew looks around the room, and then slowly and cautiously says, "Good, Dad. How 'bout you?"

"I slept well. Your mother's still in bed."

"She's usually the early bird."

"Yes, well, you know in the movies, how the cancer patient gets sick right away from chemotherapy? In real life, the side effects don't come on for about three or four days. Same thing happens every Saturday."

"Hopefully, it'll all be worth it."

There's Shirley's optimism again, spilling from her youngest son's lips like goddam honey. These drugs are going to kill the cancer cells and she's going to beat this thing. Blah, blah, blah. Joe wishes he could believe that. He feels like he's torturing his wife, making her go through these treatments so that she can die a few months later than she will without chemotherapy.

"Can I make you some coffee, Dad?"

Joe looks up, realizing he has accomplished nothing since coming into the kitchen. "Sure."

"Still take it black?"
"You'd better believe it."

Joe remains seated and listens to the trickle of water, the thud of cabinet doors and rustle of coffee grounds being scooped into a filter. A faint fragrance of coffee starts to revive him.

He straightens in his chair. "Hey, I didn't ask you. How's that girlfriend of yours managing in your absence?"

"Tara?"

"Yes, Tara." He hasn't forgotten her name, for God's sake. He just sees no point in saying it. "How's she getting on?"

Matthew keeps his back turned to his father. "We broke up a couple of months ago."

"I'm sorry, son. That's a tough break." Joe's sentiment is sincere; Matthew and Tara lived together for years.

For several seconds, the only sound in the kitchen is the fizz and hiss of the coffeemaker. Matthew tinkers with mugs, scoops some sugar into one of them and brings them over to the table. "It's better, knowing what a cheating bitch she is, instead of not knowing."

Joe considers his options for response. He doesn't want to invite any more details into the conversation than are necessary. No sir. At this point, the fact that Tara cheated on his son is already more than he cares to know. "Well, at least there're no kids. No divorce proceedings to go through, or anything."

He has obviously picked the wrong thing to say. He can tell by the disgusted look on Matthew's face. He's messed up this whole father-son bonding crap already.

"Who's getting divorced?"

Joseph and Matthew turn their heads in disturbingly similar fashion. "Shirley. How are you, sweetheart?"
"My head is killing me. Who's getting divorced?"
Matthew says, "Nobody," while Joseph says, "Matthew and Tara broke up."

"Oh, no! What happened?"

Matt kisses his mother's cheek and offers her his chair. "Is there anything I can get you to make your head feel better?"
"I'm taking enough drugs already, honey. When did you and Tara break up?"

"In July, when I found her in bed with another guy."

God almighty, why does he have to keep bringing that detail into it?

"Why didn't you tell us?" Shirley says. "I don't know. Because it was painful? Because I wasn't ready to talk about it right away? With everything you have going on, I saw no point in bothering you with my problems."

"Oh, honey. You're never a bother to us."

Joe clears his throat. What about the time

Matthew wrecked the Volvo when there were still eleven payments due on it? Or the time he nearly set the kitchen on fire with his science fair project?

Matthew passes his mother a cup of tea, brewed from one of the last decaf teabags in the cabinet. See? Why did he bother going on this quest for coffee Tuesday, when he knows perfectly well that she's a tea drinker? After thanking him, she says, "I'm probably going to be sleeping on and off all day. I think the two of you should go have a nice lunch together. Joe, take Matthew to the top of the Empire State Building or something. Do a little sightseeing on his last day here."

"We can't just leave you alone, Shirl."

"Of course you can. Having cancer hasn't turned me into a baby."

"Can we bring you back something to eat, at least?" Matthew asks.

Shirley shakes her head. "Don't bother. Since I started chemo, everything tastes like tin."

Joe studies her narrow face, her jutting collar-bone. He wishes he could convince her to join them for a meal. She needs to put back on some of the weight she's lost. And she needs to provide a buffer for two men who will surely butt heads if they're left alone. But there's no arguing with this woman. No sir, not once she's made up her mind. After breakfast, she practically pushes her husband and son out the door and onto the elevator.

In the lobby, Matthew greets a couple of Joe's neighbors. A woman from the fourth floor, or maybe the fifth, asks Matt about his plans to return home, while the gay guy from the second floor asks Joe how his wife is feeling. God almighty, how much of his personal business has his son shared with the neighbors? When they reach the sidewalk, Matthew says, "You know, Stan told me you can come talk to him any time."

"Stan? I thought his name was Sam. Why on earth would I want to talk to him?"

"He just lost his partner to cancer, a couple of weeks ago. You didn't know?"

"I was wondering where his boyfriend went." He'd assumed they'd broken up.

They reach the subway station and board a train. Joseph sits down; Matthew leans against a pole. "He's a great guy, Dad."

"My neighbor? Well, good for him."

"What does that mean? 'Good for him.'"

"I don't need Sam or Stan or whatever his name is telling me he knows what it's like to have the love of my life dying of cancer."

Matthew swivels himself around the pole so that he's facing away. It almost makes Joseph want to hug him, believe it or not. He was such a precocious little boy. Whenever he didn't like what was being said to him, he would turn his chair so his back was to his parents. "I just don't understand you, Dad."

"That makes two of us. Tell you what. Why don't we get off at separate stops, and we'll tell your mother we had a nice day together."

"Fine."

"Fine."

No doubt the kid is going to get lost in New York City on his own. He has a knack for that.

Shirley is still very much alive, but recently Joe has started imagining her as a spirit, watching over him, approving or disapproving his every move. She would not be happy with the way things are going right now. No sir. Not at all.

The train rattles on for a while, people continue their conversations, board and disembark, do not seem to notice two men intentionally turned away from one another. After the doors slide shut for the third time, Matthew asks, "Where should we tell her we ate?" He has lowered his shoulders some.

"Katz's. That's where I'm going, so we'll say we went there together."

"That's not fair, Dad. You live here. You can go to Katz's whenever you want."

"Do you know how long it's been since I had a decent pastrami sandwich?" Matt stares out the window without acknowledging he's heard. Does he really think it's that easy for Joe to go out whenever he wants? He has no clue, *no clue*, of what his father is going through. "Fine, I'll tell you what. You go there too, but we'll eat at separate tables."

"You're kidding, right?"
"I think it's a perfect solution."

"Separate tables? On a Saturday? We'll be lucky to get one." There's a brief exchange of reluctant smiles, and then Matthew sticks his hands into his jacket pockets and gets off the train with his father.

The sidewalks are bustling on this sunny Saturday, but Joe feels as if he's walking alone, inside a shadow. Lately, sounds have been muffled, smells have been muted, and that goddam shadow follows him everywhere.

Walking a pace behind his father, Matthew drops the big bomb of a question, the one that Joseph had hoped would go unasked. "What do her doctors really say?"

Joe stupidly thinks that if he walks faster, his son will fall behind. But Matt is right there, relentless, on the periphery of the shadow. "What more do you need to know? She has cancer. She had a mastectomy. She's getting twelve rounds of chemo."

"On the train, you said you don't need Stan telling you what it's like to have the love of your life dying of cancer. Why did you say that? Is Mom dying?"

Matthew has stopped walking. Joseph had hoped to send him home without the whole story. It must be the look on his youngest son's face, or maybe it's a sudden realization of the goddam *unfairness* of everything that the poor woman has been through in the last several weeks that causes Joe to blubber out his answer. "It's in her lymph nodes, Matt. And her lungs. And her bones."

"Jesus, Dad."

They're standing beside a plate glass window, in whose reflection Joe sees his brows turned inward at the same angle as Matt's.

"Mom knows the prognosis, right?"

"Of course."

"She wants to fight. She says she's going to beat this."

"The oncologist gives her six months to a year. That's if she goes through all twelve rounds of chemotherapy. If she doesn't fight, she gets three to six months."

"Jesus, Dad," Matthew says, more quietly this time. His eyelids are red, and again Joe sees him as his little boy, crying over one thing or another he deemed to be a gross injustice. At eight years old, Matt burst into tears over a magazine photograph of a girl who'd lost her legs to a landmine. "Why didn't you tell me?"

"I guess for the same reason you didn't tell me about Tara. It's painful. It's hard to talk about." They have begun to walk again, although Joseph cannot recall taking the first step.

"Do Jake and Luke know?"

"Of course not." He hadn't planned to tell any of his sons. He's beginning to wish the secret hadn't slipped out. Matthew is asking too many questions. "I don't want you to tell them, either."

"Dad." Matt has stopped walking; they're at the restaurant; it's as if the place has plunked itself right down in front of them.

"We should see if they have a table," Joe says, although it's obvious that Katz's is not as crowded as usual. He motions to the hostess, hoping his son will just shut up already and pretend the exchange never happened. She brings them to a table in the corner. Joe places his palm on his unopened menu. "I already know what I'm getting," he says, smiling at the waitress. "Matt?"

His son is staring at the framed photographs beside him with his fist over his mouth and his red eyes glistening.

Joe looks up. "Maybe we need a minute," he says.

The waitress is being very kind, very understanding. She deserves a big tip. Joe struggles for a way to distract his son. "The corned beef here is good too."

Matthew lowers his fist and a strand of saliva follows and snaps. He blows his nose onto a napkin, which he then shoves into his jacket pocket. The kid is a mess. "I know. I've been here before."

"When?"

"Bunch of times. With Mom." Matthew studies his father's face for a moment. Would it have killed the kid to shave this morning? "Before you retired."

Sarcasm escapes without warning. "My life has been just dandy since I retired, let me tell you."

"I'm sorry, Dad."

Joe shrugs. Why should Matthew be sorry that his father's life has gone to hell in the past few months?

"You know, Mom is the glue that holds this family together," Matthew says.

"Yes sir. That she is, son."

"So what're we going to do if the doctors are right? What's going to happen to us if she dies?"

Joe shakes his head. "I don't know."

Glasses of water are set down in front of them, and the waitress scurries off again.

"Dad, I know you don't want to talk to your neighbors about any of this. But you can call me any time. You know? I stay up pretty late."

Joe can't help grinning. "I know you do."

"You can call me for anything. Even if you're just lonely. I've been finding out what that's like, lately."

"Thanks, son." He looks at Matt for a second, gives him half a smile. It's the least the kid de-

serves. Then he looks up at the wall beside their table and points to one of the photographs hanging close to his shoulder, of the restaurant's owner shaking hands with a Republican senator. "Now this here is one of the best senators we've ever had."

Matthew sits up straight. "You're kidding me, right? That clown?" Then he stops and smiles. "Nice try, Dad."

"It was worth a shot."

Matt opens his menu. "Mom loves the roast beef sandwich here. She goes on and on about how good it is; then she barely makes a dent in it. I might get that and bring back half for her."

Joe opens his mouth to remind Matthew that his mother had turned down his offer of food. But he stops, picturing his wife sitting where he is, across from her favorite son, eating her favorite dish at her favorite restaurant. She must've been in heaven. She's never actually come out and said that her youngest is her favorite, but it's obvious. The way she brightens every time he calls. The way she lit up, a few weeks ago, when he offered to come help out, and then danced around the house, anticipating his arrival. The way she chastises her husband whenever he gives the boy a hard time.

Yes sir. Matthew is Shirley's favorite. That's starting to make a lot of sense to Joe.

END

A GAME OF SOLITAIRE
by June Kino-Cullen

Days go by without winning. I tell myself it's okay. It's the process that counts. Keeps my old brain sharp. The more I play, the quicker I move that red five on top of the black six, the black queen on top of the red king. Then my mind starts to wander, imagines the Ace of Clubs is burdened with a club foot, but because he was born into that pedigree of aces, he gets to move to the top of the hill and governs with a just hand. He's so good and saintly, he becomes the pope who rules over his nephew, the King of Diamonds. King of Diamonds expands his territory through an incestuous marriage to an elite cousin, Queen of Diamonds. Their consummation results in a son, Jack of Spades. Relieved that the interbreeding didn't result in any abnormalities, they name him after their favorite game: Black Jack.

On his twenty-first birthday, Black Jack gets lucky and finds a girlfriend, a ten with a heart, brains and red hair. They get engaged. But then one day, Black Jack's nemesis, Diamond Jack, from a neighboring fiefdom, shows up, spots Black Jack's girl with her luscious cherry-red lips. Miss Ten-of-Hearts notices handsome Diamond Jack winking at her. Her heart quickens. But, alas, she has already agreed to marry Black Jack. Their engagement is known throughout the land. And rules are rules. She can't just stroll over to Diamond Jack and whisper, "Damn the rules. Let's run away together." Unless of course, one cheats. But what's the point of cheating at solitaire? But then again, already steeped in a world of make believe, what's the harm of playing around? I let Miss Ten-of-Hearts sneak away in the middle of the night. She lies on top of Diamond Jack. The next morning Black Jack finds them together. Furious, he kills the competition.

Black Jack takes back Miss Ten-of-Hearts, but she's pining for sexy Diamond Jack and starts to lose the color in her cheeks. She starts to turn pink, which isn't so bad, but when she turns white, Black Jack questions her place. Not only has she cheated on him, now there's that inter-color thing. But he can't help it, he still loves her. He beseeches the goddess of cards, Lady Luck. Happy to be summoned by the gallant Jack, Lady Luck sidles up to him in the shape of a cumulus cloud and strokes his cheek, but when Black Jack asks for help about the still gorgeous Miss Ten, she gets jealous, turns cirrus and poof, she's gone. So much for luck. Black Jack stares at the pale woman next to him with her disheveled red hair, which is starting to show strands of platinum blonde. He sighs. *She used to look so good in that red dress with the slit on the side.*

Now what? Should Miss Ten be punished? Should she die? She did betray Black Jack. Then again, shouldn't women have the right to change partners just like female chimpanzees who copulate indiscriminately? Again, I stray, although tangents are loopy and fun. Back to my story. Should I stick with fairy tale plots where disloyalty is punishable by death? But so many of my stories have sad endings. I decide that Jack lets her live. He lies down with her, or is it lay down since he's a card? Anyway, he gets laid.

Several weeks later, Miss Ten announces she's pregnant. "Who's the father?" asks Black Jack. Miss Ten smiles and gives him a deep kiss. Black Jack rubs his stubble and thinks, *There's a chance it might be mine*. He decides to let her live. He kisses the top of Miss Ten's curls which by now has turned from platinum blonde to snow white. But that's another story.

A beautiful, chubby son is born, a maroon ace of clubs. Maroon? Jack scratches his head, but is relieved the baby doesn't have a club foot like his uncle, the pope. Miss Ten coos and kisses the baby; hands him over to Black Jack. "Oh, Jack, he has your eyes." He's elated until he spots a birthmark in the shape of a diamond behind the baby's right ear. Drat, this is taking a tragic path.

I've never written a romance before, and according to the Romance Writers of America and Britain, romance must have happy endings; rules are rules. Then I tell myself that in the days of old, magic prevailed where anything was possible. I make myself the court jester with a three-pointed fool's hat. Bells ringing, I prance around the deck trying to come up with a good ending. The court grows restless; dusk is upon us. Out of breath and ideas, I bow and announce that I'm done with this fractured fable and make a fast exit. As I'm running, I remind myself that, like a game of solitaire, if I keep playing long enough, I'll win someday and get one good story before my life folds.

HORSE COUNTRY

by Barbara Bottner

I've only agreed to accompany my husband Dan to have Sunday brunch with a Paul somebody because I'm terrified when I imagine him talking to a horse breeder un-chaperoned.

When unnerved, some people buy expensive chocolate. Dan buys a nine hundred pound mammal.

It's the kind of overcast day in the San Fernando Valley that screams for the New York Times, Mozart and high end yoga pants. One thing Dan and I've always been good at is Sundays. It's as if our heart rates and pulses finally synchronize.

But, there may be another heart rate joining us soon.

I'm not sure how I feel about this.

My period is three weeks late.

This is the morning I'd planned to tell him what color the 99% guaranteed blue and white pregnancy kit turned, but he got this call from some breeder who's only briefly in town. So, while he gets dressed, I make the bed, tossing my childish collection of stuffed animals in among my pillows. I don't really mind postponing the big news. Well, continuing to postpone.

I've kept him in the dark. It's where he lives, anyway. I decided I needed to process my own issues about parenting before I say a word out loud.

On the plus side is that I'm heading to the far reaches of my thirties. Which is how I tend to think of being forty-one.

Forty-two, okay.

I turned forty-three last week.

I've never been sure I could be someone's mother. I'm a writer and significantly self absorbed. But lately, I've found myself stalking infants in the supermarket. The babies like my goofy efforts but the mothers look slightly disturbed. And I worry that my intense babbling to someone else's child is getting to be over the top.

So, that's a clue.

As far as Dan is concerned, his horses *are* his kids. Were. At least this past year I've managed to persuade him to sell off ten of his eleven trotters. His stable had become all consuming, not to mention expensive. I accomplished this by begging, manipulating, threatening and weeping. Ultimately what worked was wearing high heel red suede shoes and gallivanting around the bedroom half-naked.

Ironically, it's probably because of the strenuous activities following one of those performances, that my life might be in for a massive change.

We're almost at Ventura Boulevard. Dan's flushed face reminds me that I live with a man who strategizes about anything that can run on four legs and has a mane with the discipline of a convenience store lottery player. But unlike them, his bank account is loaded with fresh cash that glows neon in his mind.

The wild and crazy guy I married rushes across Sepulveda against the light, yanking my arm to keep up with him.

"That Buick almost got me!" I complain.

"This will be fun," he says. He has perfect hearing which doesn't mean he hears me. At the next street Dan stops at the cross walk like a normal human being for once and he smiles at me. I don't want this next thought, but here it comes: he's happy. I see the pure sweetness at his core. He's beautiful.

"Imagine!" he says. I don't have to guess at what. It's always four legged creatures that make him this buoyant.

I hear myself saying 'drats,' out loud, like a cartoon wife, who aspires to be a force of nature but is only two-dimensional, has silly hair and no real core. I am Marge Simpson with a better profile.

Dan needs his games while I need him. He is the tree trunk and branches to my flitting bird who's never had a nest.

We arrive at the chic The Wine Bistro. The ceilings have old-fashioned fans, presumably from Cuba, setting off the genuine New York factory tin ceilings. The lighting is halogen and arty. Thin bread sticks and dark rolls with rosemary smell exquisite.

We often come here on Monday nights to listen to music. Dan loves jazz but not as much as he loves the track. I've encouraged him to play his tenor sax even though it's loud. I tell my pal Marlene, my budding therapist pal, it's like living with John Coltrane, the early years. I've bought him fake books and CD's and played him the classic albums I've accumulated since college. But playing music at the level he aspires to is difficult. And for Dan, being alive is already difficult.

What would happen to our nights out if little XY or XX comes along?

Okay, I admit it; I've read how the fetus develops. For the first few weeks, it's the size of a poppy seed, i.e. it's only a cluster of cells. In other words, a sesame seed is larger. So, I figure I have time to find out if my maybe poppy seed should grow.

But not that much time.

Dan points me towards a tall blond fellow dressed in sleek, casual clothing who waves, and grins broadly. Something about his eyes make my hands sweaty..

"Open mind," prods Dan as we head to our table.

"I've heard all about you," Paul's long, clammy fingers grip my hand like a vise. During his prolonged smile, I notice that he's missing a tooth.

He catches my look, says, "Dan, I can see your wife's wondering about my dental status."

"I always adore being referred to in the third person," I smile with faux sweetness.

He's not biting, comes closer. "Wrestling. I held the championship for lightweights when I was in college and I still fool around. Probably not that smart." His pungent Patchouli aftershave wipes out the lovely rosemary breadstick aroma.

"What college?" I ask dripping with honey.

He hesitates, comes out with, "Oberlin. I majored in economics. Wrote a paper with my professor that was ultimately accepted into the *Economist.*"

"Really? As an undergrad?" I almost squeak, incredulous. By the time a paper hits major national magazines, grad students' names become invisible.

"That's formidable! What was it about?"

"It must have been, what, 1980? Dealt with the global economy. We were about twenty years ahead of our time."

I lean forward, wait for him to continue the excellent grave digging.

Dan catches the tension, tries to redirect. "Nice shirt, Paul," he says.

"Should be for almost two hundred bucks," says Paul. "Sometimes you splurge, right, dude?"

Dude? Since when is a surgeon who looks like Beethoven, a *dude?*

I'd like to splurge all over him. And I don't buy the tooth story. If you're dealing with horses in the six figure range, you don't go around looking like a hoodlum ---unless you *are* a hoodlum.

Dan tries to get me and Paul to agree on something. "How can you not love horses? The way they fight to win, their sheer athleticism; it's inspiring!" He turns towards me, his broad, strong face a alive with enthusiasm and glowing. Horses are sacred to him, like cows are to people in India where, if you hit one in an auto rick or motorcycle you can go to jail for two years.

I wish I could lock up the part of Dan that gambles.

I also wish Dan knew there were more sacred things than cows or horses. Like XY chromosomes.

On the other hand, I worry that I'm too selfish to be anyone's mother.

"I *do* love the horses. But from a distance. The way I love Johnny Depp," I explain. "Anyway, honey, you agreed, to find new, *healthy* sources of pleasure," I say, using my modulated, therapy-approved voice.

Under discussion has been Dan's compulsive tendencies. Since he doesn't bet, and only buys, he insists he's in the equine business.

"Have you ever *been* to horse country? It's *gorgeous!*" Paul asks.

I look at him with savage eyebrows.

"I mean if we *were* to breed, honey...." Dan adds.

Dan's voltage tells me he's got the mind-altering adrenaline buzz on. And now I *am* getting perturbed. The Gamblers Anonymous literature I've borrowed explains how the partner of the addictive personality is prone to dizziness, palpitations, hysteria, sudden, inappropriate outbursts of anger, headaches, loss of appetite, excessive overeating and withdrawal from friends and family. Eventually, to absolute self-destruction.

"Calm down," I say, mostly to myself.

"Willie swears by Paul," Dan says, citing his trainer.

"It's Willie's crazy schemes that got us *into* debt, *honey*," I counter.

"He's done good by us too," says Dan, ever blinded to Willie's conscientious attempts to get us to purchase yet another equine.

"Willie, who drinks booze with the sort of allegiance one devotes to the Green Berets, *that* Willie? Willie who's always manure-adjacent, is miraculously going to solve *our* money problems?"

"We'll make cash from mating King! Not to mention there's a fortune to be made if his offspring became winners, right Paul?"

"Absolutely," says Paul looking uncomfortable.

"Welcome to our marriage," Dan applies my joke.

My open mind is mostly shuttered like a beach house in Arctic Winter. The days of boarding, training, racing, losing- our-entire-savings and going-into-debt are finally and only recently, over. "Paul, you should know our money is in an account Dan can't get to?"

"That's why I'm turning on the charm," says Dan, flicking his bad boy dimple at me. I wonder, is this type of personality any kind of father material?

I think of his ex-wife, Maxi. She told me they had trotters *instead* of a marriage. Maxi didn't care for the four legged creatures. She laid down the law: no horses. Then, no kids. Then, no husband.

Dan got the stable and I got Dan.

Originally I didn't have any real opinions in this arena until the night he took me to the back-stretch. There I discovered the dank smell of the hay, the Olympian animals, the Run-yonesque ambiance. I felt transported into a truly exotic land. Old black men, faces carved with untold tales, were sitting under a single light bulb playing gin, just like in the movies. I wanted to know more about these living legends but was afraid to hear their stories. I imagined them as disenfranchised black men, leaving small towns that held no futures, riding on railroad cars, sleeping in abandoned barns with paperback novels stuffed into their pockets that sold them on the glamorous life of grooming horses in the beautiful rolling hills of central California. Maybe they believed the color of their skin would finally not count against them. And maybe they fell in love with the muscular animals when their own bodies were starting to fade.

But as arthritic and badly dressed as they were, sucking cigarette butts and snorting snuff late into the night, they played hand after hand. The scene had the iconic feel of a Norman Rockwell painting.

To my surprise, I felt drawn to this exotic world. At least for a while.

Then, I was with Maxi.

I'm convinced that if Dan didn't own pacers and trotters, our life together would improve. I believe that without horses, we wouldn't have this tension; this background argument that covers us like smog. Dan wouldn't be fielding phone calls from Willie at 2AM, to talk about a pulled tendon. Maybe he'd bring me flowers or give me a neck rub once in awhile. Maybe his concerns would center on us. On *me*.

But what if my elemental-- perhaps desperate-- need for his undivided attention is unreasonable? I've never hidden it. But let's not get into

that whole bi-polar, terrifying mother story and how I grew up with so much fear I developed unfortunate coping habits, then had to pay a bloody fortune to learn to undo them. No. Been, been, *been* there.

On paper, I'm nobody's ideal version of a parent, that's for sure. But I'm working on it. I touch my stomach. In there, a cute egg with a lovely singing voice has merged with a fine, dashing sperm with an impossibly high IQ. So, I will get myself up for evolving. But will Dan?

"Paul's willing to pay us real money for King," he says to me, as if Paul weren't there.

"What's real money, guys?"

They look at each other telepathically, I guess, refusing to answer.

Even this mild conversation could easily turn into something worse. Our fights are often defined by geography. At home, it's as if we're on opposite teams, while in grocery stores, we hug. Decisions in the meat department, which kind of beef, bottom round or brisket, maybe pork chops for a change, get us holding hands. Once we arrive at the leafy vegetables, romaine or arugula--- we become so over-whelmed, we cling to each other. By the time we reach the imported cheese section, there's often necking. Organic or local. Marlene says this isn't love, it's anxiety.

She's so wrong. Frankly, I worry for her future patients. I believe that love *includes* anxiety. Anxiety is one of the building blocks of existence.

I grab a bread stick and suck on it as if it were a pacifier. I'm trying to figure out why the hell I have the sweaty palms and simultaneous goose bumps.

I try to imagine Dan focusing on a short person with a bat in his hands. Or her hands. I was a great pitcher in middle school.

Paul's ball bearing necks swivels towards me. "We'll work out those details. Anyway," he slides to a photo on his cell: "here are a few of the seventy odd acres of green rolling hills where King will run free."

The land he shows us is breathtaking. "This where you breed?" I ask.

"Actually, our property is just across the way from the photo. We've been building the barn so we haven't had time to take pictures."

Seriously---a photo of a ranch *across* the road? I glance at Dan, raise my workaholic eyebrows, but his face is ever shinier with eau du enthusiasm. Paul's already discussing the   various mares he wants to mate with King. Then he starts selling and selling hard.

"You have to get a look at this foal! I'd give you a great price."

"I like a balanced top line," Dan says, free-associating. "I don't like a heavy fronted horse. But ultimately there's always the question of concentration."

Concentration. *Yes!*

"From what I've heard she's a royal pain in the ass. Doubtful she has the makings of a brood-mare," says Dan, finally showing some spirit.

"We're done *buying* horses, Dan! We're *divesting!* Raising a foal is just another big bet*!*"

I start mumbling about the math; the cost of hay, replacing hooves, vets bills, things I have learned about but have zero interest in. I'd rather be in my bathrobe, offering my astonishingly insightful political analysis of Fareed Zacharia's monologue on the Middle East.

I want to say, 'you're a doctor. Why can't you just doc?'

Completely ignoring me, Paul mentions gestation periods. For a horse it's only a couple of months more than a human.

I can't be more than five weeks in.

"Try to remember King's glory days," Dan pokes me.

To be fair, his star steed, King, had won several purses. In his last race at Los Al, he ran with a lot of heart, but pulled a suspensory ligament and finished up the track. We had to retire him. Now, Dan wants to believe he can make money by breeding the stallion.

Breeding. There's a loaded word.

Sometimes, when I read of the crises in Africa I think, why replicate my complicated gene pool, generations of repressed Hungarians and dour Poles harboring ancient resentments? Why not adopt one of those adorable kids and give *them* a chance?

That's probably another clue right there.

 "Paul, the doc and I are getting *out* of the business. We're not considering buying at *all.*"

"Instead of a baby horse," I say, the big announcement trembling on my lips…

"What can I get you?" The tall, sleek waitress appears and cuts me off. "Have you decided?"

"I'll have quiche," I say, suddenly delighted my tell-all sentence has been interrupted. "Without the salad."

 "No *salad?*" This is fantastically puzzling to her.

"Quiche, a la carte!" I repeat too adamantly, giving her the energy I'm feeling about Paul.

 "Good choice," patronizes Paul who's never set foot here before.

Why am I having such a violent reaction to this *dude*, I wonder?

But I can barely touch the food on my plate. Too busy being vigilant.

I'm not by nature a violent person, not generally vindictive, although I have spurts of strong annoyance and the occasional episode of road rage. But I feel threatened. Dan's poor judgment and deranged hopes for sudden wealth, for appearing in the winner's circle, for being interviewed on some cable sports TV station, can lead us down the road to destruction, bankruptcy, humiliation.

Why can't my husband be more tuned in? I use my psychic powers to send him a word. *Baby.* Baby, baby, baby!

No dice.

"I can let you have the foal for..." Paul' missing tooth glares at me.

"Buying is *off* the table," I hiss.

I've been known to blow opportunities, cause embarrassment, act outrageously. I've exited a room, a job, a country with my tail between my legs----or tail-less.

The waitress is gleefully pushing a House Special desert...---a flaming chocolate brandy number. Writers are prevaricators. We get paid to lie convincingly. So, in my brightest voice, I say: "Sorry, but deserts are poison to a diabetic! I'll wait for you boys outside."

"Diabetes?" whispers Dan incredulously.

I'm on my feet mumbling about glucose levels.

It's a little brisk on Ventura Boulevard, but I don't care; it's warm compared to sitting next to the horse hustler.

Three minutes later, Dan bursts into the street. "I'm *so* sorry to hear you're diabetic! It came on rather suddenly!" He shakes his head incredulously and gives me a shattering look, or a look that might shatter someone less determined than I am. Then he turns and marches back inside.

Twenty minutes later, Paul and Dan emerge. We all shake hands in the restaurant parking lot. He's driving a rented Ford Fiesta. Really? He couldn't go for the extra bucks for a Caddy? We're saying ,oh, we're so extremely happy to have met each other. Chums, we are. "We look forward to seeing you up at the ranch. Love your sweater, my wife would be thrilled to meet you, you can get a prize foal for about ten grand," says the snake before he slithers off to his blue rent a wreck.

I take off ahead of Dan.

"You were awful!" he scolds, marching behind me through the carefully tended suburban streets.

"I was unpleasant. You haven't seen my awful."

A dog barks. A radio plays "You've Got a Friend." I sigh, try to improve my posture, a self-help project that might come in handy in the coming months.

"You can have the last word," Dan promises.

"My last words are: his eyes were bullet holes!"

"Jesus!" Dan sprints ahead of me and he's no sprinter. Then, winded, he waits up and turns around. "It used to be the odds that interested me. Favorites, long shots, Exactas. There are rules, but they're always being broken. There's order, but there's chaos, too. You never stop learning: heart-rending races with big-hearted horses."

"Poetic, dear. We really should walk more."

He ignores my wisecracks. "I'm realizing, though, it's more than that to me. It's a foreign country, a new language; it's painting *and* music. You know how you always say I should explore my creative potential? Well breeding, making a winner, now *that is* creative."

That word again. Breeding. Bingo!

We shuffle inside our house. His eyes are steady on me. I give out nothing encouraging.

"Well, I suppose I can see, he *is* a bit slick," he admits, sotto voce. "I was really just meeting him for King's fee."

"The man is a walking Chernobyl!"

"You're *way* overstating the case," he slips his arm around me amorously. "Hmmmm." He slips his hand down my ass.

"I can't do this now, Dan."

He gives me the full on sex voltage, heat coming out of him as if he's a wood burning stove. I don't respond: I'm all business, so he tackles the situation again. "Okay, okay, if you're that certain, I guess we can sell King. I think we can get thirty-five grand for him."

It would erase our debt. I suck in air as if I've been underwater too long. "Are you making a true commitment, Dan? Even with all of that racetrack poetry inside you?"

His mantra is "whatever you say." The man just wants to get laid but his words still make me hopeful.

"No breeding *at all?*"

"*You* are what matters," says Dan.

He strokes my hair. "Comon," he says, and leads me into the bedroom.

"Hold on, there, sailor...."

"You have something better to do?" He has the special effects ability to transform into a human super nova when he wants to. He pulls me into his chest.

Old longing.

He kisses my neck. I hate that I'm this easy to get.

We're under the sheets, now. It's hard for him to talk while making love, like his emotions are in some sort of crawl space that we both have to get into. But at least we *do* get there sometimes. All of this love pours out now. His skin is medicine to me.

Then, what *is* that--- a tentative sound--- tapping? Drumming on the front door? Then, more forcefully, insistent knocking. We go limp; someone's selling roof tiling, religion, college-bound kids hawking cookies--- eventually they'll leave. But they don't. We freeze like guilty children.

"*Yo!* You guys!" That voice is *so* damn familiar. "It's *me*, Paul! I forgot to leave you the papers!" He's about ten feet away from our naked bodies. "Hey, your screen is broken!"

"Tell him to get the hell out of here," I growl.

But Dan's flipped open the blanket.

"I can fix this screen for you," Paul offers.

I holler, "get *lost!*"

"And the papers---it would take all of four minutes to go through them!"

"Really?" Dan asks,

I lunge towards him, grasp his giant leg. He extricates himself, mutters "I'll be right back," jumps into his jeans and heads towards the door like a frantic mosquito. I suddenly wonder why didn't I heed my aunt who, after meeting Dan told me to keep looking around "and if I you're lonely, get a cat!"

I never liked cats.

In the living room, Paul's managed to get Dan to read the papers. Something happens to me; a force, fierce, focused, unafraid, opens my mouth which shouts: "I'm coming out there, Dan. And I'm *naked.*"

Dan and Paul roar. But I'm not being funny: I mean to be Kali, the Indian goddess, passionate. strong, destructive. As in, "Kali has had enough!"

When I was young, I was bold. True, everyone was; we were changing the world. We made love in public, got arrested in foreign countries. We did radical theater, yelling at the audience that they were Capitalist pigs. We did those things. *I* did those things, I remind myself. I tell myself, 'you are not just a woman stuck in suburbia. You're not a cartoon. You're not Betty Boop. Jane Jetson. *Or* Marge Simpson. You may not be a goddess, but at least you can be Lucy from Peanuts.'

I head for the living room thinking if I am to bring someone into this world, I need to be fearless. I open my robe, drop it in a full frontal display.

For an instant, Paul's speechless. Then he utters an almost sacred *"wow!"* He quickly realizes that *that* reaction is 180% the wrong one so he jumps up streaming nonsense words, grabs his papers and races out the front door.

My turn to laugh.

"What was *that* supposed to be?" asks Dan.

"That was me saying *enough!*"

"I never committed to anything!!" he exclaims.

"You ran out of the bedroom on me."

Dan's eyes have gone soft and cloudy. "I don't know if I can do life without horses," he mumbles head in hands now. His body folds down.

"There *has* to be something else!" I say, wondering if this clue will register.

Outside there's vehement chirping, another bird dispute that happens all the time in the San Fernando Valley.

"We're the destination for all the birds with issues," he says, than a tear starts streaming down his cheek. "I gave up the stable. I've lost everything that matters."

"Everything?"

"I mean everything that isn't us," he amends.

If only he'd look up and study my face for a moment. Read my mind. But his eyes are closed.

"I'm doomed...."

"We're all doomed, Dan, we just manage to forget about it."

Then, under his breath, he starts humming an Eagles song, The Sad Café. He sings it perfectly, a tiny a cappella gem.

Some of their dreams came true,
Some just passed away
And some of them stayed behind
Inside the Sad Cafe.

These words account for so much in both of us.

Maybe a dad with an addictive streak is not ideal. Neither is a mother who is prone to sudden weeping. But somehow I can see us together, this little pink XY or XX person and her sad café of a dad who, watching her grow, will become less melancholy. He will adore his child, I'm sure. Anyway, who knows what the cures are for the human heart?

We fall back onto the bed. Dan rolls over onto my stuffed animals, picks up my maroon elephant. "I can't believe how many creatures you need to keep you company when you can't sleep."

"They love me," I say. "They love all of us."

"All of us?" he mutters, starts drifting into asleep.

"All of us."

I don't tell him that my bears, rabbits and I lie awake and together, we stare at the ceiling, asking questions without answers.

Big questions.

THE SLEEPING PERSON EXHIBIT

by Alexis David

It was raining when we went to the sleeping person exhibit and when we came out both our wool sweaters became damp and maybe between our legs too. I remember you said the sleeping person looked like a child, even though he was a man in a business suit.

"I felt the exact same thing," I said and decided I liked this external and internal dampness. "But, who's this artist? They remind me of Marina Abramovich," I said, trying to look in your eyes, but your glasses were covered in specks of rain.

"Possibly," you said, "More mysterious."

We had not heard of this artist. Their name was R.L.. Hernandez.

The next day, I texted you that I wanted to go back to the museum. My hands were shaking. I couldn't tie my tie. You hadn't sent any follow up text after the museum. But, you responded, "You should!" The exclamation point gave me hope in a lot of ways. I shaved my beard. I bought a new sweater at J.Crew.

But you didn't say we should go together and I wondered if I'd see you again. Your damp wool reminded me of the sheepdogs from my parents' farm. But, I had always felt exactly like a sheep dog. And you seemed so much higher, like a wolf or an asteroid.

We had met online. You said you loved conceptual art and we spent our first meet up talking over warm beers and the different artists we liked. I used to drink a lot of beer back home and when you suggested "The Tooth and Hair" pub, I thought you had googled me—I thought you knew that I was from the UK and picked the most English pub in Toronto.

You mentioned the British artist, Hamish Fulton in the conversation and it felt like another drop. I was impressed. I had liked the idea of his walks and his photographs. I had always liked his name too. I had the feeling that you and I would never get past this beer and conversation stage. We had a coziness, but it was a very deliberate platonic connection. Maybe we got close too soon so there wasn't any time for the weird tension that can build up to sex. Women who I almost have had sex with get in my dreams and in the vapors over my kettle. Your friendship was actually quite refreshing. Romance can be exhausting and time consuming and dangerous.

So when I got to the sleeping person exhibit again, I wondered if I would see you. I had included the time I was going: "Going to museum at noon." It was a statement that was a question. But, I didn't see you in the few strangers who walked around, softly, holding pamphlets to their chest, whispering to each other or taking photos of the other art work. Photography was not allowed in the sleeping person exhibit. The flash would disturb the sleeping person.

I walked into the dim room, painted with a really sad and lovely yellow. And in the middle was a raised platform with a single square mattress. I think that yesterday the business man looked so much like a child because no one sleeps in single beds except children and maybe nuns or priests.

The room had the white noise of people whispering and there was a fan going on in the corner. The kind a mother would prop up on a hot night, after the daughter asked for one.

The sleeping person today was a very tall woman with very red cheeks. She looked Russian, but like the old way we think of Russians. Not, the new way, where they are actually quite beautiful and contemporary. This woman had on a hand-knitted sweater and she had dark hair that had been braided, but I could see from the rubber bands near the bed that she took them off to sleep.

The rules of the exhibit were that anyone could take a nap, but the person waking up had to ring the chimes and anyone standing in the yellow taped triangle on the floor would be the next sleeping person. I think this was to discourage lines and to discourage people from sitting and waiting. The curators were afraid of the hostility similar in the Marina Abramovic "The Artist is Present" exhibit. People were eager to connect with her and so oddly, were mean and awful to those in the line. It was ironic, since the line could have been a chance to connect with a stranger, which was the point of the exhibit. It showed how much we care about Gods and celebrity and heroes. We think that certain people have the exact thing we need and no one else.

There were these little tiny stools around the room to sit and watch the sleeping person.

I sat down. I think I liked the exhibit because I liked to feel the vulnerability that comes with watching people sleep. It's a strange inclusion into their life. When I was little, I'd watch my father sleep on the couch and his face looked like a still bath of emotion. Or like a statue or maybe someone that was a step away from death. It was actually quite frightening to me and I had the habit of blowing air on to his face, so his eyelids would react. I needed to constantly reassure myself he was alive.

In the corner of the exhibit was an attendant who brought in new sheets for each person. But, the sleeper had to change the sheets for the next person. This added another weird and beautiful moment of intimacy. A stranger prepares a bed for another stranger.

The Russian woman made me realize the divinity of sleep. Sleep was a gift from the gods. Hours in the day where they would take care of the work of our world.

I stayed on the stool for an hour until she woke up, changed her sheets and rang the chimes. A middle aged man was in the triangle and he smiled when he heard the music. He took off his blazer and the glasses he wore. He looked like a professor and he was one of those people whose face, with the absence of glasses, looked like a weird owl.

I wondered if the date would come here again. I guess I wanted to share this man's sleep with her. He looked like he was from India or Pakistan and he pulled off his shoes to reveal long dark socks. Then he took off his socks too. There was an audible change in the people watching, like he was letting us in on another layer of secret of his life: his bare feet. He slept with a small smile on his face and I felt a real sense of happiness from him. His feet looked like his face without glasses, in that they were exposed without the presence of the hot socks. He looked like he only needed a good book to be happy. His life had been full of so many interesting thoughts that they shaped his mouth into a smile.

My date never came back to the exhibit and so I stood behind some kids who looked playful and rambunctious. They didn't look like they would hold out for the sleeping part. They kept saying, "Is it real? Is she really sleeping?" I wondered then if it were real. I read the artist's statement. It was in Helvetica on the wall. The artist R. L. Hernandez had been born in Portugal but now lived in New York. There was no photo of the artist but I googled the name and I found a photo. It was my date.

I had just gone on a date with the artist of the sleeping person exhibit. And now, looking back at our interactions, with this knowledge, it clicked. Of course you were R. L. Hernandez. And, I wondered if maybe your whole life was curated experiences. You had curated those beers and this exhibit. You had curated the statement to not include your photo and to not say your full name and I knew then I could never love you because you were trying to be someone in control of everything. Like you were the God of Sleep. And, so I started to cry. There were other sadness in my life, what I had left in England, the memory of my father when he was alive but sleeping and suddenly, I was back in England as a child weeping inside the bathroom, looking down at my flannel pajamas and thinking how I really wanted the blue ones, but my mom got me the red ones. We can't control anything in our lives.

I inched up closer to the mattress and I was on the triangle. The walls at the museum had gotten so intensely yellow and it smelled faintly of hand sanitizer which was a cruel reminder that outside this space, everything was sanitized. I wish I could tell those kids that it was real. It was absolutely real. And, I knew then if I had kids of my own, I would never tell them these stupid myths about Santa and the tooth fairy. I would always be on the inside with them; whatever I knew, they knew too. And this decision, resolved something deep within me, fixed a skewed internal alignment.

And then the sleeping person awoke and he rang the chimes and I was in the triangle and he looked at me happily, as if sleeping here would cure me. As if I would be my dad

sleeping on the couch. As if I would finally get the blue pajamas. As if I would understand my date somehow. Not really know her, but understand something deep and essential about her. Like, I could enter this platform and sleep on the bed and I would have the experience of a long marriage with her and when I woke, the marriage would be turned into the memory of dream.

The man fixed up the sheets and then he sprayed some lavender spray, which I hadn't realized was available and it felt like a gift and like everything would be okay if I just took off my socks and lay down in my new sweater and slept, like a child, in this museum, in front of all these people. As if this would be enough.

About the Author:

Alexis David is a fiction writer and poet. She holds a MFA in fiction from New England College. She also has a BA from Hobart and William Smith Colleges, where she went to school as an Art Scholar in Creative Writing. She has published in My Next Heart: New Buffalo Poetry (BlazeVOX 2017), Green Mountains Review and Ghost City Press, among others. She writes in a glass room while looking at trees.

OUR LAST MONTHS
by Judith Helen Goode

My wife is dying of cancer.

We have been together thirty years and stayed in love for all of them. We share ideas, politics, world view, sex, fun, family. Have I left out anything? If so, we share it.

I fell in love with Charlotte's voice first: she was a commentator on radio station WBAI in New York. Her voice had such a range: Intense, serious, saddened, amused. I listened intently to each iteration. I always listened to her commentary, of course, which I applauded. Often it had a feminist theme; always it was political (the political is personal). This was at the height of the Second Wave of Feminism, in the 1970s.

Then I met Charlotte in person and my authentic life began. She was with someone but she broke it off for me. Soon we moved in together. Our lives began to mesh. I still think her voice is the most wonderful thing about her. It's low and perfectly modulated. Naturally, I love her body and have been on a years' long effort with her to drop extra pounds, which she did. She is now at her ideal weight—or was before the cancer.

She saw me through my struggles with the politics of academia. Hers were less contentious because she teaches at a small, progressive college and I taught at a huge state university. I am retired now so I can write full time. Charlotte is still teaching, although she is on leave now. She is well known as a feminist scholar and writer. I am somewhat known as a fiction writer, especially in literary circles. We have always supported each other in our professions.

What I have been describing is, yes, the ideal marriage. (We only married because our tax accountant told us to; neither of us cared about marriage. In fact, Charlotte didn't believe in marriage. I was neutral.)

My wife is dying of cancer.

We live in a loft in Soho. I would prefer a less trendy neighborhood but when we bought the loft, Soho was considered far downtown. We actually have two lofts across from each other, one for living and one for my writing studio. Charlotte has a trust fund and I have a generous pension so we pretty much did what we wanted when it came to the interior of the lofts.

We eat well, often out or take-out. Sometimes I cook a soup or a stew. Charlotte doesn't really cook, except that she makes salads. We have many friends and many cousins on Charlotte's side, also siblings, and grand nieces and nephews on both sides.

My wife is dying of cancer.

Charlotte and I just came home from her immunotherapy treatment. She has done chemo, which is nightmarish. Immunotherapy is easier. But just getting into a cab to go uptown is tiring. Her body has weakened. She went straight to bed. Later I'll bring her a tray of something delicious to tease an appetite out of her. This becomes more and more difficult.

Sometimes we sit on our roof garden (ours is the top-floor loft) in summer, late spring, or early autumn. We have a gardener but we also like puttering around in the garden ourselves. Often we don't talk. Sometimes we talk about the disastrous administration and our frustrations with it. Each of us knows the other's history, going back to childhood. Instead, we talk about what our families are up to.

And we talk about what my life will be like after. Obviously, this is painful but it must be done. Just like my psychotherapy, which is mandatory according to Charlotte. I'm one of those lucky souls who never needed therapy... until now. I like it. It's another view of life. And death. So I will be continuing therapy. I'll see friends and family—a lot. There will always be someone with me to prevent suicidal impulses. And my life will be a requiem for Charlotte.

I'll pay attention to diet and exercise. I'll even go to the gym. I'll take time to relax, just the way we have always done together. As I relax, I'll think about her and all she's given me. I'll be grateful for the life we've shared.

My wife is dying of cancer.

We try for normalcy: it's essential for our sanity. Charlotte often stays in bed in the morning in our upstairs sleeping loft. I come downstairs to the kitchen, which floats in the center of the large space that serves as dining room and living room. This space is the length of the loft. I nosh as I prepare breakfast, which is often only for me.

Once when my sister was visiting she tried to make sense of our refrigerator. She took everything out, including the spoiled take-out, and managed to make room for it on the island. Then she wiped down the inside of the frig, threw away the spoiled stuff, and arranged the good stuff as she thought we might like it. Within a few days, the frig went back to its normal state of chaos.

It isn't that we weren't grateful to my sister for the spic and span frig, our lifestyle doesn't include many curated sit-down dinners. Between

Charlotte's teaching-meeting schedule and my readings schedule our daily lives were as chaotic as our frig. We thrived on that medium; we were engagé.

Naturally, as we got older, we haven't quite kept up that pace but we're busy. We often have company—friends, students, family—and Charlotte has a young assistant, Kim, who comes every morning "to organize my life," as Charlotte says of herself. I myself am slightly less frenetic in style because I spend large swathes of time on my computer wrestling with a novel or a short story.

My wife is dying of cancer.

Always but even more now we put a premium on the time we spend together. It comes first. We used to go to bed at the same time so we could tell each other our day. Now our day is usually a trip to the oncologist for Charlotte's immunotherapy session. Then Charlotte goes to bed and I sometimes nap with her. But I get up after an hour and go to my work. Immunotherapy is easier on the body than chemo but any exertion, even just taking a cab to the doctor's office, is tiring for Charlotte.

She has made her will and signed a DNR. The book she has just written (her third) is in its final stage, and Charlotte's assistant—bright young person that she is—has read the draft and made any corrections needed. Charlotte is slowly getting through the corrected draft to give her okay. Charlotte's editor is very understanding about the missed deadlines and slow pace of the writing.

Just now, Charlotte surprised me by coming downstairs and into my writing loft. "Let's go up to the roof," she says. "I feel better." I say, "Yes, of course—I'll make the drinks." I make a seltzer with just a dash of Campari for her and a gin martini for me. I follow her up the stairs, carrying the drinks and some nosh on a tray and let her hold the door for me. On the roof, just before six pm, the temperature is 75 degrees and breezy. We sit at the built-in table and circular bench and enjoy the late afternoon sun.

Charlotte's book is a kind of memoir of her work as a feminist scholar and writer. She also writes about being Jewish. Susan Faludi was just here to give some commentary on the book, and I think this energized Charlotte. Susan has also become a good friend, and friends are especially important these days.

Charlotte has many friends. The number of visits we've had since she's been sick has been almost overwhelming. Everyone wants to see her, to touch her. Besides friends, there are all those cousins of Charlotte's. For the most part I like the cousins, among whom I prefer some over others. They've been surprisingly comforting in this period. Comfort has become a scarce commodity chez nous.

My wife is dying of cancer.

The wind blows gently as the sun goes down. I don't think there's any science to prove this but I've noticed that on windy days the wind seems to abate at sunset. We talk about Susan's visit, her work as an activist, and her commentary on Charlotte's book. On good days Charlotte gets quite a lot of work done. On bad days, not much at all. Today was a bad day but Charlotte seems to be rallying. Could she be going into remission?

We speculate. Charlotte says she feels lighter, less burdened by pain and nausea this evening. Would she like to go out to dinner? I ask. Maybe, she says. She would like to go down to Chinatown and go to our favorite restaurant there. Miso soup sounds good to her. Anything that pleases you, I say. But we make no move to get up. It's so lovely out here on our roof garden.

I wonder how many people have wished what I'm about to wish: that we could push the stop button right here, stop time, stop the progression of our lives? Many, I would guess. But time is a bully…. Normally, we take a leisurely walk down to the restaurant. I assume we're going to need a cab. But Charlotte says she wants to walk. Are you up to it? I ask. She tells me yes. So I grab the cap I wear since I've gotten bald and we're off.

It's a glorious evening—New York at its prime time; everyone is out. I can tell from her expression that like me Charlotte's loving the city. I worry that the crowds will tire her but no, she's enjoying herself. Seeing her this way, the old way, makes me feel almost giddy. I hold her arm more closely. We progress on the street.

At the restaurant, we order a selection of the dishes we used to get. Then we enjoy the hot fragrant miso soup the waitperson brings us. We're so much in the moment, so spontaneous, so without a care this evening. We've not stopped time but instead nudged it just a hair back so we can treasure this good time. It's apart from the bad days with two spaces in between—as in the old days when writers followed a period with two spaces….

My wife is dying of cancer.

Not wanting to spoil a good thing, we walk a couple of blocks, then hail a cab home. That night we make gentle love and sleep through the night. In the morning Charlotte gets up with me and takes her tea to her writing desk. I've urged her to type her work into her computer but she still insists on writing it longhand and giving it to Kim to type. I urge her to take a lunch break but instead she has Kim make her a sandwich and bring it to her desk.

"I want to take advantage of the day and get some work done," Charlotte says.

I can't argue with that. Over the next few weeks, Charlotte seems almost her old self, working part of the day and even eating a little more than before. As far as food goes, I'm always eating—every time I go into the kitchen I have a nosh. Although I wouldn't mind losing a few pounds, my weight is pretty much stable.

Charlotte, of course, has lost weight during her illness. She is the thinnest I've ever seen her. It seems unfair that she gets to be thin only because of an illness that will kill her. But that is the grisly truth of cancer. During these halcyon weeks of remission, Charlotte goes to her favorite dress shop and buys a couple of dresses that fit her. I tell her that she looks ravishing and she smiles with sad eyes. It's hard to be genuinely happy with the shadow of death hanging over us.

Yet we're happy when the grandnieces and nephews arrive. We enjoy listening to their news, what's happening in their lives. When they ask about how we're doing, we always tell them the same thing: "We're functional." They smile at our choice of words. Over the past few weeks we've been able to upgrade that to "We're well." When they look quizzical, we explain "Charlotte's in remission."

In general, we don't talk about Charlotte's illness to anyone but the oncologist. Then we go into specifics: how she's eating, how she's sleeping, if the current medicine cocktail is working, etc. We like the oncologist. He's clear and straight forward. When we asked him about how long Charlotte has, he said months, not years. We accepted that as the rules of engagement.

We take this opportunity of remission for a month in the Hamptons. The sea air is invigorating and the beaches are glorious. We go to the ocean side, then cross to the bay side, which is still water and not so cold. We float like blimps, luxuriating. On the way home, we stop at a farm stand and buy fresh vegetables and fruit. At home, we make a huge fruit salad and indulge our senses. Then we go to our writing.

My wife is dying of cancer.

Charlotte gets a lot done in the Hamptons, I less so. I'm somewhat stymied by our life prospects and tend to brood while Charlotte progresses at lightning speed. This is partially because she's reading proofs but it moves quickly. At about three we take a nap and then head out to the beach for our afternoon swim. The water is delicious, not warm enough to be soupy and not so cold it takes your breath away. I make a foray into the ocean and ride some small waves in. Charlotte sits on the beach smiling at me.

By the time we go home we're thoroughly satiated. We congratulate ourselves on our last-minute trip to the Hamptons and on our luck finding this airy house to rent. On the way home we stop in the village of South Hampton and buy swordfish for dinner, a treat for both of us. It's wildly expensive but very fresh and absolutely mouthwatering. We make a salad of fresh greens, tomatoes, and vinaigrette. My eyes tear to see Charlotte eat.

Our days are blissfully the same and soon it's time to go back to the city. Once we're home, Charlotte begins to decline. I'm tempted to look for another house in the Hamptons but Charlotte really isn't up to it. We lay low. We have a constant stream of visitors, however, as we did before we went away. Some of these visits are tearful goodbyes from people who live on the other side of the country or abroad.

We have a wonderful if occasionally sad visit with our Hungarian friends, whom we met in Budapest last winter. Milo is a sociologist and Magda is a novelist. We have politics and literature in common and it is a thoroughly satisfying visit. We all have a moment of tears when they leave. Then we watch a mystery on TV but Charlotte folds before it is over.

Charlotte's friend Lizzie from Boston has been staying with us on and off and now her visit is prolonged. She helps Charlotte in the bath and combs her kinky curly Jewish hair. I sense that the time is approaching. I shut myself in the bathroom and bang my fists against the basin. Charlotte and Lizzie are in the kitchen and don't hear me.

We have a cleaning woman but we also hire a home health aide. Lizzie can't always be here to help Charlotte bathe and dress. The home health aide is a young vigorous woman who can hold Charlotte up in the bath and wash her. She is trained to do that kind of thing. I would help but I have a bad back. I once tried to put on blush and lipstick on Charlotte and made a mess out of it. We had a good laugh.

Luckily Charlotte finished her proofs in the

Hamptons. She wouldn't be up to it now.... Our days get shorter even though it is still summer. Charlotte can't make it up the steep stairs to the roof so when she goes to bed I go up to the roof with a lonely sandwich.

I go to bed early and get up before Charlotte is awake (the pain pills make her sleep more than usual)). Then I can get in a few good writing hours before I go and visit Charlotte during her long morning in bed. I bring her herbal tea and toast with marmalade, which she may not be able to finish. She takes a stab at it because morning is when she typically feels best.

I lie down next to her and prop myself up on a pillow, of which there are several because Charlotte likes throw pillows on the bed. It took a little bit until I got used to it, all those many years ago when we moved in together. We had periods of adjustment to each other when we were each relatively young. And of course's there are the stages of Charlotte's' illness.

We like to talk in the morning in bed when Charlotte wakes up. We talk about all the things we used to talk about: politics, our friends and family, our feelings, how I'll wake up alone when she's gone. I tell her that all I see is gray after. No color, no joy. You'll heal, Charlotte says. Only enough to write your requiem, I say. And again I tell her: my life will be a requiem for you.

No, I want you to live again, she says. That won't be possible, I say, because you're my life. You have to look at things from another perspective, she says. What perspective? I say. My only perspective is that I'll be without you. But friends and family—you'll have to keep up, she says. I know, I know, I say. I'll do my best. There's a pause. Good, she says softly: she's falling asleep again. That's when I usually get up and go downstairs.

There's a half a loaf of challah in a basket on the island. I pick at it mindlessly. I'm thinking about what to put on Charlotte's tray when she wakes up at about eleven. That's her pattern now at night. She falls asleep early, around

seven, and wakes up again around eleven. The pain wakes her. I have her pills ready and a glass of water.

Sometimes I have to hold her until the pills take effect. Sometimes she cries from the pain. I sing to her then—Beatles songs, which are her favorites. "Will you still love me when I'm sixty-four?" We won't make it together to sixty-four. Maybe you'll meet someone special, she says on occasion. No, this is it, you're it for me, I say.

She doesn't argue—she knows better. She knows how it is with us. Like some animals we mate for life. When one mate dies, the other roams the forest alone. That's what I'll do; I'll roam Soho but not alone. I'll have the mandatory friend or relative with me. But it might as well be alone, considering my state of mind.

The pills have reached their full effect. Charlotte says she wants to play Scrabble. I get the board and set it up on the bed. It's fun at first but she begins to fade fast. I put away the Scrabble and ask her if she wants to go downstairs. She tells me yes and that it's time to make the pull-out sofa bed in the living room. The upstairs sleeping loft is no longer a reality for her.

I go down and make the sofa bed. Our cleaning person irons the sheets at my request. Wrinkles in the sheets are uncomfortable for Charlotte's tender skin. When I go back to the sleeping loft I find Charlotte crumpled in a ball at the bottom of the steps. I call out her name and she says I'm all right—don't worry. I help her to her feet. We walk slowly into the living room and I situate her on the soft sofa in an alcove of the loft.

I ask her why she was coming down from our sleeping loft. She said I wanted to do it one last time. Well I said it's done and please no more experiments. No more experiments she repeated. I ask her if she wants anything and she says tea and toast. Oh you're trembling! She says. I was scared I say. I'm so sorry she says. I'll recover, I say.

I bring the tea and toast to her on a tray, tea properly brewed in a teapot and lightly buttered toast with the goose berry jelly Charlotte likes. We sit and crunch on the toast, talking about our work. I try to pretend that we haven't reached a new stage in Charlotte's illness. At least she's eating something. But she barely makes a dent in the toast and says she wants to go to bed.

I pull the covers back for her and help her get into the bed. We talk for a while longer, me sitting beside her on the bed, then her eyes close. I go across to my writing loft. It's basically for a few minutes of not thinking about Charlotte's illness. I don't expect to write. It's after midnight. I sit, looking at my computer screen saver, which is a picture of Charlotte and me on the beach at the Hamptons a few years ago, before the cancer.

Those were days when our concerns were each other, our work, our activism, and our family and friends. Our health was a given. I have asthma, which is under control. Charlotte had a difficult menopause, with violent mood swings and crying depressions. When she emerged from that it was with a new peacefulness—at least on the personal side. Politically we were both in the fray, Charlotte especially in feminist politics.

Some years ago, the New York Times Magazine ran a cover story on prominent feminists, including Charlotte, Kate Millet, Vivian Gornick, and the late Ellen Willis. It was the first time that the mainstream media recognized the prominence of feminist activism and scholarship. The cover was a photo of the four looking determined and self-possessed. We were all proud of Charlotte and her compatriots. Remembering this recognition of Charlotte's life's work, I think about the loss Charlotte's death will be to the movement.

I sit for a little longer and then go back and get into bed beside Charlotte. I'm just falling asleep when Charlotte puts her hand on my arm. I wake with a jolt and ask her what's wrong. She says she can't sleep. I check my watch and tell her it's time for her pain pill. I get up and bring it to her with a glass of water. Now comes the twenty minutes until the drug takes effect. She begins to writhe. I stroke her hair.

Somehow the time passes and she becomes calm. I assume that the nights of sleeping through are over. I calculate what time it will be when the next pill is due: five am. I consider getting an alarm clock and putting it beside the bed. I decide that's the plan and go up to the sleeping loft for the clock, which I bring down and set.

Charlotte is asleep but it takes me a little while to sleep again. Even before five Charlotte is awake and writhing. I tell her ten more minutes. I have the pills beside me and after ten minutes I give her one with water. Twenty minutes for the pill to work. I suggest a cup of herbal tea. She says yes and I get up to make it. I bring her the tea and hold the cup to her mouth. She sips, I put the cup down, then lift it again. We go on this way until she's had enough.

I'm wide awake, she says. Shall I read to you? I say. Yes, please, she says. Her book is in the sleeping loft. I fetch it and open it to the bookmarked page. The book is a novel by one of her former students. It's good for up to forty pages, she says, citing the number of the page where we begin. I read, only mildly interested in what I'm reading. I typically read nonfiction.

Soon, Charlotte is asleep. I'm not, although I'm exhausted. I'm worrying—something I don't often do—about this stage of Charlotte's illness and what the next stage will be. Or if there will be a next stage. The oncologist could only estimate Charlotte's remaining time. I was surprised that I had to hold the tea cup for her but assumed that it was because of the pain.

We have discussed hospice and Charlotte says she will only do it for the last week or so. She'll know when it will become too much for me. We have everything planned, as well as you can plan for something like this.

The next morning, Charlotte throws up her tea

and toast. So at least for today it'll be seltzer and soda crackers. We have those items on hand. As I said, we have planned for everything. Today she sleeps later than usual and wakes up crying from the pain. I have her pill ready and sing to her for the twenty minutes it takes to work. It's a rough twenty minutes but we get through it. She's going to need a stronger pill. I call the oncologist and make the request. Then I call our pharmacy and ask them to notify me when the prescription is ready. At seven pm I walk the three blocks to the pharmacy and realize that I haven't been on the street since our last visit to the oncologist. It's jarring but also stimulating to be among the crowds.

I'm sequestered here with Charlotte in our lofts. But Soho is always popping, mainly with tourists. The nice thing about our roof garden is that we're in the thick of things but above them where it's peaceful. I could have waited for the pharmacy to deliver the stronger pill but I know Charlotte will need it for her next dose. I reflect that the time is getting near. Cancer doesn't wait for people time. Soon when I go out I'll be coming home to an empty loft. But no—I'll fill it with visitors. I won't want to be alone. Not for a long time.

Two weeks pass with Charlotte comfortable on the stronger pill. After that it's injections but that'll be at the hospice. It happens sooner than I expect: one morning Charlotte says, It's time. I suppose the hospice stay will prepare me for the empty loft while Charlotte is still alive. She brings nothing with her—she says she'll wear the nightgown they give her. That way, I won't have to take anything back. Charlotte has already given away most of her clothes, which are high end and valuable. They don't fit anymore. She's kept only the two dresses she recently bought and her several pairs of house pajamas.

We both cry a little when I leave her at the hospice to go home for the night. It'll be our first night apart since my last book came out and I went on a reading tour. That was when Char-

lotte was still teaching, before we knew about the cancer. The next book—a collection of short stories—will come out after she's gone.

The empty loft is a shock even though I've prepared myself. As soon as I get in the door I turn on the radio, which is always set to National Public Radio. But I hardly listen to what the program is. I have called Lizzie and she is on her way. Tomorrow she'll go with me to the hospice. For now, we've agreed that she'll stay with me until the end. She talks a bit too much for my taste but I'm glad she's here with me so the loft is empty only of Charlotte, which of course is everything.

At the hospice I get into bed with Charlotte and spend the day until they kick me out at nine pm. I read to her and sing to her and we talk. I spend every day like this with her. Then I go home to the loft and Lizzie, who has been at Charlotte's side throughout. She comes with me to the hospice but leaves us alone for most of the day.

When I get home at night Lizzie has made a meal for us. I eat without appetite but with gratitude. Charlotte and Lizzie were college roommates at Cornell. She is devoted.

Charlotte is on a morphine drip that she can control. Depending on her pain level and consequently her morphine intake, she drifts in and out of a light doze. We talk around these lacunae. Mostly I hold her: I want to be her protector on this final journey she's taking.

We have a week together this way. Then it's over. At least I'm holding her when she goes.

My wife died of cancer.

THE COLDNESS OF PEARLS
by Deirdre Barragry

Harry was so punctual he might have been mistaken for someone who wanted to be there. Twenty minutes early, as if about to interview for the position of a lifetime or embark on the holiday of his dreams. *If only.* He'd come by bus, both to kill time and to submerge himself in the wash of mundanity before the meeting ahead. He was bemused to find a tear of affection welling in response to the familiar asthmatic grunt of the Number 84, the tongue-biting ramps along newly-widened Fern Avenue, and the navy houndstooth seats worn to threads at back and base. He'd let the bus lull him away from his spinning mind as it clambered around each bend, even finding nostalgia in the orange rivulets running from the spilled cans of the youngsters at the very back. This week's "youngsters' were last year's "inconsiderate oiks". This had been the route of his early twenties, from his parents' hushed semi-d to the School of Medicine and on to nights under Georgia in her bedsit over the fruit-shop. The smell of overripe bananas still stirred him to this day, occasionally causing him to have to scurry through the fruit aisle of Tesco Express.

Harry chose to alight at the credit union, but as the 84 began to trundle away from him he suddenly felt abandoned and had to fight his instinct to flag it down with a shameless display of arm-flapping and climb back on. He'd intended to walk this last part of the journey at a relaxed pace, but thoughts of Georgia quickened his step until his bladder took precedence and made him jog.

Harry perched deflated on the edge of an overstuffed armchair in the foyer, irritable that something could look so plush and yet be so unyielding. It was stuffed excessively firmly and he'd soon developed a both literal and figurative pain in his rear trying to sit on the velvet dome, before giving up and shuffling forwards on his heels. He crossed his legs one direction and then the other before inspecting his nails and glancing again at his watch. *Busy for a midweek evening*, he thought with a sniff. *Off season tourists and lovers.* He ran a hand over his newly soft jaw and jiggled a foot. He'd missed a smear of polish on the top of his left loafer. Harry hissed and fished a crumpled tissue from his jacket pocket to buff and blend it away. A tipsy couple in their twenties wove past him as he crouched, noisy and underdressed for the time of year and not a coat between them. The bloke, in a short-sleeved shirt so tight it looked like it had been misted onto him with an atomiser, had a beefy arm around his date's ribs. She was tentative in her strappy sandals and laughing too hard to walk straight. It took them a second try to negotiate the exit, her squealing as she stumbled on the lintel.

Harry shook his head and returned the polish-stained tissue to his pocket. His diamonded socks were showing. He stood and pinched the knees of his trousers to adjust them downwards and sat momentarily before rising as if stabbed in a glute. He flung his hands behind his back and clasped the fingers of one with the other, taking decisive strides to the line of pictures above a spray of flowers on the mahogany table. The delicate scent of lilies was incongruous with the yellowing black and white photographs of sea dogs and trawlers. Harry glanced down at the powdery stamens and their earwax-coloured pollen and pressed the tail of his tie to his chest. *Crabby Jack (1886 -1943) never had to worry about such things.* Harry checked his watch again.

One last dinner together was all she wanted. Opinions on how he should respond had been divided, his own among them. He'd flailed between acceptance and refusal since taking the call before caving in. Three weeks on, he was still flailing. He studied Crabby Jack and willed his pulse to slow. He caught a faint reflection of himself superimposed over the old sailor and considered wryly that he looked more ghostlike than the long-dead mariner. He tried out a smile but it was tense as a tetanus victim's and he swiftly dropped it.

Georgia sailed through the door at eight on the dot, wafting her unconventional fragrance and leading with noiseless browned feet. She startled him with a kiss on the cheek, not waiting for an invitation. Unbidden she fixed his tie, fluid in her ritual despite so long a separation, and with a bright side smile and a flicker of eye contact, led the way to their usual table. The Inn was packed, the intimacy heightened by the low ceilings and density of diners. Harry followed with his nails pressed into his palms and the rising heat of panic and desire.

Harry remained mute while Georgia ordered for them both, her forefinger roaming the menu as she made her selection. She smiled sweetly at the waitress, her eyes crinkling as she stacked and aligned the leather-bound menus and wordlessly returned them. Georgia played with her hair and sat back to study Harry. He looked good, apparently. He didn't feel it.

Starters appeared and broke the hanging silence. Harry watched Georgia's steaming soup bowl descend in a slow arc and land on the table. His own had barely contacted the starchy tablecloth, when he found himself pushing back and standing, and then fleeing to the bathroom.

He collapsed into the echoing tiled whiteness. Harry gripped the knot at his throat and yanked at the noose again, staring at the pantomime in the mirror. He looked like an irate turkey, and he might have managed a nasty laugh if he hadn't been choking. The knot yielded, finally, with a satin whirr. *Why did she always have to do his tie so bloody tight?* Harry braced against the marble sink, squeezing the cold ceramic, and cleared his gummy throat. The eyes rising to meet his were reproachful and bloodshot. He knew he shouldn't have come tonight. But he couldn't refuse her invitation, under the circumstances. He'd never been good at saying 'no', and they both knew it.

There was still time to duck out. Harry pinched the bridge of his nose. His soup must be clotting by now, the green of minted peas forming a tideline on the white earthenware. Georgia was out there, sipping hers with the dainty slurp he used to find endearing, while he holed up in the bathroom bunker of the Primrose Inn. He grappled with a brass tap. It groaned and ground into his palm. Harry soaked the corner of a hand towel and dabbed his face. The Primrose Inn took great care over these extravagant touches, the boutique soaps and the stack of pristine hand towels. Fresh. Folded. Frivolously abundant. Harry had always liked the place. It was cosy, upmarket but not pretentious. Not unlike how he used to view his life with Georgia, the comfortable combination of two former general practitioners with reasonable financial acumen and modest inheritances. He smoothed his mussed hair, what was left of it, and tossed the damp towel into the hamper. He would never come here again. He tugged sharply on his jacket cuffs and braced himself for the wall of heat, noise, and contentment on the other side of the bathroom door.

The fish tank's azure aura lent their usual table an unearthly glow. He followed the tractor beam back to the alien landscape of his marriage. Georgia was studying a clownfish, her cheek in her palm, slowly tracing a finger of the opposite hand across the glass. The clown-fish tried to nibble it. Her dimple deepened. She looked up as Harry approached. Her eyes and teeth glinted blue, and the pearls at her throat reflected the light.

"Better now?" she said. She laid a toned arm along the back of his chair and pulled it out a little for him to slip into it.

He hopped his chair tighter to the table top – it might stop him falling through the floor. He could have done with a seatbelt or some duct tape. Georgia planted a hand between his shoulder blades and leaned behind him to say something to the waitress. The tenderness burned him. He wanted to slap her hand away. And then to press it and beg her one last time to change her mind.

Through Harry's lamb and her salmon, Georgia talked about her friends and her golf. She'd recently attended her sister's retirement party. Everyone, especially Sharon, missed Harry at it. It wasn't the same without his legendary air guitar skills. They all sent their love. And the gang were just devastated when they learned he wasn't to be her guest at the Lady Captain's Dinner.

So this was how she was going to play it. Cheerful chatter and avoidance. Harry sawed at his meat inexpertly. The knife snagged and mauled the flesh. He cut the served slices into ridiculous little scraps with frayed edges. Georgia beckoned to their waitress with the ready smile and asked her to bring him a sharper knife. But it wasn't the knife that was blunt. Harry was falling into power-saving mode.

He repositioned his hold on the knife. What was left of his inner optimist was done for. The most it could hope was that this might all be the product of some interaction between his selection box of meds and a case of merlot. That any moment now, he'd wake up hungover in that vast sleigh bed of their marital home, cocooned in security and Egyptian cotton. With Georgia on one side and the dog on the other. He'd open a window to let in the morning air. She'd complain of the draught. He'd have eggs for breakfast with a statin chaser and bring Georgia tea and the papers.

Georgia deftly folded back the salmon's glis-tening skin. "And Chloe and Mark miss you too and said to tell you to get in touch. Don't be a stranger and all that. You know, if you're in the area, or, well, want to talk or fancy a cuppa."

If he wanted to talk. If he wanted to talk about what? The weather. His new apartment, with its spotlights in the ceiling and hardwear-ing carpets. About how his world imploded one November afternoon when his wife told him she didn't want to live anymore.

Because that is precisely what she'd said, after inviting him into the false shelter of shar-ing a pot of tea and watching the rain teem down. She didn't want to get elderly, she'd explained as she raked the hair by her temples with her nails. She'd seen enough death and enough disease to know which of the two she feared more. It was her life, her decision. She wasn't looking for any second opinion about her assisted suicide. She wanted to depart on her own terms, before her looks faded further and her body broke down. Any attempt to open a debate would be futile. She hoped that Harry would not be so selfish as to attempt to dissuade her from leaving the world in pragma-tism, rather than waiting for desperation to set in. There was mention of Switzerland and something about counselling. Then she'd smiled with her eyes and squeezed his knee. Harry doubted that Chloe and Mark could ex-plain away his failure to prove himself worth living for, over a plate of digestive biscuits.

Someone in the restaurant popped a cham-pagne cork. The shot of success and celebra-tion. Harry wondered if he'd ever feel happy again. He'd settle for less, somewhere midway between happiness and emptiness would do.

"They'd love to see you," said Georgia. She poured béarnaise from the sauceboat and it bled into her roasted root vegetables.

Harry chewed without tasting and watched her eat. He'd hoped she was sick in some way. Mentally, physically, spiritually. Any category would do — anything at all on which he could pin her determination to leave their life and hers. No, she wasn't depressed, no more than you might expect after a dignified career spent fighting disease and decay. She had nothing else to tell him. Her calmness had unnerved him. A good old-fashioned breakdown of his marriage would have been less painful. Another man he might have come to understand in time. At least that way there was a chance that after much soul searching and getting blind drunk at the golf club, some memories of happier times might survive. It was one thing he'd learned as a G.P. — life can get messy at all levels, from cellular up. People would have been kind to him, sorry for him, instead of morbidly fascinated by the totality of his wife's solution to the age-old burden of becoming of age-old. He would never escape its shadow. Georgia's decision razed everything to the ground, the destruction so total that only a charred outline of life as he knew it remained, ashy dust too fine to hold. Had there been a point to the decades of arguments and promises and days out and celebrations, or were they just ways to fill and mark time? How long ago had Georgia swapped building for maintenance?

"I've missed you, too," she said, resting her freckled wrists on the table.

He could see her out of the corner of his eye, seeking his face, but he refused to give it to her. To be fair, she didn't protest when he moved out. She had wanted to spend time with him, ticking off her Bucket List together. He couldn't and wouldn't do it. She'd made a clinical assessment and concluded that she didn't want to see what came in old age, so sure was she that she wouldn't like the view. She couldn't bear to face it and yet she made him wonder endlessly if he was weak for passively letting his clock tick down to nought. Harry had railed against her rationale with abundant affection, and then tried bargaining. He'd finally resorted to anger, and when still she would not budge, he'd left.

Harry wasn't a fool. He could see how the prospect of catheters and sickly fortified drinks from a carton held limited appeal, but surely there was quality left. She went scuba diving for the first time in her life not a month ago, for God's sake, in the Seychelles of all places, and was still a graceful woman. Harry didn't relish disintegration either, but until that wet winter's day, he'd been confident they would weather it in companionable acceptance, perhaps even joke about it. *If you're happy in your nappy, clap your hands.*

"Have you had any further thoughts on the trip?" said Georgia, her voice rising at the end to a girlish tone.

Fatbergs congealed in the gravy around Harry's sad, rosy islets of lamb.

"Well, there's a return ticket reserved for you if you want it," she continued, "and Sharon is booked on the same homebound flight. I'll email the booking details. I made reservations at the Hotel Avalon for two nights, it looked decent enough. There's a heated pool."

Two nights, of which she'd be staying just the one.

Harry set his cutlery down.

Georgia studied him, her lips pursed. "Do you hate me?" she said, her tone less assured.

Harry rubbed his cheeks and heaved himself around in the seat to face her. Her skin was dewy, she was radiant, fish-tank blue. The beach holiday had suited her, softened her lines, and rounded her curves. She looked fresh, and different. He realised with a pang that she was strange to him. Her decision to side with the dead had given her a new lease of life. He wouldn't be on that plane to Zurich. He suspected she knew it too. It would come as no surprise when he didn't show up at the airport. Sharon could fend for herself.

"Do you?" she repeated. "Hate me?"

There it was, a flicker of fear. His wife, with the balls to sign herself up for a scheduled appointment to die, feared the judgement of the man she didn't care to get old with. She fidgeted with her pearls. Harry was so in love with her the day he bought them. He'd been sure they would delight her. Couldn't wait to present them to her. Georgia always had a fondness for pearls. She said she liked the way they were always cool to the touch, no matter how long they lay next to her skin.

Her lip trembled as she reached for his hand, but he furled his fingers around his knife. Only one of them would have to learn to live with the consequences of what left his mouth next. Harry looked at the mole on the offered inside of Georgia's wrist and sucked his teeth. He was gratified to see her afraid, asking instead of telling. He could ruin her last days, condemn her to replays of harsh words bitterly delivered. Either way she'd still be dead by Thursday.

The clownfish blew him a bubble, on the watery side of the glass. It had more in common with his wife than he did. There was only one way this could end.

About the Author:

Deirdre Barragry is an Irish writer, currently resident in Dublin. Having lived and worked in many different environments and communities both within Ireland and around the world, he remains endlessly curious about the things that make us different and the same.

GOFER ALL OR NOTHING
by Katrina Johnston

The speciality at the Hampton Grill is huge cheeseburgers with wedge-cut fries. I'm on the normal day shift now. Hooray! Lucky me. Compared to the night-time slogs, the dinner rush is not so daunting. It seems like sanity. Maybe it will always be like this – smooth sailing.

There are no more rowdies after the bar closes and spews out drunks. The tables tend to be neater during the day. The bathrooms too. There are less unpredictable messes and fewer fights. I suppose the day shift might be busier, but I don't mind. There are two negatives – the servers. They are bossy snits. It should be easier. But it's not.

We're the only restaurant for several acres of rural farmland. Locals, transients and truckers make up the majority of our customers.

Sarah and Sandra are the servers who claim to be identical twins. They don't look exactly alike to me. Sarah is slightly shorter. Sandra has a longer nose. Both of them think they're gifts from heaven. They do look similar, but that's as far as it goes.

I'm the flunky and the errand slave. I go for this, I go for that, and I go for whatever the cook, the servers or the management require. I clean up messes.

Today.... Sandra, and not the other one, was busy being royal. Both Sarah and Sandra treat me like a minion. They're only three years older; 24 to my 21.

Sandra bellowed: "Melanie! Don't forget to bring a case of coffee creamers."

I was heading past the the walk-in, going toward the kitchen, lugging a box of frozen burgers. I pretended not to hear. I began unloading and stacking the soup bowls. Sandra pounced again. "Where's the case of creamers?"

"Get it yourself, I said. But very quickly I spoke again. "No wait. I'll do it." I wanted to keep her mollified. I had good reasons. The manager had explained that I might score a portion of her tips.

That's Paul Tomlinson and he's okay. Much earlier, he had poked his inspector's nose into the kitchen and tsk tsked over the fryer. "The cooking oil is despicable," Tomlinson said, but no one paid attention. He ran his bony fingertips along the counter. "Degreaser needed here and everywhere. And by the way..." and he turned to me, "...Melanie," he said, "I am considering that all personnel should share gratuities."

"Really?"

"Yes, you're a valuable part of this team."

I grinned."Thanks," I said to him, as pleased as a turtle in the mud. I tried not to show real enthusiasm. If Sandra and Sarah understood that they'd eventually have to divvy up their tips with me, they'd probably be snottier than ever.

Then Tomlinson said: "Okay. I've decided. Twenty-five percent."

"That would be amazing," I said, and I started thinking that any percentage was better than a big fat zero.

So, Sarah and Sandra have to be extra congenial with our customers if I'm to get anything in the way of tips.

.The Hampton Grill is in the middle of the prairies. My parent's grow canola. I keep two goats at home. We have a mixed farm. I call our goat shed a barn, but it's really a pre-fab shack. We have three chickens. Used to have four chickens, but one of them was sacrificed last month. It was my birthday.

I'm seriously thinking about finding a way to consign this place to history. I can't even locate the town of Hampton on the tourist brochures. There's no action anywhere.

I'd like to bust right out and move to Southern California. I dream of beaches.

In California, I'd visit the art studios. I'd find some wealthy buyers for my charcoal drawings. I'd shop my portfolio around to the best galleries. Even if at first I couldn't get noticed, and I ended up going broke, I'd find my way to work it out. I could doodle for the tourists. I dream about it every day. I want to get away to taste my freedom.

I'd have myself a blast because a lot of creative people live in San Francisco and I want fame and the inspiration of other artsy types.

My job here is not rewarding. Creativity consists of strong profanity bounced around the kitchen. The twins like to swear. When the temperature goes up, the cursing goes up too.

I suppose they're pissed about the so-called deal of sharing tips, but that's the way the burger sizzles.

I hurried to the walk-in fridge to find a box of coffee creamers.

Today, it's just me, Sarah, Sandra, and the cook until 3:45 pm.

Sarah cornered me. "We need more ketchup." She was fiddling with the fryer's on-off switch.

A few seconds later, Sarah said: "Melanie, for pissy sake, clear the pathway." She jabbed my shoulder with her elbow. "Move. Tote the dishes back and run 'em through the sanitizer. The bins are overflowing."

I wanted to strike back: 'Don't tell me what or when.' I wanted to shove her out of my vicinity.

A rumour is swirling.

Holly Dewell is coming to Hampton. They say she might be staying overnight. I wonder if that's truth? She's my favourite country singer. I mean she's everything.

Tomlinson returned after the post lunch clean-up. He began by hovering at the grill and scribbling notes. Then he scraped a spatula of heavy grease and tsk tsked once again. "It's the most unusual circumstance, you might have heard the gossip," he said to me. "Holly Dewell is planning a pet intervention. Going to rescue Rialto in all his flabby glory before Ms. Wickstrum goes into a facility."

Everyone in Hampton knew about Ms. Wickstrum and her famous cat. My family is well acquainted. She's a neighbour, so I knew all this.

Ms Wickstrum isn't able to keep her trailer. She is going senile. She has to go into Rest Haven, but first she has to find a placement for the black and white tuxedo cat she calls Rialto. He's a super heavy beast. A picture of the cat and an accompanying descriptive story are featured in last year's Guinness Book of World Records for the heaviest living feline. Poor, dumb pile of flab. He's over 38 pounds. Rialto lies around like a puddle on the floor. He sprawls upon a cushion until Ms. Wickstrum remembers (if she does and if she is able) to haul him to his litter box. He doesn't go outdoors. As far as I understand, he doesn't move.

I was stunned. I tried to keep a serious expression on my face. My mind was whirling with excitement over the possibility of seeing my singing idol, Holly Dewell. I was supposed to be rinsing dishes.

It was crazy news to me that a famous singer was concerned about the plight of Ms. Wickstrum or her cat, but I knew a lot of social media stuff about Holly Dewell's career. I follow her online. She's the very best.

I realized I was going to see her; somehow here, no matter what it took.

I've got most of her CDs. Her lyrics express love and reality. She sings as if she knows everything about me. I don't share much of my feelings about being such a fan with the folks around here, but Holly's songs make me shiver. I crank up the volume. Sometimes I cry.

I'll go and find her.

I'll make it to the airport. I'll get her autograph. I'll discover what she's really like. But she'll only be in town for a brief stopover before she carries on to Vegas.

I don't connect with anyone here in Hampton and it's far too long ago that I had very many friends during high school. Most of them have moved.

This is the second most important aspiration for me. I mean.... More friends. My first goal, always and forever, is to find a way to make it as an artist. Painting and drawing and sketching have been my wisest and my dearest allies. But I could use more human contact in my life. Even I know that.

Tomlinson cornered the cook over by the fridge and they began discussing something in a very serious manner. I eavesdropped.

"Ms. Dewell is going to be an honoured guest," Tomlinson told the cook. "We're expected to provide for her. She doesn't care to stay at a hotel. Wants a private residence."

"So where's she's bunking-in?" The cook sneezed three times, "Camp grounds?"

"Hampton Chateau."

"That old mausoleum? The run-down place back of Drayton's?"

"Yes. One and the same. A room has been renovated. The amenities are connected."

"I suppose she might want a pool, a sauna, and a concierge?" the cook said.

"No, not all that. The private residence insures the singer might retain her anonymity. The rescue of the cat is supposed to come out as an exclusive and at a much later release to the press. After it's all done."

"She'll be wanting food. Is that right?"

"Sushi. "

"Sushi?" That stuff looks like bait. I don't do Japanese."

"Better learn. However.... Maybe.... I'll have to send an employee to the Ferntown mall. There's a seafood place. Yeah, right, give me steak and fries in any other circumstance. She wants sashimi, shrimp, tempura. Yeah that's what her representatives have specified. We should supply a good variety."

The cook shook out a ragged tea towel and drew it through his fingers. He flicked the cloth with a decisive whack that split the steamy air. "Don't do Japanese," he said again. "What kind of beverages does this lady wish to order?"

"Wine – Sireana – Cabernet and a vintage port. Something prior to 1958. No juice or soda. No desserts."

Tomlinson turned towards me. I flinched like I'd been stung. He wasn't smiling. "You willing to help me Melanie?" He was examining me from head to toe, and I felt like a suspect under criminal surveillance. "Into the office," the manager said, gesturing like I was a feather duster. I obeyed. I followed him.

Technically it's called the 'office' but the room is an alcove with a rickety table and a couple of chairs. After Tomlinson closed the door and we sat, it seemed he was about to announce an investment scheme. "Melanie," he said. "I want you to go and buy the wine and the port and the sushi for our guest." He pushed two twenty dollar bills across the table. The cash is for your initial expenditure. The rest.... ring it up on debit." He skidded a bank card at me. I caught it before it skittered to the floor. "Go to Ferntown."

"What? Mr. Tomlinson...." I said. "Sushi? Ferntown? You can't be serious?"

"See.... Like this. We don't prepare seafood at the diner. I don't know of anyone who serves up any kind sushi way out here."

"Uh huh?"

"You'll have to fetch the food. Take the bus. Go to the Japanese place. I think it's called Komaji's. I'm too swamped to drive south right now. Get a sampler. Make sure it's elegant... sashimi, tempura, shrimp, and perhaps another? California rolls? Bring the items back in the carry cooler. Keep the sushi packed in layers of ice and the cooler gel packs. It's gotta be ultra fresh."

"It sounds way too complicated," I said.

"It's not," Tomlinson said. "I have faith. Don't forget. Ms. Dewell's agent has ordered a bottle of port and a brand name too – the finest. It's called Graysons. Here, take my cell for all emergencies." He slid his phone over to me. "Don't forget the cooler."

I began to sweat. How was I supposed to go all the way into Ferntown on the mid-day bus and haul supplies back to Hampton before 2 pm on Friday? That was the time that Holly Dewell's flight was expected to arrive and I'd end up losing out. I'd probably get back at 4:20 pm and that was far too late. Even if I managed to complete the errand, I wondered if Holly Dewell would answer the door at the residence? Did she have an entourage of security personnel, a body guard – her own staff gofer? Would they welcome me if I came to visit?

Hey, I might be a hero? Maybe, I should go for it. I had to go for everything and take every single chance to get to meet her.

***

The bus was packed.

At the liquor store, they didn't have the wine. I

had to guess at other varieties. I found two bottles of Sauvignon and a Merlot and the Graysons. The cashier wouldn't ring the purchase until I excavated my ID. When I finally stepped outside, the taller bottles were clinking awkwardly against the shorter one. That load was packed in a less-than-helpful paper bag. The cooler was a nuisance. It is a rather large and squarish box. It's heavy even when it's empty. I hurried because I didn't like hanging around the liquor outlet. At Komaji's, I ordered the expensive choices. I was rushing. I was nervously heading back to the bus, intending to catch the 1:45, and trying to keep steady, balancing the cooler and the liquor. I had to hold on carefully.

A sky-blue Ford pick-up swung around the corner. It raked over the curb while I waited for the light. I stumbled back. The bag containing the bottles dragged itself from my right-hand clutch. The bottles hit cement, shattered, splashed my pant leg and the bottom of my jacket. Instantly, I smelled like a wino vagrant. The cooler box bashed against my shin.

I sent creative profanity towards the driver who had not slowed or stopped to check on me. I wouldn't cry. I couldn't. My curses went nowhere.

I trudged on. After a few minutes I waited on the sidewalk. I called Tomlinson. I told him where I was. I explained about the booze and about nearly getting killed.

"Go again, Melanie," he said. "Go and buy the liquor one more time. Come back as soon as you might." Then he laughed. I heard him sigh. "Go directly over to the Chateau. Do not pass Go, do not collect $200."

Was he trying to be easy-breezy by attempting his own brand of funny, or trying hard not to swear at me?

I did what was necessary, resenting all the while that I'd be so much later. I'd have to wait for the final bus departure. I wouldn't get back into Hampton until it was almost dark.

***

The smelly bus rolled over Hampton road at 5:27 pm and it curved around the jagged rocks along the newly paved thoroughfare – 5:32 pm. At the "Welcome to Hampton" sign – 5:44 pm.

Once I'd alighted from the bus, I checked. It was heading onto 5:48 pm. Outside the residence. I was gasping – 5:51 pm. I pushed the doorbell with my elbow.

I heard the yowling of a cat.

The fatso.

He was just beyond the door. And the famous Rialto was screeching high soprano. He is known for his flabbiness, not his voice. Apparently he is not a tenor nor an alto. He was sounding miserable, screeching like the Scottish bagpipes, discordant noise.

Holly Dewell opened the door. "Hello."

Except for the yodelling animal, she was alone. I twitched.

"Wow," I said feeling overwhelmed. "I expected a body guard, maybe an enormous dude with muscles or with dark glasses – a secret agent type."

She was very beautiful. Her teeth were white perfection. She was shorter than I'd expected, but she had such a friendly way of welcoming. She pulled me inside, her very own right hand guiding me. She had a brilliant manicure of peachy frosted elegance. She reached beyond me to close the outer door. I twitched again.

"I've sent my associate and my manager away," she said. "They've gone ahead. They're arranging a Vegas production."

I said nothing. She winked at me. Yes, she winked!

"This place is so darn deserted," she said. "It's weird. I crave my own company whenever I can arrange it, but this has been adventure. Well, I mean.... Creepy. There's a loss of privacy when everyone wants a piece of me. I'm alone in here except for this diva, singing pussy cat."

My knees felt like jelly. I held out the cooler and the bag. "Here's the food and drinks," I said. I stuttered.

The fat cat kept on yowling.

"Come all the way inside and shut that inside blinds," Holly said. "Thanks so much for bringing the supplies." She indicated a side table. With a sigh of relief, I placed my burdens on the table.

Rialto was just beyond the entrance way. He was in the living room area, but only just, like someone had dropped him there because he was too large to tote further. He was on the rug, screeching like a loud and annoying toddler, a lumpy puddle of fur having an ultimate tantrum.

Holly pointed a finger at the cat. "The reality of this animal rescue deal is driving me crazy," she said. "Please...." she went on, "Come on. Pull up a chair and sit in comfort. I'm all alone with this crazy squawker. What's your name?"

"I'm Melanie." I stammered. "Why do you have Ms. Wickstrum's fatso here? I mean, wouldn't someone else be more inclined to take charge of the logistics and his transport?"

"It was supposed to be a humanitarian gesture," Holly said. "A high-profile public stunt. A story. We've arranged to have the cat delivered here and then tomorrow the animal is to be shipped onwards to a rescue place in Nebraska. It's called Soft Landings. They adopt. They're sending an assistant in the morning. Someone will put him on a train, then a diet, make sure he has a responsible owner and a good life. My agency informs me that the elderly woman who has been keeping him is the same person who has fattened him up."

"Yeah," I said. "That's Ms. Wickstrum. A catastrophe."

Holly laughed.

And then I took a deep breath and continued talking, but way too jittery. "Ms. Wickstrum's sort of become a legend here. The cat is infamous."

"I understand," Holly said. "The squawker. Until tomorrow anyhow.... Acchhhh.... He won't stop this horrible mewling and it's so damn loud, and now he's squeaking too. That's a new sound. He sounds so.... pathetic. Can you hear the squeak?"

"Hungry." I said.

"You think?"

"Always."

"But, I gave him food, and more. Seven packages of Kitsy Munch. The packages were stockpiled for this exact purpose. I've got nothing in the fridge."

"Rialto would like other treats, something different than a dry cat food."

"Hey, an idea. You say you have a quantity of sushi?"

"Right?"

"Fish!"

"Sashimi – shrimp – others."

"Give it to Rialto. Maybe that will shut him up?"

We grabbed the cooler, snapped it open, tore away the wrappings and discarded the ice. Then we set the sushi down before his royal flabbiness on a flat sterling silver tray.

Rialto was laying supine, his face towards the ceiling, his paws curled over his expansive girth. He sniffed. He stopped crying. He had to work it out. First, he moved his torso tentatively and his stomach followed, squashing against itself in a sort of hideous orchestrated undulation of rolling over. He craned his neck, reached for the tray. He sniffed again. We laughed, but it really wasn't comical.

"So distressing," Holly said. "Pitiful."

And there was nothing beautiful to watch when Rialto began to consume. He ate like a hog; slurping, gorging. A long pink tongue wrapped around half his face as he struggled with his own dexterity of getting slices of food

from tray to mouth, greedily sucking and chugging down each morsel. We watched the vanishing. Piece-by-piece, California rolls and all. He ate until the tray was empty. Then Rialto closed his eyes and purred and fell into a fat cat doze.

I looked at Holly and she looked at me. "Peace," I said.

Holly rubbed her hands together. "Finally." She sighed. "I'm really praying that he sleeps right through the night. Except, we've got no dinner. I hope you'll stay with me and keep me company in case this guy vocalizes once again. He might ramp it up."

"Sure," I said. And we moved away from the cat and sat down on the big orange sofa chairs further back within the room.

Holly brushed a hand across her forehead. "Are you from this area? What do you like to do?" she said. "Are you into music? Sports?"

"I like *your* music," I said. And I felt overwhelmed. "I'm an artist," I said, feeling shy. "I do sketches. Sometimes, I do over-washes. And I also do some fill-ins using watercolours."

"That's really amazing stuff," she said. "I'd love to see your work, but I guess you don't have it on your person. And you've been so kind to bring the rescue. I'm sure starving," she said.

"I know a local restaurant. It's about ten blocks along the highway, just a few steps north."

"I'm not going out in public," Holly said. "I hope you understand. I tend to get mobbed. A side-effect of the biz. I've got fans. Too many sometimes. Could we phone and get something delivered?"

"Yeah," I said. "Do you like cheeseburgers?"

"Cheeseburgers?" She nodded. "Plenty. And french fries."

"Cool," I said. "I can use my bosses debit and his phone."

"I only eat the classy low-cal items," she said, "to reinforce a positive public image. Please don't tell my publicist, or my trainer. They worry about my image."

I called the Hampton Grill. We ordered enough take-out for two very hungry women and one obese yowler.

"And while we are waiting," Holly said, "Tell me more about your sketches and your paintings. Did you go to art school?"

***

After a while, we heard the doorbell.

Sandy and Sarah stood on the threshold.

"What do you want?" I said.

"We've come to say hello to Holly Dewell," Sarah said. "We've come to welcome her. We've got the food as per the takeout order."

I could smell the onions.

"Well, hand it over," I said. And I used my own imperious voice, trying for new confidence, like I was the chairperson of this particular celebrity encounter. "I'm in charge."

I really liked telling Sarah what to do.

Holly had ducked beyond the curtain in case the visitor was some sort of maniacal fan, or perhaps many fans who might have found her country hideaway. But when she realized it was only the food we'd ordered, Holly came to stand beside me. She reappeared and smiled briefly at each twin. I felt her presence near my shoulder blades.

Holly put a protective hand at the side of my upper arm. We faced the twins together, and said in unison: "Thanks." I took custody of the bag of food. I could really smell the burgers now.

Before I realized what was happening, Holly had reached over my head and pushed the door, effectively shutting away the anxious faces of the twins as if they were flunkies twice dismissed.

"Bye," Holly said. And the door swung closed.

They fell away from my sight. The last image I retained was one of Sarah and Sandy's mouths gaping.

"I'm ultra hungry," Holly said, and she grabbed the bag. "You were telling me.... What kind of scenes or visions do you dream up? How often do you draw? Do you use graphite sticks and pen and ink?"

***

We talked and we ate. Occasionally we checked on the sleeping fatso.

"Hey," Holly said, "Do you think I should have given those two girls some kind of tip? They're sisters, right?"

"Did they earn anything?" I said.

"I'll have to get my agent to add a generous bonus. Those girls probably depend upon their tips. My agent will send a gratuity over to the restaurant in a day or two. What's the name of the place?"

"The Hampton Grill," I said. "It's the only place along the highway."

"So, beside my tunes – what other kinds of music do you like?"

***

She was like a friend.

Holly told me about performing in Nashville and in Austin. She's been to England six or seven times. She's held major concerts in North America.

We talked until half past twelve. After that I checked my watch and it was 1:45 am. Additional minutes kept on skipping along. When I realized it was edging close to 2:00 am, and I had a lengthy walk to get myself home, I mucked about to find my jacket.

Rialto, the enormous, squishy, squashy brute, kept on sleeping like he was a little fish-aholic. If he planned on waking and singing opera, Holly had enough leftover cheeseburgers to satisfy a horse.

"This kitty cat is kind of sorrowful, Holly said, looking down at Rialto. "In a sprawly, lumpy and pitiful fur-ball way.... he is handsome. Well, I mean, he may be considered handsome, that is... if and when he's silent. I hope they take good care of him and feed him sensibly at the rescue place."

We both gazed down at Rialto until tears welled in Holly's grey-blue eyes. "Poor baby cakes," she said. "I swear he's snoring." Holly reached down and she stroked Rialto's head. "Listen."

Luckily, he did not reawaken. We held our breath and we listened. "Yep, that's snoring" Holly said. "Listen.... It's like a sweet and spiritual tune."

"Dreaming about sashimi."

Before I ventured outside, Holly said: "You've gotta come to California. Stay with me."

"You're not serious?"

"Oh yeah, I am. I think we'd have some amazing times. I mean, we are friends already. We'll go to Sausalito. I'll take you around to the art galleries. I've got many connections," she said. "I know a lot of folks who will open doors for you. You might be famous. Could you handle that?"

"I might go for it." I told her. And then she slipped a business card inside my pocket. "Here's my 411," she said. "Please call me. Do it very soon. Say you will! I'll arrange a meeting."

"Well sure."

She gave me a hug. "It's like we're long lost sisters. We could be.... We could be twins."

"I don't think so." I laughed.

"But we are both artists and we finish each others thoughts and we laugh. It's meant that we would meet this time, and share our good experience."

I went outside. I turned around and I waved, but shyly. I stepped into the night that was full of countless stars hanging over Hampton. Sequins on the clouds.

I started walking home, passing through the intersection. I took a shortcut around the jagged rocks along the boulevard, walking down the centre line. There was no sign of traffic and the wind was warm.

I could hardly see the moon, but it was shining all around me and I wasn't dreaming now. I was humming something from Holly Dewell's playlist. Something sweet and soulful. I couldn't recall the name of the song, but I knew the lyrics word for word for word and those words nearly make me cry.

(end)

About the Author:

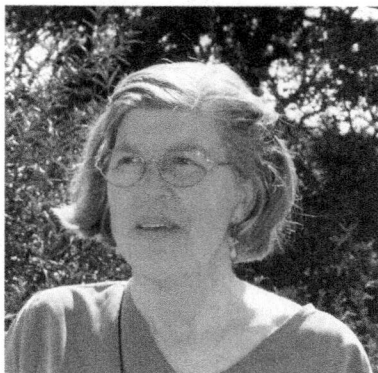

Katrina Johnston is a recent Pushcart Prize nominee. Her short stories appear at or on several online magazines. She lives in the beautiful environs of Victoria, BC, Canada. The goal of her writing is to explore and share with others whatever that she finds.

SORRY BETSY

by Mimi Karabulut

I take a seat, but this table is all wrong. It's too old for the room. The room has a modern feel to it, but the table is creaky and worn and chipping at its corners. I want to sit somewhere else. I want to protest the meeting. I want to tell them they haven't been trying hard enough, they need to do more, they need to fix her, but I stay quiet. It's not like I have the gumption to speak up anyway.

We have something important to discuss, they say, so I sit at the decrepit table and lay my head down.

White coats trickle into the room and swirl around the table in waves of pristinely bleached uniforms. I feel them bumping and nudging around one another, around the table. More arrive, and now too many doctors are in this minuscule room and they're crowded around me and this ancient table, a table that rocks as I breathe in and out. I hear it THUMP-THUMP, THUMP-THUMP, THUMP-THUMP, and I need to get out, get out of this room with all these people. More enter, and now the door is blocked. We're trapped in this room, and I don't know why there have to be so many people, I need to get out because I can't breathe and I'm stuck in this room with this rocking table.

I cover my face and breathe. I lean to my side. A stranger touches my shoulder, I shake her touch off. Since when is it polite for strangers to touch me? Since never.

I turn to raise my hand supposing that's the thing to do. The table THUMP-THUMPs and rests.

"Yes," the head doctor says.

"Can we try for a heart transplant?"

"In your mother's condition, it's inadvisable to operate."

The table THUMP-THUMPs.

"But you can do it, right?"

"We would have to wait for the heart. That could take months and it is likely the lack of oxygen to her brain affects her present functioning."

A doctor shifts his feet and nudges the table into my chest. The table relaxes with a THUMP-THUMP.

I perk up.

"There's got to be something we can do. She's only 58. What's Plan B? C? D? This is the best hospital in the state. You can bring her out of this. You said it yourself, you've been practicing for 22 years and you've never lost a patient."

The head doctor takes a deep breath and his eyes shift down.

"I'm graduating in the fall. You said you'd do everything to make sure she saw me walk."

He raises his eyes and says, "When you brought her to us on Saturday, we were cautiously optimistic that she would recover."

"And?"

"Let's have Betsy explain from here."

I know what this means. I shudder and force the table to THUMP-THUMP, THUMP-THUMP, THUMP-THUMP, and then yell, "No! All Betsy knows how to do is put her hand all up on my shoulder. She needs to learn some social boundaries."

I glare at Betsy who shyly smiles at me. What kind of social worker smiles at a girl waiting for her mother to wake up after four days? I smash my fists on the table and the head doctor's face pivots. I don't understand why his brows twist. I'm standing and rocking the table, THUMP-THUMP, THUMP-THUMP, THUMP-THUMP.

"We've done everything we can for her."

THUMP-THUMP, THUMP-THUMP.

"Pardon?" I say.

The table pauses.

"She would have needed a heart transplant a month ago to have a chance to live. Without life support, her heart can't function on its own."

"So then we get her another heart."

"The waiting list is too long. We can keep her on life support, but we have more pressing concerns," he says.

My anger pauses as I shirk into my seat. I grip the table for support.

"Your mother has been non-responsive to reflex tests."

Betsy touches my shoulder. I shake her hand off and grip the sides of table and begin rocking it back and forth, back and forth, until its rhythm knocks the ground for every breath I take. It's a THUMP-THUMP, THUMP-THUMP, THUMP-THUMP with a quickening pace and they glance at each other with those eyes I know mean nervous but I only want them to know that they need to do more to bring back my mom.

I close my eyes and rock the table again and again as I say, you need to bring her back, you need to do more. I repeat this again and look up at the somber white coats and whispers to nearby colleagues and solitary hands over their eyes. I don't want their pity. I want them to save my mom.

"Are you familiar with DNR?" the head doctor says.

I stop. The room is dead. I say the words they need to hear. I leave.

My little brother is crying on the floor, blocking the entrance to Mom's room. I go to touch his shoulder since that seems to be the thing to do now. I rub his back instead. I don't want to be another Betsy.

They gather us in her room. My mom will die soon. I'm not sure what to do. Do I stand and watch? Do I cry in the waiting room? Do I hold her hand? But her hand is swollen. The edema is severe, they cautioned me.

Our hands form a circle over her body as I'm reminded that my Aunt is Catholic. We watch my mother as the nurse narrates the oncoming heart attack, but I hear the table thumping faster and faster, desperately grasping for life and trying so hard to work, but it's going too fast. I need to calm its rhythm but our hands are locked and so I turn my head towards the room — and the nurse calls Mom's time of death. The THUMP-THUMPs quiet. The room is silent. The white coats are gone. The meeting is over. My mother is dead.

About the Author:

Mimi Karabulut is a writer in Chicago. She's appeared in 121words and is working on her first book.

MR. DARLING CONFRONTS A VISION

by Andrew Mitin

Mr. Darling

> James to his wife and father
> Jim to his friends and co-workers and
> Jimmy to his mother

was not a morbid man, or rather a morbid young man, since he is merely thirty-four years old and may have aged either somewhat or else significantly depending on how long this writing is delayed, in any number of ways, from reaching its audience and so Mr. Darling may very well be in his late thirties by now or even in his fifties, or else, God forbid

> both for his sake and
> the sake of his family

on his death bed, regardless of his present age, if not already many years interred, and so his brief forays into the realm of the macabre would surprise many people, most especially his mother, who has never yet tired of calling her son Jimmy

> never James or Jim
> at least at the time of this writing.

Mr. Darling is an affable man, smiling brightly whenever engaged in conversation. He always looks his interlocutor in the eye so that whoever is on the receiving end of his kind attention feels they are more witty and appealing, more erudite and charming than they are and this allows Mr. Darling to move through his life among people who are genuinely glad to see him, whether that be Rachel

> his wife, first thing in the morning or
> his co-workers throughout the day
> his father, when he was alive and
> his mother on special weekend days with

visits to

> extended family
>> at holidays
>> for weddings and funerals
>> which have begun to occur more fre-

quently than celebration days and

> Rachel again
> in the evening and at night.

James prepares his breakfast, which consists of coffee and a piece of fruit, usually a banana, and is lauded for this because Rachel doesn't care much for coffee, enjoying instead berries blended with Greek yogurt, a packet of instant oatmeal, some wheat germ and a dash of apple cider vinegar with the Mother to start her day. She enjoys even more the freedom to make this herself, as she sees fit, either with flavored oatmeal or plain, one or two dashes of the Mother, sometimes with blueberries and other times with raspberries, and, mostly on weekends but sometimes during the week, Rachel Darling blends

chocolate ice cream and
berries with
    roasted pecans or
    raw almonds

because she's been good all week and is getting her work done and James loves her and leaves her to her life while he pursues his own, in just the right ratio, so when the Darlings come together they find themselves renewed

each in the other
    every evening and
    again at night.

James was impressed and encouraged. He looked forward to driving to his parent's home where the day would progress in much the same way such days had always progressed, even after the addition of Rachel. Hugs all around and the news of the week followed by the meal. They would take their seats then one another's hands and bow their heads. There was consistency in the home of Mr. Darling Sr.

benevolence was there and
expectations too

that James rarely fell short of because Mr. Darling Sr. knew men, having grown into one himself, and he knew what was in their hearts when he saw what they did and he knew James would also do what men do even as he instructed his son to do what was right. Then James would find a way to tell his father what he'd been reading. Mr. Darling, Sr. was given the latest news about Alfred Stieglitz or Diane Arbus

1864-1946 and
1923-1971 respectively

and the novels of Geoff Dyer and John Berger, both alive at the time of this writing, and his new-found fascination for the Minor Prophets, a fascination instilled by Mr. Darling, Sr., who was the first to show James that discussing one's reading habits was a legitimate form of conversation. After Mr. Darling, Sr. suffered his first heart attack James became cautious

around him. While James could reconcile the logic of heart attacks and could recall numerous instances of hearing about them, most frequently while seated in wooden pews on Sunday mornings, he could not reconcile the fact that his father could possibly be one of those whom the pastor beseeched from other such seated parishioners for prayer. Mr. Darling, Sr. became attracted to the Psalms. The Gospels gave him comfort and hope and though he danced through the rehabilitation process, a process his doctor's had become increasingly encouraged by, which greatly encouraged the family, Mr. Darling Sr. fell ill with pneumonia and

(Passed into the bosom of the Lord) said the minister
(Went to be with Jesus, whom he knew and Who knew him) said Mrs. Darling
(On to his next life) said his cousins and siblings and
(Away is to where and who cares exactly) said James who

was angry at having to reconcile his father's mortality and was tired of scratching at hope that he would somehow survive his life, which was feeling more and more like a death sentence, and lamenting the hours he could have spent with his father

at rehab appointments and
helping around his home and
in conversation at dinners and
in conversation on the road
(Doing any-fucking-thing any-fucking-where)

but that James had spent doing what he couldn't remember now, but had had something to do with

watching the Spartans and
reading books or
taking pictures
    that wouldn't turn out better than they had.

Jim is inquisitive and encouraging. He makes his rounds through greenhouse sections every day so that when he approaches no one is surprised or too much elated because they expect it, the same way they expect their paychecks

once a month
on the last working day of the month,

when some will meet up for a cocktail at

Reno's East or North
    never West
or Crunchy's
    sometimes the Peanut Barrel
or else Dagwood's

because it isn't on campus but is so very close to campus and Jim will laugh easily and even get in a line or two that will genuinely cause some in the party to remark to themselves that

I had a good time and
    after all
there are worse places to work.

Jimmy is deferential and dotes upon her. He is conscious of her proximity and never fails to be within earshot if she suddenly needs something or has suddenly remembered an interesting anecdote from her daily routine, when she'd asked for sliced ham when what she really wanted was smoked turnkey, but didn't feel strong enough to admit her mistake aloud and in front of casual acquaintances who were waiting their turn in the deli, or when she'd happened upon Jimmy's old bus driver in the parking lot of Tom's Foods and he'd asked after him, not because he remembered the diminutive boy amongst the hundreds of boys during the years Jimmy rode the bus or the thousands of boys composing every year he'd driven for the district, but because Jimmy had been an acolyte in the church where the Darling's attended and where the Sanders' had attended and it was good, Mr. Sanders believed, to ask after one's own, or when, as Jimmy is beginning to fear, his mother will suddenly stop fixing sandwiches or relaying her anecdote and seek him out with wide eyes in alarm and disbelief, hoping to relate one final anecdote about how

(Isn't it funny
a thing that's never happened
to me
is suddenly happening
now)

before falling into the kitchen counter and collapsing onto the linoleum. This thought and thoughts very much in keeping with this thought are beginning to assail Mr. Darling at all hours and in varied manifestations, regardless if he is

Jimmy
Jim or
James and

he is feeling increasingly anxious about it. Perhaps it is the fault of all the funerals of late he wonders and believes to be the case, hoping this belief will cause the hallucinations to leave him in peace. However, eight months after his own father's funeral, and after two similar services that saw members of his wife's extended family so interred, the visions have not only not abated but have ramped up to such an incredible degree that Mr. Darling

believes he is going crazy.

The visions began innocently enough and were separated by long swaths of time to make them seem like mere aberrations rather than an opening salvo, the first twinge of future labor pains or like a small cut

on the foot while swimming or
on the hand while picking berries

whose penetrating object was a mystery, but would later make the limb gangrenous. By suggesting these visions began innocently is not to say their subject matter is innocent, nor is the term meant to imply these first hallucinations are in some way contrary to the normal run of his daily thoughts, that they are born of some mysterious spirit, or are the result of foreign substances ingested against his will or without his knowledge. No, these early visions are simply the result of Mr. Darling functioning as a normal human being when decisions and actions from his past rear their unflattering heads in the present and remind him of his old self in the hopes that the future Mr. Darling will be better for it. In effect, Mr. Darling's conscience is beginning to affect recall. His earliest memory of having acted in a way that now seems unthinkable to him occurred when he was fourteen. Jim had recently made out with his girlfriend, a prolonged affair that excited and terrified him to such an extent that he didn't move, but remained where he was, doing what he was doing, without so much as moving any further muscles

    either in his neck or
    the muscles in his hands

to change their positions on the young girl's hips or move them off her hips to some other more titillating locale. He was as though caught in a searchlight and any movement would lead to his capture or else, should he advance any further, the spell would be broken and the young girl would realize it was getting late and that she was afraid of being pressed too much against

    the town's feed silos
    those same silos

climbed by a fellow townsperson later that evening or else early the next morning where he hesitated upon the small metal grate that acted as a kind of landing to consider the light of distant stars now dead before plummeting off

    feet first
    into
    a pool of unrecognizable mush

only feet away from where the young couple was being inducted into the amorous affairs of men and women. But it wasn't the first thrill of sexual adventure that had stricken Mr. Darling's conscience with shame, nor was it the fact that a man had taken his own life, and in such a horrific manner, leaving it to an elderly couple, who enjoyed waking early with tea and walking the breadth of the town Mr. Darling had grown up in, to find the pulpy remains of

the hopeless jumper so close to where Jim and Esther had been that now Mr. Darling

    subconsciously equates
    sex with death and has
       ever since
    been wary of the one and
    ambivalent of the other

then more obsessive about the other. No, it was the memory of the evening a few days after the authorities had identified the jumper and released Daniel Harwith's name to the public, mentioning only that his body had been found early in the morning by Mr. and Mrs. Schouland and omitting the fact that Mrs. Schouland had thrown up upon hearing her husband first gasp then shriek at the gruesome discovery of

    Mr. Harwith's ankle bones
    swaddling his ear lobes.

Jim had, for motives that to this day are confused because misremembered, knocked on his parent's bedroom door and confessed to having kissed his girlfriend. Mr. Darling, Sr. waited for him to continue and his mother said

(Oh Jimmy, she's such a nice girl) and

Jimmy wasn't sure if this was a delighted phrase, encouraging him to continue with her or if he'd done something wrong by kissing the nice girl and because of his

    Desires
       that were just beginning to announce
themselves
       and instincts
       that would make a mess of things until
developed
she had become something other than a nice girl
       and so

Mr. Darling performs his rounds every morning and is being reminded of past actions that strike him now with repugnance at himself and at the world whose furrow he's found himself within. He enjoys the emptiness of the greenhouses at this early hour before the parking lot is filled and before the plant's unrelenting demands for water compel researchers and their graduates, undergraduates and technicians to fill the hallways with duties of their own and requests for Mr. Darling to find more pots or look at faulty irrigation systems, or else determine why a pesticide application has done nothing to eradicate the pest problem after twenty-four hours and after the economic threshold had been passed a week earlier, a term mostly used in industry where such things as economics are the driving factor in maintaining healthy plants and not in academia where plant material is grown, not for profit, but for genomes or to test certain chemical reactions upon their delicate foliage and root systems. Before all of this becomes the minutia that make up Mr. Darling's day he has these moments walking the somber hallways, reflecting on yesterday's job performance and anticipating the coming day's. It is within these

> quiet reflections
> unguarded

that Mr. Darling looks out a clear pane of glass to see grass freshly mown

> stretching toward the light
> of a warm spring sun and

suffers a wave of chilled panic at the quick memory of knocking on his parent's bedroom door, a decision

> (No, no)

that led him to break up with his first girlfriend because, he had said, he had a dream about a brunette. Jim felt this had been God-sent

> a sign
> an omen
> a portent of catastrophe

that proved His displeasure at his having been with Esther, but Jim couldn't confess this last proof, not having discovered this as a possibility to extricate himself from relationships until he decided to forgo sexual intercourse

> choosing to abstain from the sexual expression of

> Affection
> desire and
> love until
> appropriately wed

explaining to Esther that his feelings for her did not warrant such physical expression because she was not his soul mate

(But it would be awesome to still be friends).

Mr. Darling comes to and the grass is green, the sky a brilliant blue. He laughs to himself about how seriously he took that momentary memory and goes about his day. He continues his days until four months later, when the football team is preparing to open their 7-6 season against UAB under a new coach, the school's fourth in eight years. Mr. Darling climbs into the peak of a greenhouse to replace a number of vent arms whose teeth, because they are made of aluminum and not steel, have worn down over time and will no longer catch in the gear boxes, rendering them useless in opening and closing the vent to insure optimal growing conditions. While drilling holes and securing brackets and fitting new metal arms into new metal gear boxes, he falls into the rhythm of work that does not require strict attention to what he is doing. His mind begins to wander. He thinks of his mother

> how she will fare after the death her husband
of Rachel
> who is slogging through an entry-level government job
of the coming semester
> when students will return and fill the campus with
> > heavy foot traffic
> > limited parking spaces
> > crowded bars and
> > varied reports on police blotters when

like the onset of a premonition, these meandering banalities cease mid-rumination and he sees himself as he is

> precarious

on a sixteen foot extension ladder
working over his head
    alone
then as he isn't, but might very well soon
be:
      slipping from his secure position
      foot maniacally seeking a stable landing
        he believes is there but
        had never actually been there
body weight shifting right while
his left hand releases the trellis support and
    he falls backwards
    continues to fall backwards
until his torso becomes parallel to the
benches
    loaded down with the green tufts of sugar
beats
    then past parallel
as his left shin is recruited to be the hinge, it
having suddenly been thrust into such an absurd position
    straining now
    snapping and
    (No, oh no!)

Mr. Darling is left dangling upside down and shrieking at the far end of the research facility. He drops the drill he's been working with and grips the sides of the ladder. He catches his breath. The climb down is slow. When both feet are safely on the ground he finds he can't stand, his legs are shaking too much, and he bends beside a bench, soaking his knee in irrigation run-off. The drill no longer functions, the bit has shattered. Other instances like this occur while he is at work, but none manifest such a physical reaction of his nervous system. Occasionally, while in

    budget meetings and
    meetings with his staff that

he isn't particularly interested in, which he leads but doesn't contribute much besides setting the week's agenda and listening to

    rudimentary complaints
      commiserating non-verbally
      in the way that seven years of marriage
has taught him

his leg will spasm as though startled awake or
his head will toss as if shaking off a pest or
    in exasperation of more requests for mon-
ey
      for student labor and supplies
      greater quantities of compensatory
time
        regardless of university policy's
strict limitations of such
      or else how incompetent certain depart-
ment's budgetary analysis is or
      how stupid a twenty year old has been
over the weekend
        resulting in a full-time staff member
having to interrupt a family dinner
      to do the job right, the result of
which is
        the conclusion being that work
time is deemed more valuable than
      family time
        which cannot possibly be the
case
        but of course it is and

in this instance the hallucination has less to do with his own bodily injury
    although these were occurring with more regularity as
    each succeeding scene builds upon the last
    gaining in coincidence of misadventure and horror

as though such scenes initially began a coping process that has become feeble to their task than with that of his loved ones. Particularly his mother, Mr. Darling's first beloved before Rachel Darling, who has wakened from her sound sleep on more than one occasion, the first time being six months ago, two months after the passing of Mr. Darling, Senior. At first she believes the shrieking occurs within her dream, but she isn't dreaming of anything particular that she remembers upon waking at which time she thinks the screams are coming from outside but the windows have been closed for weeks and the furnace is busily clicking on and off then she knows the shrieks are coming from the sleeping mass beside her. She is horrified and without any subtlety or finesse she shoves her husband's shoulder blade then pulls her lover's love handle at which point his right arm comes flying over his right shoulder, swinging above his wife's head

> missing it by inches or
> closer since

Mrs. Darling's eyes haven't adjusted to the dark and she can't be certain just how close she's come to being struck, and strikes the leafy iron work of the headboard, eliciting further shrieking of a more direct nature with an intensity and intentionality that was lacking in his prior shrieks. When Rachel asks him

> not then, but later that morning
>   when they have sat down together
> she with her smoothie and
> he with a left hand finger between the thin
pages of Malachi
>   his right had covered by an ice pack

Mr. Darling thinks

> (I know what I've been so terrified of
> being the proximity of my life to
> the closeness of death
> mere centimeters within my chest
> beating and beating until the beating
> stops
> And I can claw and I can scratch and
> I can pull my hair out and dig to the ribs
> the valves are a tyrant unto themselves)
but he says
> (I don't know what I dreamt)
and he says

(Perhaps I'd've remembered if I hadn't been wakened to searing pain in my hand)

which, truth be told, didn't hurt him as much as he let on but merely surprised him, a fact he wanted to cover up, first because he felt an injury would somehow warrant him a free pass when not discussing the subject of his nightmare and second because he heard the shriek he emoted and didn't know he'd been the one to cry out. When he realized this was the case, even in his groggy state, he felt he needed a

reason why it had come out so childish and feminine or

> if not these descriptors then
> one more in keeping with an antonym for
masculine surprise and

Mr. Darling did remember the dream. At least he remembers the subject if not the content:

> the terrible demise of Mrs. Darling, his
mother and

even if Mr. Darling does not remember the exact scenario in which he sees his mother's final instance as a living being, he can recall now

> quite clearly

the many more that will follow in the proceeding months

> stroke
> heart attack
> car accidents
>   in town and country and
>   upon mountain roads
>   at night
>   in snowstorms and rainstorms and
>   thick fog
> crashing into guard rails
> into on-coming traffic
> then through guard rails and

plummeting into deep ravines, the metal mass searing off hundreds of tree limbs as Mrs. Darling screams for Jimmy to help her

> for God to save her
> for her husband
>   (For God's sake!)
to help her

or else innocently sipping iced tea at a coffee house and being obliterated by a careening cement mixer, whose driver has had a

> stroke or a
> heart attack

or sipping that same iced tea and being shot in the head by a stray bullet or one intended for her from the gun of a deranged person or one in full possession of his mind, because it's never a woman who kills in this way, at least not that's reported nationally, and wanting to make a political or religious or socio-economic point as interpreted by media outlets both locally accessible to the heinous act and as far from it as an academic campus halfway around the world, this woman has lifted a handgun. But on this most recent early morning, Mr. Darling has not shrieked and so has not wakened his wife, who continues to sleep peacefully beneath the dark covers beside him. He is up, inexplicably, after only three hours of sleep. Though he feels refreshed and alert, surprising considering the early hour, he knows he will fall asleep again in a few minutes, but after lying awake for nearly an hour with no sign of sleep returning, Mr. Darling gets out of bed, quietly closes their bedroom door behind him, fills a glass with water and turns on the television. The sudden flash of blue light shocks his susceptible pupils, as though he has just looked directly into the sun and when he slowly acclimates to the pixel twitches

> by slowly turning his face
> away from the wall
>> slowly
> and toward the screen

Mr. Darling believes his eyes have still not adjusted and have, in fact, had their physical make-up altered in such a way that he sees his father standing before him. Mr. Darling rubs his eyes, believing the apparition to be merely a

> sun spot or
> the afterglow of the last
> television image yet

when he returns his gaze to the place where his father stands, what Mr. Darling believed was an after-image or a sun spot

> (Perhaps a remnant of shadow)

is once again the stature and bearing of Mr. Darling Sr. He is dressed in the television's blue light serenely admiring his son, whose breath catches, whose hand clutches the re-

mote and turns the screen to black. In the darkness now, spots of illumination precede his glances across the opaque living room. Mr. Darling thinks these spots are early symptoms of a tumor, that he's heard of these occurring and wonders if he is beginning to experience those symptoms that would necessitate a visit to the doctor's office and if such a visit would be preferable to that of visiting another sort of doctor, one who would ask Mr. Darling what he thinks these hallucinations mean and prescribe him a dose from some unnameable chemical combination that will cease his experiencing his dead father in the living room. When he thinks how the presence of either doctor will keep Rachel up nights and how she will mourn his pre-death with

> sorrow-filled looks and
> unpredictable kindnesses and
> probably anger
>> directed at him and
>> at their God and
>> at the world
>>> which
>>>> more than likely
>>> has something to do with
>>> the abnormal growth
>>>> thriving
>>>> in her beloved's
>>>> frontal cortex

he chastises himself for having such unmerciful thoughts and sees again the stature and bearing of his dead father. He appears more like a tree than Mr. Darling remembers, not that his father had once had flesh like rough bark or smooth or that his hair was coiffed in such a way as to denote a bird sanctuary, or even that his limbs were more limb-like than not; it is more that Mr. Darling can't exactly remember what his father looks like, only what he felt when

> he hugged him and
> what he smelled like when
>> he kissed his father's hair and
> what he sounded like when
>> his wife

Mr. Darling's mother
made him laugh and

this lack of detail in the stature and bearing of his father has joined with that image of a birch tree symbolic to Mr. Darling as an image of childhood that his brain frantically seeks for and decides upon when confronted with the apparition it can't rationalize. It is a misfire. But with the sudden lack of bright stimuli, the emotional distress experienced by Mr. Darling over the past six months and his immersion again into total darkness, his mind must be given some sympathy for continuing to inter- pret visual imagery in the absence of corre- sponding visual input. Mr. Darling

closes his eyes
then opens them and
his father remains. He moves his eyes in rapid succession
left-right
up-down
rolling and crossed yet

his father still stands, observing his son's be- havior with a wry grin, a feature of Mr. Darling Sr. who was often in a good mood and who

while suffering from
the shock and pain of

his first heart attack was still able to question the route his wife was taking to the hospital and to forget about his own mortality or else to spite it said

(The country miles are the straightest)

and these are the words Mr. Darling hears his father say to him in that moment of darkness and quiet. He stares at his father, who stares back wondering, quite reasonably, whether James has lost his mind by hoping such a tactic could possibly rid him of his presence. Mr. Darling reaches a terror pitch of panic at not being able to will this specter away and he shouts

(What then)

and his father reaches out to him

(What)

as the breeze proffers a tree's limb and

(No, oh no)

Mr. Darling leans forward in his recliner to bat away the vision's extension. He closes his eyes and flails but his ears are not stopped and he hears his father's voice

(There is nothing)

unmistakable and clear and Mr. Darling claps his ears and shrieks. Mr. Darling falls against the floor and Rachel is standing now in the hall- way

(There is nothing)
stunned and
watching from the doorway

not wanting to get too close to James' flailing arms or his writhing mass as he begins to lo- cate himself on the pre-dawn living room floor. When he calms and begins to breathe normal- ly, Rachel rushes toward him

falls beside him
petting his forehead
(Sweetie, there's nothing there) and
he grips her tiny hand
(I should) he says and
she endures while he crushes it and he says
(I should have) and
weeps.

ARMISTICE

by Halle J. Carter

Now that most everyone has gone, Lexa can hear what's going on in the tiny kitchen off of the living room. The TV is up loud enough that she has to strain to hear them, but she'd rather listen to SJ stroke her own ego than watch yet another episode of *House Hunters International*. She risks sliding her gaze down to Shay, who sits slumped beside her. Her shoulders are tense and her eyes are narrowed, focusing on the TV alone. She's been there all night, not even looking up when Morgan and the others showed up with liquor and gossip. Four days, maybe five, have passed since her breakup. She's done little more than sink lower into the cracked leather of the couch as the week crawled by.

SJ's voice rises over the drone of the HGTV host, sounding velvety and smooth after her overindulgence on their "special occasion" bottle of wine. She has a way of making everything a "special occasion", even if it's another slow Thursday night and they all have class in the morning. Morgan stands over there with her, swirling the tip of her brand-new acrylic nail in her gin and tonic and smiling at SJ the way she'd smile at someone young, someone who needs it. Lexa doesn't think SJ needs it, but maybe she's wrong. SJ laps it up, after all, basking in the attention and letting Morgan trace her fingers over the lines on her palm.

Shay keeps throwing a clouded glare their way

and cranking the volume on the TV up. Each time she does it, her grip on the remote grows tighter, her knuckles blanching to the bone. Lexa is concerned for her, and rightfully so. She looks ready to snap in half. But SJ, as usual, is only concerned about SJ. She's discussing *The Importance of Being Earnest,* using phrases no one can understand and stringing long, complex thoughts into hurried, enthusiastic sentences. Her chin is high in the air, her eyes are hooded slightly. She's pleased with herself. She always is.

Lexa opts for the lesser of two evils and diverts her attention onto the TV again, trying to tune SJ out. SJ's not even a Lit major; she's *English with a concentration in Film Studies* as she's so fond of announcing whenever she gets the chance. That's almost worse, since she tries to analyze every movie they watch. Even *Gran Torino*, which is Shay's breakup film for whatever reason. They've watched it at least five times over the course of the week, neither of them having the heart to tell Shay no when she suggests they watch it again. Lexa can probably recite the entire film by heart, and SJ can pinpoint where the score swells to show the change in the protagonist's motive. Or something like that. Lexa has grown used to letting SJ talk until she feels she's said her piece.

They aren't what they used to be. Something had changed when the three of them had moved in together last year. SJ drinks more, Shay glares and fumes over every slight disagreement, and Lexa tries to figure out where it all went wrong. But none of them change. None of them threaten to move out. They just exist and try to ignore the fact that they haven't laughed together in weeks, let alone eaten dinner around the communal table they once valued so highly.

Lexa rises to her feet, every muscle in her body aching to move, to get out of the dark haze that surrounds what she once would have called home. Three pairs of eyes turn to look at her, one cut into mean slits, one drunken and wide, and one glazed with self-important indifference.

"I'm…" Lexa fumbles for an excuse. "I'm going to walk down to the strip."

Shay turns back to the TV the moment the words leave her mouth. Morgan laughs a little bit, as if she can't believe Lexa is wasting her time. SJ is the only one who acknowledges that she had spoken at all.

"Knock yourself out, Lex." Her shoulders roll in one of her signature, slow shrugs.

She tugs on her jacket and sets off, the rickety metal stairs clanging with each step as she charges down to the street below. Their apartment is above a convenience store that considers SJ a valued customer for the amount of cheap wine and margarita mixers that she buys in a week. During the day, they can often hear the country music from the store's speakers drifting up to their living room. But now the store is closed and locked, the signs dim and the aisles illuminated only by the whitewashed glow of the streetlamp in front of it.

Lexa turns away and heads down the road to the corner where their street intersects with Beacon Street. The chain of bars that everyone calls "the strip" is located there, sandwiched between restaurants no one can afford and memorabilia shops no one goes in. Behind the tall, colonial buildings, the spire of the library bell tower scrapes against the void of the night

sky. Lexa often catches herself looking at it when the group goes out to the strip together, a painful reminder that she has an essay due next week or an exam coming up. It's not all drinks and gossip and taking to the streets at 1 AM for no reason at all, no matter how much she wants it to be.

Beacon Street is unusually quiet for a Thursday night which, normally, would form a hot pool of unease in the pit of her stomach. But tonight she's glad for the quiet, glad to be listening to cars rumbling past and old rock music wafting out from dive bars, mixing with the scent of beer and cigarettes. Anything's better than HGTV and SJ's voice. She flashes her ID at the bouncer, though she's not entirely sure which bar she's decided to go in. It ends up being the sports bar that's only popular during football season. The walls are wood-paneled and are shrouded in faded pennants and jerseys from players no one can remember. Black and white photos of the football team crowd the wall behind the bar. The bartender is one of the players, the linebacker from the 1968 championship team. It was an interesting story the first time Lexa heard it, but it lost its luster, like almost everything in the bar, the third time he'd tried to tell it over a commercial break.

He isn't the bartender tonight. Instead it's a dark-haired, broad-shouldered guy whose baby face doesn't meet the rest of his strong build. Lexa slides into one of the barstools and waits for him to speak first.

"Can I get you anything?" His voice is small and self-conscious, but strained with professionality.

"Just a Pacifico, if you have it," she says, not bothering to let her eyes wander to the case of cold beer bottles behind the bartender's spread legs.

"Is Corona okay?" He gestures down to the case, the glass silver with condensation and filled only with the cheap, tasteless beer for those already drunk, on their way to football games or house shows, not women drinking alone on a Thursday.

The feeling of his eyes on her, icy though his face is kind, and the thought of how she must look, alone in a bar only good for one season that has long past them by, casts a cold shadow over her chest, solidifying the growing irritation which had been waiting to overtake her all night.

"Yes, fine, whatever," she snaps, waving a hand dismissively at him.

He snaps open the bottle, the cap clattering on the counter separating them, and slides the beer over to her without looking up.

With his eyes still trained on the bartop, he says, "Just so you know, we were set to close in fifteen minutes before you waltzed in."

Lexa snaps her gaze up from fiddling with her wallet and tries to recreate his frigid stare from earlier. He still doesn't look up and that alone sets a cold, cruel fire ablaze in her chest. "Who cares?"

At that, he does look up and despite his huge build and somewhat rude demeanor, it's all too clear in his smooth features and young eyes that she had pushed too hard.

"It's four twenty-five for your Corona," he says finally in a polished, controlled voice. When they lock eyes on accident again, he dips his gaze first.

She hands him her debit card and mulls over the beer for a moment. When the iron taste of guilt creeps up the back of her throat, she swallows it with the foam of her beer. The bottle cap sits in the middle ground between her and the bartender, bent at the middle so the red print of the card is stretched thin. She pushes it around with one finger, her other hand smearing the condensation that's formed on the brown glass of the bottle. She replays the sound of her voice in her head, *who cares who cares who cares.* It doesn't sound like her, not the Lexa from last year that she had loved the best.

"Hey." She tries to channel the old sound of her voice. "How long have you worked here?"

He doesn't look up from wiping down an already clean glass. "Why?"

"I used to come here all the time with my friends," Lexa takes a swig of her beer and looks over the rim at him, trying to soften her eyes. "I feel like I would've remembered you."

"I doubt it." Despite his watery eyes and soft features, his voice takes on the same clinical coldness that's always at the surface of SJ's.

She narrows her eyes at him, sensing the same sharp, accusatory burn in his own eyes when he finally looks up from the glass.

"What makes you so sure?"

"Because I would've remembered *you.*" The grim line of his mouth quirks a bit at the edges, threatening to spread all the way into a smile if he would allow it. "I started two months ago."

"Oh."

"You wanted to know," he says. He studies her for a moment, but Lexa can't ascertain his intentions. "Not a regular anymore?"

The beer doesn't taste as good when she brings it to her lips again. After a long, bland swig, she says, "Not with my friends."

"Oh. That's too bad, I guess." He stands in front of her now, leaning forward on the bar top. His smile is polite and doesn't show his teeth.

When she speaks again, it doesn't sound like her. "It doesn't matter to me."

His face grows unreadable again, the youth of his features shrouded by mistrust and offense, so much that she can't take it. She pushes back from the countertop, the feet of the bar stool screeching in protest, and doesn't look him in the eye. Striding off toward the door, she feels his eyes burning on her back.

"Have a nice night," he calls. The worst part is that he sounds like he truly means it.

Beacon Street is just as dismal when she pushes past the bouncer and stands on the edge of the sidewalk, the toes of her Converse dangling over the drain. There's nowhere left for her to go but home, so she turns her back on the sports bar and sets off down the road. If she's lucky, they'll all already be in bed by the time she returns.

When Lexa emerges from her room the next morning, SJ is up and sitting at the kitchen table nursing a cup of coffee and squinting at the fine print on the side of an Advil bottle. She's never up this early, not if she doesn't have to be. Lexa skirts around the table on nimble, quiet feet, but SJ doesn't look up at her. When she finishes reading the label, she pops two of the pills and downs them with a swig of coffee. Her eyes are squinty and unfocused, but they hone in on Lexa as she moves around the small kitchen.

"Where'd you run off to last night?" The question isn't coming from a place of genuine interest. It sounds like she's circling her prey, trying to catch Lexa in an iron trap.

"I told you." She doesn't look up from slicing her apple. "I went to the strip."

"Must've been fun." SJ snorts into her coffee mug and offers Lexa a knowing smile.

"Mhm," Lexa moves to settle onto the couch with her back to SJ.

"Wait hold on," SJ's voice stops her as she moves out of the kitchen. "Sit down. I think we need to talk."

They haven't had a real conversation in a while now. Their words are all double-edged swords, each one delivering a decisive blow and serving as judge, jury, and executioner. What used to flow so easily comes in stuttering gasps, tinted with the desire to undermine each other, to force secrets to come into the light. Lexa can't remember the last time SJ was frank with her, or the last time that she wasn't spitting venom right back at her. But now she's extending an olive branch, her eyes soft and her voice lacking its usual fanfare.

Lexa accepts the peace offering and sits down across from her. "What's up?"

SJ leans forward, coffee forgotten, and steeples her fingers. "Obviously things have been a little...weird around here recently. There's a lot that we need to talk about, but right now I think we need to focus on Shay. The breakup really hit her hard."

"I'm surprised you noticed." She'd tried to bite it back, but the remark had slipped out all the same, borne of instinct. It cuts like glass against her tongue and she flushes as soon as it leaves her mouth.

"That's exactly what I'm talking about." SJ points one long finger at her. "Look, you're probably not my biggest fan right now. And honestly, I'm not yours either. But this is *Shay* we're talking about."

Lexa glances at the door to Shay's room, covered in pictures of the group altogether and birthday notes from a few weeks ago. There are gaps in the collage from where she took down pictures of her and Justin. She insisted a few times that their breakup wasn't permanent, but the pictures came down all the same. There's one of the three of them the day they moved into the apartment, arms tangled around each other and eyes eager and bright. Shay hardly ever looks like that anymore. None of them do.

"What happened to us, Sarah Jane?" Lexa presses on, despite SJ's strangled noise of protest over the use of her full name. "Remember how excited we were to move in together?"

"Nothing's ever as good as you think it's going to be." SJ takes on her most impressive voice, the one that she uses during debates in class. Then she stops, schools herself. "Maybe we're all better friends than roommates."

"Who says we can't be both, though? You were my first friend here."

SJ cocks an eyebrow at that, but it doesn't seem as challenging as it would have if she'd done it last night, or even five minutes ago. Right now she looks like Sarah Jane, not good enough and trying too hard, the girl Lexa met freshmen year. But it's gone the moment she shifts her features again, back to SJ and all her cool indifference.

"Yeah? You were mine too." SJ sighs. "Let's start with Shay. Then we'll figure everything else out."

Lexa looks down at the tabletop, tracing a finger over the cracks and stains from when they all used to sit around and talk for hours. "The lease for next year is coming out soon."

SJ tenses up, the muscles in her jaw hardening and her shoulders rising from their usual slouch. She reaches up under the curtain of her hair and twirls the cartilage piercing in her right ear, a nervous habit that Lexa hasn't seen her do since freshmen year.

"Well…" SJ drops her hand back down to the table and looks up from under her lashes at Lexa. "We'd better figure everything out before then."

She gets up from the table before Lexa can say another word and dumps the remnants of her lukewarm cup of coffee down the drain. Lexa hurries to her room while her back is turned and takes her time getting ready for class, brushing her hair even when it's smooth and soft and changing her shirt three or four times. She can feel SJ's presence in the living room even from here. Her stomach churns with the impossibility of it all, all the things left unsaid between them.

When she returns from her room, Shay is sitting out there as well. She's on the couch, her knees pulled up to her chest, and is altogether ignoring SJ at the table. SJ isn't sitting, instead standing with both hands on the back of her chair and staring at the back of Shay's head like she's trying to decode it. Lexa kicks the door of her room closed with her foot. It echoes through their tiny living room like a gunshot and SJ slides her eyes to meet Lexa's for guidance.

Clearing her throat, Lexa takes a seat on the couch beside Shay, the dried out leather feel-ing like snakeskin against her bare legs. Shay turns bored, burnt-out eyes on her and tilts her head to the side as if Lexa has offended her just by sitting down so close to her.

"So we were talking," Lexa begins, ignoring the way Shay's eyebrows shoot to her hairline when Lexa gestures between herself and SJ. "And we think we should all do something tonight. Just the three of us."

"Uh, yeah," SJ settles on the armrest on Shay's other side, effectively boxing her in. "Just like we used to."

Shay sighs and chews on her bottom lip. Finally she shrugs, "I guess we could watch…"

"No, we're not watching *Gran Torino*," SJ holds up one hand to silence her. She pinches the bridge of her nose and straightens her shoulders. When she speaks, her voice is steely and waspish. "Look, sitting around watching TV isn't going to help. You need to get out there and take your mind off of everything. You can trust us, you know? We're your friends and we want to help."

The claim sounds brittle, made false by the irritation that laces through her words. Shay picks up on this as easily as Lexa does and turns her lifeless gaze onto SJ.

"You're my *roommates*." That word has never sounded worse. "If you want to help, fine. You can start by not telling me what's best for me."

"We just thought…" SJ's almost begging.

"I don't care," Shay cuts her off. Lexa hears herself in those razor-sharp words. Then Shay pushes off the couch and retreats to her room in three quick strides.

Lexa sinks low into the couch, the leather still warm from where Shay was sitting. The implications of her words sit heavy in the air, straining the small space between Lexa and SJ. SJ throws herself onto the couch next to Lexa in what Lexa assumes is supposed to be companionable defeat. Shoving herself away, Lexa pushes her hands through her hair, the sting of

Shay's words throbbing even at the roots of her hair.

"Way to go, Jay." The old nickname burns on her tongue.

"Oh, please," SJ sits up a little straighter. "She's just being dramatic. She'll come around."

"You didn't have to talk to her like that." Lexa's voice rises and she almost hopes Shay can hear her. "You always go in guns blazing and you never think about how what you say could affect someone else."

SJ shoots her a reprimanding look. "You're being awfully self-righteous for someone who dips out of here any chance she gets."

Lexa doesn't have to look over at her to know that her nose is jutted into the air. Cold, dry anger pulses through her, so poignant it makes her head pound. "Yeah, because we're just one big happy family here, right?"

"That's not even what you want," SJ counters. Lexa skitters her eyes over to her but doesn't look at her directly. "You couldn't care less if we all moved out tomorrow."

"Maybe we should. Maybe you're right about us. Better friends than roommates, or whatever," Lexa waves her hand to dismiss this whole conversation and brings it up to rub the corners of her eyes. Her head still pounds and she vaguely registers she needs to be on campus for class soon.

When she braves another look at SJ, she expects her to glow, basking in Lexa's admission that she was right. But she looks drowned and washed out. SJ fixes a narrow, icy stare onto her and takes in a deep breath.

"I guess so." She rises from the couch and circles around to her room, not sparing Lexa another glance. "We only have to make it until the end of the month, right?"

"Right." The word sounds hollow and tastes sour. SJ disappears into her room without another word and Lexa wonders if the sting in her eyes will still be there when she returns from campus.

Her class isn't for another hour, but she sets off towards campus all the same, wandering aimlessly before ending up in the campus coffee shop. She spreads her Accounting notes on the table in front of her to give the pretense of productivity, but none of it remains in her mind long enough to matter.

Her phone buzzes against the table, sending little ripples through her untouched mug of tea. It's SJ's name that illuminates the screen. The message is on their roommate group chat. They usually only use it for notices now, but Lexa has never deleted it so their old inside jokes and ugly pictures still appear when she opens the message.

Going to the Red Hat tonight. You guys are welcome to join.

Lexa has to read it a few times to make sure she's processing it correctly. It isn't an apology, but it's the closest she'll ever get out of SJ. It's another olive branch, all she and Shay have to do is reach out and take it. For a moment, it feels like three months ago and Lexa turns back to her notes with a clearer mind.

SJ is alone at a table in the corner when Lexa steps into the bar, her eyes refocusing to adjust to the dim lighting and sharp smell of liquor. SJ's shoulders are hunched, as if she's trying to protect herself from the laughter and music that surrounds her. One hand clutches her screwdriver so tightly that Lexa can see the blanch in her knuckles from here. Her eyes are wide and her features are loose and open. With her free hand, she twists her cartilage piercing with two, red-nailed fingers. SJ doesn't worry, but Sarah Jane did.

Lexa moves toward the bar and orders a PBR, deciding to make her sweat a little bit longer and hoping that Shay will arrive before then. She still doesn't know what she wants to say to SJ. Last year they never ran out of things to say, jokes to make and gossip to swap, old stories from the days before they'd met, days that seemed far-off and unreal now that they *had* met. Lexa still feels that connection, that dull, persistent burn of fondness for her, buried underneath the unfamiliarity that now reigned in their apartment. She doesn't remember when they grew apart, just that one morning she had woken up and sat at the breakfast table and realized that there was nothing left for them to say. They had run in separate directions, Shay to Justin, SJ to bars and parties and Morgan, and Lexa to anywhere else. And somewhere along the line, when they all turned back to look at home and each other, they found that there was nothing left.

She casts another glance back at SJ. The soft, humming burn grows stronger in her chest, always there and waiting to return if only she had seen that they had wanted it to return, too. Just as she's about to turn back to the bar and order, SJ snaps her gaze to her and meets her eye. The hard worry in SJ's eyes melts away and she stands, her stride slow and relieved.

"Hey," SJ says. She tests out a full smile, flashing the pure white of her teeth, not the slow tugging of her closed lips that she usually wears around the house. "I wasn't sure if you would come."

"No Shay?"

The smile slips low and SJ doesn't recover it. Her eyes glaze over again, dark and hard, as if she's shut the steel door of a safe and locked it tight. But when Lexa looks her right in the eye, there's no anger there, only resignation and a tint of defeat that Lexa didn't know SJ could feel.

"No."

They both glance over at the door, as if the sheer force of their combined hope will materialize Shay at the door, walking towards them with open arms and the beautiful, sly smile that had once intimidated Lexa. The door remains closed. SJ slides onto the barstool next to Lexa and runs the tip of her finger around her glass, smudging the faint red line of her lipstick with each loop.

"Well," she sighs after a beat. "There's no reason why you and I can't have a drink together."

Something instinctual makes Lexa's heart close up with the same hardness that shielded SJ's eyes, the same feeling that had kept her eating breakfast in her room and at the library late at night just to avoid being home. But SJ's eyes have already started to warm again, so Lexa tries to dig deep for that same warmth, that old fondness that has always been waiting for her, until she can't go any further into herself.

Lexa raises her beer, her fingers forging paths through the silver condensation, "To you and I, then."

They clink glasses and over all the rambunctious laughter and choppy guitar music and loud, slurred voices, Lexa can only hear that soft, light ping. They drink in tandem, watching each other over the rims of their drinks. In the same moment, their eyes snap away again, toward the door. Each time it opens, Lexa's chest flares with the hope of salvation, the naive thought that it could all be how it was, that they can turn back time and forget what they've done to each other, what secret, cruel thoughts they've hoarded close to guarded hearts.

Lexa tries to hold onto the sound of her glass clinking with SJ's, the bright smile SJ had unfurled for her when they'd locked eyes across the bar. She tries to merge it with her old favorite memories, but it's all tainted with the same notion that they can't go back, can't erase the long stretches of silence, the nasty text messages and handwritten notes taped to the fridge or the dishwasher.

It's SJ who finishes her drink first, pushing the empty glass away from her with practiced flourish. Lexa feels SJ's eyes on her and against the initial reaction to snap her gaze in the other direction, Lexa turns and looks back at her. For a long, exhausting moment, they search each other's faces, desperately trying to find anything to latch onto, an olive branch, a light to guide them home.

Lexa breaks first, returning her gaze to her half-finished beer. Out of the corner of her eye, she catches SJ deflating, proud shoulders slumping, bright eyes turned down to the grimy bar floor.

"Have a good night," she says in a small voice that couldn't possibly be the SJ from Thursday, grand and blustering and honey-tongued.

Lexa does not watch her walk away, does not look up from the scuffed bartop, does her best not to think about herself in relation to SJ or Morgan or the bartender or Shay sitting alone and miserable in her room, about the closed doors that will await her when she finally finishes her drink and walks away.

About the Author:

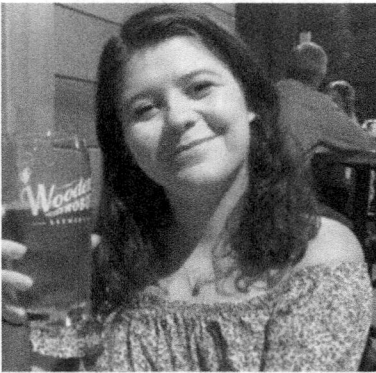

Halle Carter is a recent graduate of the Creative Writing Program at Appalachian State University in Boone, North Carolina. She currently teaches high school English in Charlotte, North Carolina. Her passions outside of writing are politics, food and wine, and film.

ON THE WAY TO FLORIDA

by Thomas Genevieve

Holly knew Keith would blast the air conditioning the entire trip, and he did. Smiling, she pulled the sweatshirt she brought in anticipation over her head. There was a certain comfort and satisfaction in knowing the other's tendencies.

The time read 12:10 when she tapped the passcode into her phone. They'd been on the road for a couple of hours already, which meant they were due for a stop.

She scrolled to check the messages and pictures still being posted from the party: a multi-celebratory jubilee that was in honor of Holly's completion of graduate school, the commencement of her and Keith's permanent empty nest, a belated fiftieth birthday she had asked no one to acknowledge the previous year, Courtney's graduation from college and her acceptance to, and start of, grad school, Nicholas's recent twenty-fourth birthday and the job offer that was moving him some thousand miles away from home, and, as Keith toasted after he imbibed what seemed like a case of Budweiser, in honor of him, "for putting up" with all of them.

The trip was to be a punctuation on a time in their lives. Holly didn't want to say goodbye to her kids at an airport. She thought it would be better for them to drive south together—drop Nicholas off in Atlanta and Courtney in Gainesville. This was their longest road trip since Courtney and Nicholas were kids—a trip that preceded much change in the following years.

After tomorrow morning's tears, Holly and Keith would leave their youngest behind and depart for Savannah and later Myrtle Beach. Though they laughed when Holly deemed it the "romantic leg of the trip," both were looking forward to it. The Spanish moss, the beach, the breaking of her cleanse.

As usual, due to Keith's indifference, Holly planned everything. The only input came while they were lying in bed, as he leaned over to look at her laptop.

"The Carolinas," he said.

"What about them?"

"We'll stop there on the way down."

"Which one?" she asked.

"Any of them."

Laid-back Keith just wanted sovereignty over the music in the car. Holly offered to put whatever he wanted on her old iPod—she didn't dare relinquish space on her phone—Keith preferred a CD wallet of his favorites, which in the dozen or so hours on the road, he had deejayed with predictability. She also knew he'd underpack the CDs, and she could eventually cite redundancy as an excuse to play her music off of her phone.

While scrolling through social media, she found herself missing life back home, but she then reminded herself no one was really around during the end of July anyway. For most of her friends, the middle of the summer was also set aside for family vacations or three-day weekends at the beach. Their hiatus from routine would end, though, by the close of summer, and after Labor Day everything would be back to normal. Until then, the running group was a bit small. A new recipe might not get shared or sampled. Book club was postponed until there was enough for a quorum. And if you wanted to do yoga, you had to go by yourself.

Holly, in partial repose, socked-feet on the dashboard of the Ford Explorer, had the urge to stretch her legs. She took another sip from her favorite tumbler to extinguish the hint of desire to break her cleanse—a cleanse she started following the party and planned to break once they were in Savannah. She tilted the mirror on the sun visor to meet Courtney's eyes.

"Hey, back there. How about giving your dear old mother some attention, since, you know, you're abandoning her soon?"

Courtney plucked out her earbuds. "Is someone a little cranky because she's hungry?" She emptied the crumbs from a bag of chips into her hand and ate them in playful defiance.

Holly stuck her tongue out at her daughter. "I'm actually not," she said. "I'm feeling pretty good and Savannah's not too far away."

"You haven't even dropped your daughter off yet, and you're already thinking about the rest of your vacation without her. Who should feel abandoned now?" Courtney said.

"Okay, okay. Put your earbuds back in," Holly said with a guilt-inducing inflection.

"Well, maybe I was just sick of hearing the Steve Miller Band again," Courtney said.

Keith responded in defense. "This is only the second time I've played them all trip."

Holly returned to her phone. She didn't want to think about the moment she would say goodbye to Courtney. Since Courtney did her undergrad in state, driving out to see her for dinner or bringing her home for the weekend was always an option. There were also breaks and summers when she knew Courtney would be around the house quite a bit. Holly understood distance and new commitments would not allow for that anymore.

How's that for quick? Holly's friend Kathy wrote in a text.

Jill's response chased it. *I know! I'm already thinking about what we're gonna do for her.*

Completely lost, Holly hoped she'd gain some insight from Instagram or Facebook. When the screen loaded, there was her answer.

Paige, the youngest and newest member of the group, who began working with them only in January, had posted a picture of a modest-sized engagement ring on a demure band of gold.

I didn't even know she was seeing anyone, Jill texted.

Holly inserted herself into the conversation. *Neither did I.*

There were several pictures of the ring at various angles. Below one of the pictures, someone she didn't know referenced the name Tim, prompting Holly to send another text.

Kathy, do we know anything about this Tim guy?

What? Lol. Kathy wrote, quickly following it with, *It's our Tim!*

Holly felt everything around her slow down and

then come to a standstill while she processed the news. After an indistinguishable lapse of time, Holly noticed a series of messages after Kathy's, *Did anyone see that coming?*

Most in the group chat thought it was obvious that something must have happened between Paige and Tim due to the way they acted around one another, but an engagement, considering they had all known Tim for such a long time, seemed shocking.

Holly typed, *This can't happen*, but then changed it to, *Are you sure it's Tim?*, before erasing that one as well. From a distance Holly thought she heard Keith's voice, causing her to pick her head up from the phone.

The car was stopped. All the cars around them were stopped.

Keith annunciated every word with an annoyed tone. "I said: Can you check your phone to see if there is an accident?"

#

It was 12:56 when she read Jill's text about throwing the party the week after Labor Day. Kathy, in turn, volunteered herself and Holly to handle the food. Under the pictures of Paige's ring, congratulations continued to stack.

Yes, Holly, too, might have briefly suspected something had happened after watching Tim and Paige at happy hour one Friday, but she thought it was merely a projection of her own insecurities. And even if something did happen, a relationship, let alone an engagement, should have been out of the question.

There was no reason for Paige to go for a man twelve years her senior. And Tim? He said he never wanted to remarry. He also said he didn't want to have kids, something Paige had expressed was missing from her life. She was also way more outgoing than the reticent and occasionally reclusive Tim and was very active on social media—which in the past Tim had scoffed at as "a huge turnoff."

Since Paige started working at County Medical Center, there was rarely a social event she didn't attend. "Let's invite Paige," Holly heard herself say, now regretful she initiated Paige's inclusion into the pack. Holly was just being nice. She remembered what it was like when she first started, a time of great turnover, when there seemed to be little to no camaraderie on the staff. Through years of reflection, Holly concluded her isolation was one of the main reasons she herself had slept with Tim.

In the middle of that thought, she was aware "slept with" was disingenuous. So would be the classification of those two months as an "affair." In just a few weeks of meeting Tim at his condo after work, sometimes even before, and on her days off under the guise of a long run, an addiction for daily contact had developed.

Keith's cluelessness became an obvious boon to the situation. Tim's arrival happened to come during the autumn, a time of year Holly had been conditioned to expect football, a ready-made distraction, to be on every night of the week. She said she needed to go in earlier or stay later. There were no other questions asked. What she initially justified as a growing distance between her and Keith—exacerbated by the influence of her new interests—she soon interpreted as love. Or, as Judy, her old therapist, said a few years later, "the theatrics of love," a conclusion Holly eventually accepted to be the case.

And it made sense, because as feelings whetted, the more ethereal they seemed. In a dream-like state, Holly viewed the experience outside of herself, as if playing the lead in one hell of a movie—a role that brought great catharsis to her life.

But rather quickly, the satisfaction from those moments with Tim waned, and once they dressed, she felt it was a tremendous injustice that they couldn't go out to dinner or spend the night together. She restrained her reveries and withheld her promises, waiting for Tim to be the effusive one before she requited. Over the course of those two months, their fictional life reified into an achievable reality—into the changes she'd thought she could make. The changes she felt cajoled to make.

Other than guilt, nothing at home enticed her to stay. As a middle schooler, Courtney became implacable, her whining insufferable. For Nicholas, high school made him distant and unpleasant to be around. And Keith was simply Keith.

"Unedifying" she'd imagine herself saying to a lawyer when asked the grounds for divorce. That she had changed, and he didn't. That change is good, but he didn't have it in him to do so. He teased her about the documentaries she watched, about the news sites she frequented, and about her newly-acquired preference for wine over beer. His prejudices were slight but still present. And although they agreed to be apolitical, she knew how he voted when the curtain closed. What she came to perceive as ridiculous masculine tropes were a non-negotiable reality, reinforced by her then circle of friends, the wives of Keith's friends.

"Mom, are you even listening to me?" Courtney said from the backseat.

Keith laughed.

"I love how you give me shit when I—"

"I was listening," Holly said. "You were talking about," she hesitated, "some guy Brianne hooked up with."

"That was like twenty minutes ago."

"She doesn't listen to me either, sweetie," Keith said.

In all honesty, Holly wanted to say, I don't give a shit about which one of your friends was sleeping with whom, or who was probably going to break up with whom because someone took a job far away.

Holly watched the heat rise off the cars in front of the Explorer. She grabbed at her sweatshirt as if she were going to remove it, but stopped. She knew Keith's subsequent quip: "Too hot now, Goldilocks?"

The wilted lemon wedge lying in an inch of water at the bottom of her tumbler reminded her of how badly she needed to pee.

"I don't want country hits of today," Keith said, responding to the disc jockey's promise with a familiar rejoinder she'd heard for years. He scanned the dial in search of a classic rock station. "There are no more hits today!"

Only haunting fragments remained from those dark autumn evenings. The take-out and leftovers. The stale dishes piled high in the sink and abandoned on the counter. The sounds of televisions from dimly lit rooms holding the only conversations between humans.

Once it ended, she hardly saw Tim at work. What they had attributed to fate, she now saw as circumstances aided by stratagems to purposefully align the stars. Regardless of who did the avoiding, in the years that followed she threw herself into her kids and her work. An influx of new people at the center brought new friendships that became the foundation of her current social life, which successfully distracted her from thinking about what once could have been. By the time Courtney finished high school, Holly went back to get her MS in nursing.

It took many sessions before she told Judy about Tim. Years had passed, so what could it hurt? Judy justified the relationship: Holly and Keith's loss of common interests, her first full-time job since the kids were born. Most of Judy's strategies proved effective, silencing Holly's self-reproach. A few sessions later, Holly admitted everything else.

That she told Tim she loved him. How Tim made her denounce her love for Keith as something belonging to an immature person she no longer was. And about the fantasies of Keith dying in a car crash and the liberation it would bring.

"Those were just thoughts," Judy said.

"But your wishes are who you really are," Holly said.

"No," Judy said. "That doesn't make any sense. I could wish I were a movie star, but that wouldn't change the fact that I am a therapist. Fantasies don't define who you are. I could daydream that I live in Hollywood and date Brad Pitt, but it doesn't mean I love my kids any less."

Who's not making sense now, Holly wanted to say.

What she never told Judy was about the fantasy of all three of them dying in a car crash. She never told her how every night as she lie awake next to Keith, she enumerated everything she needed to pack to get by for a week or two, mentally rehearsing like her departure was an evacuation that needed to be practiced. Between patients at work she outlined the letter she'd leave behind. She was ashamed to tell Judy, but she had decided to not only leave Keith, but the kids as well. Not forever. Just until she got settled.

Holly was never certain where Tim's concerns about the kids came from. Or his comments about how fast the relationship had accelerated. She never learned if these sudden apprehensions, which seemed more like objections, were covering for other fears like her age and their constant proximity each day at work, or, the inevitable relationship he would have with her kids. As far as Holly was concerned, it didn't matter; she committed the sin without reaping any of the pleasure.

She looked over at Keith, hoping he couldn't hear her thoughts. He was busy flipping through the CD wallet, perhaps thinking he'd discover another CD hidden behind one he had already played.

Several New Year's Eves ago, after an evening of drinking and under the weight of her burden, Holly thought she might have confessed. The next day, though, while Holly feared the worst, nothing indicated that she had.

If it weren't so swamp-like outside, she would have opened the windows for some real air; maybe she'd step out and walk amongst the cars. Do anything but sit with her own thoughts.

"Is there something to eat in here," Holly asked.

"No," Keith said.

"Why wouldn't you pack some snacks?"

Keith smiled in satisfaction. "You told me not to."

Courtney leaned into the front seat and placed her phone where Holly had no choice but to see an exploded oil tanker.

"Here's the reason we haven't moved in forever."

#

Wearing a blue hibiscus sundress she never owned, Holly stood holding Courtney's diploma, while Courtney went to take a picture with one of her friends. Next to Holly, in a checkered shirt and striped tie, his suit jacket slung over his shoulder due to the hot May afternoon, was Tim. It was obvious Keith felt awkward, so Tim being Tim, excused himself to get the car. Faded oil drops stained Keith's knit polo shirt below the buttons, the same shirt she remembered from years ago when she told him to throw it out. To preempt awkward pleasantries, Holly looked him up and down and feigned her most convincing look.

"You look fantastic. You haven't changed a bit."

Holly glanced at her phone and estimated she lost over a half hour contemplating a life she had not lived. Nine text messages waited for her, but she was not interested in checking them. At some point, she needed to text Paige. But more importantly, she still had to pee. She resented the tumbler she now squeezed between her legs, the pressure from her bladder irritating her even more since Keith put in AC/DC's *Back in Black*. Holly was convinced "You Shook Me All Night Long" was an anthem for imbeciles.

Keith must have turned down the air, causing her to unconsciously pull off her sweatshirt.

"Can you change this?"

"Hey, I thought I was the DJ, Goldilocks." He had his smart-ass smile on his face again.

The realities of the engagement worsened with the inevitable—the engagement party, Paige's excitement leading up to the wedding that Holly would most certainly be invited to, the pictures of the honeymoon. And then there'd be Paige's pregnancy. She was already 35, Tim already 47. There was no way Tim talked her out of children. If Paige posted a picture of a rum cake that fell apart, Holly couldn't fathom how many of the baby's firsts would wind up on Instagram.

There was also the issue of whether Tim would tell Paige about the two of them. There was also the possibility that he had already told her. Though gossip didn't seem to be Paige's thing, if word got out, everyone would think Holly was a big whore. At the very least, Tim's confession would also prompt Paige to ask the obvious questions, and although Holly knew she was the best lover Tim ever had, he was never going to admit that to Paige. He needed to neutralize any threat, no matter how distant the relationship, because of the work situation.

A threat. Holly scoffed at her initial notion. Paige had a fifteen year advantage on her. Fifteen!

How could a woman be more confident, more knowledgeable, and more certain of how to make herself happy than any other time in her life—all keys to any strong relationship—and yet her stock had gone down? Is this what Judy called the third act of life? Being forced to watch someone live the second act you should have lived?

She couldn't stay at CMC. A new job. It was the only solution. Her experience and the masters degree would make her marketable.

Yes, she'd leave the center. She didn't know what to tell everyone though. Could she lie and say she was offered more money? If she left and the word had had gotten out that she had

been with Tim, everyone would surely draw their own conclusions. The idea of starting over was also a horrifying prospect.

"You used to play this one all the time when we were little," Courtney said.

"You know I love *Darkness on the Edge of Town!*" Keith said.

"You're only playing this because Mom's about to cave on her cleanse."

Holly had slumped into her seat before the opening verse of "Badlands." She didn't think he'd pack that CD. Of course she was glad he didn't put on Kiss or Blue Oyster Cult, but of all times, she didn't want to hear this album right now.

Keith turned up the volume. "Come on Court, you know the words."

Holly peeled her phone from the case to clean the dust and crumbs. She wiped the screen with the sleeve of her sweatshirt. A claustrophobia that went beyond being trapped in the cabin of a motionless car closed in on her.

"This is the time of life when you know who you are," Judy said.

Holly fired back. "Or you just know your limitations and are too exhausted for the drama."

"No, a person is just better at acceptance at this stage of life."

"You mean surrender," Holly said.

"No. Acceptance."

Holly was annoyed at Judy's flat-shrink tone. "That's bullshit."

"Why do you think it's bullshit?"

"It's bullshit to think I come week after week and the only strategy you have for me is to ignore everything."

"No, it's not ignoring. You confront and move on."

"I don't take my car into the shop to have the mechanic say, 'You need to work on your acceptance and then move on.'"

"That's not a very accurate comparison," Judy said, still not changing her tone.

"Why not?"

Judy paused, giving Holly hope that she had stumped her. "Because life's more complicated than a car."

Holly tapped in her passcode and scrolled past the new messages to find the last one Paige had sent. Holly typed "Congrats!" and sent it. Holly then wrapped the phone in the sweatshirt and tucked it between her and the door.

The saxophone cut out and Keith started to mimic Springsteen's overwrought humming.

"I need to pee," Holly said.

"Go in the tumbler."

"I can't go in the tumbler."

Keith began to beat the steering wheel with the palm of his hand as the song prepared for its crescendo. He looked at Holly and said, "When you got to go, you got to go," before belting out more lines. "*I wanna find one face that ain't looking through me!*"

Courtney joined him.

"*I wanna find one place. I wanna spit in the face of these badlands—*"

Both sang with Springsteen-like inflection. Courtney used Holly's headrest for a percussion. The Ford Explorer shook as the two sang the coda.

Holly could bear the sun and make it to the shoulder. She'd get out and walk around the parked cars and cross the interstate, their muted joy fading with every step.

THE END

About the Author:

Thomas Genevieve is a teacher living in New Jersey. He has been writing fiction, with a specific focus on short stories, for about six years. His work appears or is forthcoming in Brilliant Flash Fiction, the Broadkill Review, Genre: Urban Arts, the Green Briar Review, and the Sierra Nevada Review, among others. When he is not writing, he maintains a steady diet of the cultural arts.

A PITSTOP ON THE ROAD TO REDEMPTION
by Mark Kaye

In the centre of the town square stood a fountain in the middle of which was a statue of a giant conch adorned with twisted ivy and grape vine. Water poured from the top of the conch to a basin of coloured tiles that depicted three figures sleeping on a hillside. Food and wine jugs were scattered across a table and over the grass. Under the conch an inscription read: *No place on earth compares to this/For sheer delightfulness and bliss.*

Roisin Daly passed the fountain without consideration, walking straight to the café situated at the far end of the square facing the beach and beyond that, the ocean. Sitting down in one of the wicker chairs she lit a cigarette and stared across the square, past the fountain and towards the palm trees that lined the shore. She daydreamed of rivers of oil, milk, honey and wine, pouring down from the mountains to the north and polluting the ocean with their luxury.

To her left an elderly man sat, in khaki shorts and a green button-down shirt, drinking a small beer. He turned to face her and smiled. 'The ocean is beautiful today isn't it?' She returned his smile and explaining that she did not speak Portuguese, apologised to him. Turning away, she began to count the palms. 'The ocean is very calm today, there is almost no wind.' He said again, this time in English. She looked over

the bay; the ocean was rough and turbulent and away from the beaches it beat against the cliffs. Momentarily mesmerised by the swill of the water that appeared to move violently and without direction, she forgot to respond to the old man. 'Well, how does it look to you?' 'We must be looking at different oceans, I'm afraid it looks very rough to me' Roisin responded. 'Yes, on this side of the bay the ocean is very rough, but I am looking at the other side of the bay where it is calm and beautiful. That is where I spend most of my time, I don't like the roughness here, I am only here today as an exception.'

'But', she said, 'this town is so wonderful, the square, the beach, the palm trees; it's beautiful.' 'Yes' came the response from the old man 'this place has palm trees, but it is not paradise, be careful not to be deluded by it. You should try the other side. There are no bars or places to drink there, but it is really beautiful and very peaceful.' At this he finished his beer and stood up and without crossing the square left up a cobbled side street towards the ancient quarter of the town. As he went he sang to himself *'without worry, work or care, the food is good, the drink flows free... it's true without a doubt, I swear, no earthly country could compare; under heaven no land but this, has such abundant joy and bliss.'*

Watching the old man saunter away, Roisin ordered another beer and a Jameson whisky. She stayed and drank until the sun began to set at which point she moved inside and took a seat at the long chrome bar. Inside the bar the staff themselves were as drunk as their customers, some bounced from the floor to the ceiling as they poured, without spilling their drinks, until their bodies became sore and tired and they retreated into the bathrooms to move powdered goods from their jean pockets to their noses.

Roisin looked around her, observing the staff and other patrons. The café was teeming with people, of all nationalities, in various states of inebriation. She considered their stories and the events that had brought them to that place. She was quickly made anxious by this and so started on the café itself. It was a large space but crowded with old furniture so that there was little standing room other than a corridor between the tables and chairs that led to the toilets. A small stage had been built in the left back corner at the end of the corridor between the tables and a small space was reserved for dancing. Despite the strength of the sun outside, little light penetrated the stained-glass windows. The long chrome bar was populated with draft beer taps and boxes of straws and napkins. The shelves on the back wall were filled with various spirits and snacks. Hanging on either side of the shelves, framing the bar space, were paintings of seascapes done in the Dutch style. The painting that hung on the left depicted a fishing boat struggling against a violent storm, white foaming waves beat against its sides, while the characters on the boat struggled with their nets. The one on the left showed calm waters and the sun shining through fluffy bubbles of cloud. Ships moved gently through the waters without leaving marks in the water. For a lack of wind the sailors were rowing, struggling against the weight of their ship and the density of the still waters.

Roisin turned her attention again to the people around her. She watched the patrons and the bar staff become twisted and ugly in their drunkenness. Then, looking into the mirror behind the bottles of whisky and gin, saw her own face, which was also now twisted and ugly. She tried to remember why she was there, in the place west of Spain, the place which was apparently not paradise. She thought about the hospital, the clinical white walls that stood proudly void of soul or character. Her last time there had been the third time in that same hospital in two years. She remembered her mother's voice whispering to her father, 'how can this keep happening to her again? Why is she not getting better? Something needs to change, something needs to be done. I cannot go through this again.' She remembered how the blood had dried along her wrists and hands, creating crusty streaks across her fingers. She thought about how it looked like tiger fur.

Looking at herself again in the mirror, then at the faces of pleasure on the patrons around her that poorly masked the anguish in their souls. She became disgusted with them and with herself. She finished her whisky and moved swiftly away from the café, across the square and down onto the beach where she sat and cried.

'It is as I said before, this place is not paradise. It is actually more like purgatory.' She looked at the old man who was sitting next to her again. He was not as old as she had first thought. He wore his thick black hair slicked backwards and a large dark beard that appeared singed and yellowed at the tips. He smiled through his teeth 'If you don't mind me asking, why are you here?' She considered the question for a moment. She had not intended discussing the matter with anyone. 'I have been unwell for a while now. I guess I was fed up of being sick, so I left to get away from it.' She said eventually. 'And did you?' The man asked. 'I thought so. I don't know. The place looked so beautiful at first and I was having a lot of fun, but now the ocean seems brutal and the people ugly.'

'You know what my mother used to tell me?' The man asked. 'No matter where you go, the only thing you will always have to take with you, is yourself. That is the one thing you can never get away from'. 'She sounds like a smart woman your mother' Roisin responded. 'I guess its maybe time I started thinking about that.' 'You should travel to the other side of the bay.' He told her. 'There it is better.' 'How do I get there?' she asked. 'Well, it isn't an easy journey, I know from experience. I suppose the first step is being prepared to make the effort to get there. As you saw today, many people here never work up the courage to try. They stay, in the purgatory of this town, and bury their pain in beer and one another's bodies'. 'Can you show me how I get to the other side? I am sick of this place.' He pointed to the end of the beach where the beach met the cliffs, towards a passage in the rock.

Roisin thanked him, got to her feet and walked towards the passage. When she came upon the cliff side she saw a large golden gate, guarded by two angels clad in bronze plated armour. One held a large key and a leather-bound volume, the other a large shield and a spear tipped with fire. Their wings, over which clung silken feathers of glorious white, quivered under a restrained power like that of V8 engines. Around her, people buried their heads in the sand, others chests of photos and objects from their past lives. Roisin, recognised the angels.

She had heard about them twice before, on the last two occasions she had tried to take her life. The first had been from a mental health practitioner, the second from her grandmother, who had suffered her own difficulties in her time. She knew that the angel on the left, holding the key and bound volume would test her knowledge. Did she understand her condition, did she know herself well enough? The second angel, holding the spear, would test her resilience and her determination to apply her understanding practically. She had been, for a considerable period of time no, avoiding both. In her very human way, she had been too afraid to leave the security blanket of depression that she had used to soften the impact of the world's hard edges. Emptying the contents of her pockets and purse into the sand, she moved forwards towards the angels. She had found it finally, that drive of the convalescent determined to free themselves from the shackles of illness.

About the Author:

Mark Anthony Kaye is twenty-seven, from Birmingham, UK and currently lives in Portugal where he works as a freelance political reporter. His work has appeared in Bellville Park Pages, Peeking Cat Poetry, Transition Magazine, 34th Parallel magazine and Five2One Magazine.

FEVER

by James Christon

1. Inside

The wood panelling denotes how old the world is around him. How history resides in the classrooms like bottomless pits found by scuba divers. Dan takes a deep breath and unwillingly ingests an obscene amount of wood dust. He takes a sip of water to keep himself from coughing.

His other classmates are all in the act of leaving the room. Dan is the only one to remain in his seat. He was unusually tired on this Monday afternoon, so he decided to sit a little bit longer to gather the energy to get out of his chair. Some people gave him nods, others exchanged chit chat, but it was all done quickly. Within a matter of minutes everyone but Dan had moved out of the room.

The last person out seemed to have forgotten about Dan as they turned off the light switch as they were walking through the doorway; their arm darting out underneath the closing door and slithering back away into the world beyond the door.

So Dan was bathed in the grey darkness of an empty classroom on a dull Monday. He wasn't too bothered by the darkness. It was still light enough for him to see the details of the room, but still lacking in enough light to give off the impression that the room had been shrouded by an obscuring haze.

Dan is putting his things in his backpack. His laptop must go in first so that it gives the rest of the contents a backing spine from which to build off of. His books and notebook go in as an organized pile—a stack turned turned degrees. He look around the room as he puts his stuff into his bag. He swings his bag around his shoulders and walks out of the room.

Outside the classroom the hallways are also empty. He thinks that he really must have taken a long time putting his stuff away for the room to get to its currently barren state. The wood panelling of the walls are polished a deep brown. The hallway smells dusty when there's no people milling around. His footsteps are the only sounds in the building it seems. Down at the end of the hallway, he can see the grey outside world. It looks like it could rain any second.

2. Outside

The doorway falls back from his view as the sky drapes the limits of his vision. There's a soft haze of light on the horizon, like a nightlight underneath a bed. Out across the street, Dan can see the streetlamps casting the dead trees as black outgrowths from the dark ground. The light is duly reflected by the asphalt and Dan can just barely make out that there is a street below the immensity of the sky.

And the sky is immense. The moon hangs as a single slip of a slightly lit nail. It provides no illumination except for the soft glow that surrounds it. The stars shine bright, but only the brightest shine above the mists of the city. The sky is dark and expands all around Dan's head. He can feel it rubbing against his recently ruffled hair. A cold breeze knots its way through the night and onto Dan's face. He clutches his coat closer to himself.

The leaves that remain on the ground are frozen, stiff, and brown. Dan notices the leaves as he stares at the street with wide eyes. He can still feel the roar pushing against him. The way the night roars in his ears with silence. There aren't even crickets outside anymore. Dan can't get himself to look up at the night sky for more than a few seconds, and has to pull away from the view as if it were too bright to look at.

3. Party

Dan arrives at the party and there are people smoking cigarettes outside. They stand on the porch. Their embers shed a little light across their tight lips. Dan watches them watch him. He wonders what high school they went to. He wonders if he smokes one tonight if he'll get cancer later tonight. If the strain of carcinogen that might be fatal to him is found resting in a cigarette resting in a box resting in one of those person's pockets. If it's waiting like some beast of prey just waiting to be disturbed. If these kids will snap at Dan if he asks them for a cigarette, or if they're already noticing him.

Dan is watching them for quite some time before one of them says "Hey man." in a friendly tone, aware of how out of it Dan is.

"Sorry." Dan's friend says as he usher Dan inside, "He's been smoking a lot tonight."

The group of smokers chuckle. The one that was talking before says "We've all been there before."

Dan, with his friend's hands on his shoulders, glances around the world outside the door into the party: It is dark outside. The streetlamps only cast so much light and the smokers' faces are covered in a smudging darkness. Dan thinks that if he knew these people beforehand, he might be able to distinguish them now in this dark haze.

His eyes find their way back to the door to the party that is constantly growing larger. He realizes after a second that it isn't the door growing bigger, just himself getting closer to the door. He can tell that the door is white and wooden. The doorknob is golden. Four vertical rectangles detail the door. The door that he is getting closer and closer to. . .

4. Break

Dan wakes up and the sky is grey in the window above his head. He's been home from college for two days now. He's been tired and jet lagged both days. The fatigue has seeped into his bones. He can barely get out of his bed in the morning, and he even begins to wonder if getting up is really even worth it. It's just a break after all. He will have to say goodbye again.

Last night he ended up at a friend's apartment. They talked about high school and reminisce about the times they used to share. It felt like a warm glow at first, but the further he drifts away from that night, the more Dan realizes that there isn't anything inherent separating his *then* from his *now*. It still rained back in those old days and it still rains now. So he tries to keep his mind occupied and stays up late playing video games and reading books instead.

He will get up from his bed and go through the next two days. But Dan will forget one day of this break. The day Dan will forget entirely for this break, almost as if someone had come in and snatched the memory from the holds of his brain, is the day he went and smoked pot with another friend. The weed was supposedly "next level" but it just seemed adequate to Dan. They smoked it out of a pipe in his friend's playroom, which was on the second floor of his house and overlooked the cold and narrow street that dead leaves fell into. This was a room that Dan spent entire nights in on weekends. This night, this night he will forget, he will end up sleeping on a couch that his body will find surprisingly familiar. The blue light of televisions backlit the smoke falling out of the window.

On this day that Dan would forget, Dan could feel the warmness creeping into his chest, and he could feel his head beginning to raise step by step as if it were on a tire-jack. Dan stares out the window for a long time. So long in fact, that his friend begins to ask him if he is alright. Dan keeps silently staring into the silent street. Dan's friend notices that Dan's face seems almost completely barren of emotion. It's as if someone had just woken him up and he was still trying to figure out what he was seeing.

Finally, Dan says something.

"I'm somewhere else" creeps out of his mouth like a thought creeping through his head. Dan's face changes. It looks as if he sees something he recognizes: a person perhaps. Dan is still looking into the street. Dan has a look of concentration on his face as if this person were trying to say something to him that he just couldn't quite make out. The friend doesn't think much of it other than it being a high thought and an odd sort of stoned concentration. The friend smokes some more.

Dan continues to look into the wet street. The past rains made the street so dark and so black that it almost looks like a wet mirror reflecting the night. He stares and stares and stares.

5. Party Lights

. . . and there are people there. And they're touching each other. And they might touch him. They might reach out with their hands that have touched other people and they might touch him. He might feel a hand brush up against him and he would freeze. And he would

know that he could hear that roar. A roar he had felt walking through the night and a roar he would hear again, later in the night.

He would hear it now. He would feel it coming on and he knew people would stop and look into his chest. They would move past his black coat and his dark blue shirt and they would see into his chest. He would hear it echo in his head and echo and roar until it was too late. And then they would look at him.

And then they would try to make him part of their ritual: they would reach out and grab his skin and plaster it to the walls of the party. They would make him feel ok here. Someone would reach out and touch his arm to make sure he's all there. He would never be able to leave. He would never know anything other than them again.

He didn't want their hands to reach out from the black and grab him. He wanted to rest in amber lights. He crowded around the measly strung up lights in the corner that gave off a light that seemed to shake and shiver. Like the light itself was sick. Dan's vision would begin to warble in that light as Dan began to shake and shiver.

///

"It's tearing me up man. It's like I'm here, but I'm not." Dan says later in the night, sitting on the cushioned couch. He thinks he has been talking for longer than he actually has.

The shadow does not look at Dan. He does not respond to Dan.

"I can feel it. It's tearing at my head!" His eyes are wide and reveal the white that surrounds the ghastly windows. "I can't feel anything else when it's there. I want to scream but I can't." Dan throws his hands over his head. He can feel his eyelids pressing into the corners of his eyes, where his eyes meet the chalices made of bone. His fingers are pushing against his head firmly. He is squeezing.

The couch no longer feels soft and comforting to Dan as it does restraining: he sinks into the foam, but the shape he impresses into the couch holds him into that spot. He tries to shift but only creates a continual sensation of sinking into the once-comforting foam. The shadow looks down at Dan's moving form.

Then, it says something:

"I had a nightmare once."

Dan does not look up from having his hands clutch his head.

The shadow continues:

"I was in a darkened room. It used to be lit, but something had caused the light to retreat from the room. I remember thinking that the light had fled. It had not been removed, it had ran away.

"But I was still in the room. I was looking around trying to let my eyes adjust when I realized that the room was more of a hallway than it was a room. But there were still desks and chairs piled around the sides of the room as if it were a classroom. I wasn't scared yet. It was cool to explore the darkened room: I felt familiar with the place. I felt like I was exploring it from a new angle.

"But then I must have walked too close to something for I felt a scratch upon my skin. It crossed over all of the boundaries that are on my skin. He cut through my clothes and went straight to my skin. It was on my stomach and it trailed upwards, slowly. It crossed over all the lines that were on my body.

"I walked away quickly from the scratch, but as soon as I moved my legs caught on something else and I felt another slow scratch against my calf. That was when I started to turn around to look for a door out of this room. I saw one behind me that had my attention. It was the only door that I could make out in any detail, it had one of those handles that's like an L pressed against the door.

"So I start walking towards the door to get away from the scratches, but each time I take a step, more things catch on my skin and begin

to scratch me. And then I realize they're getting deeper and slower. The thing that was scratching me was pressing harder into my skin, and drawing its limb more slowly across my flesh.

"I reached the door and flung it open. Inside, taking up the entire room, was a bed. It was dark. The room was lit by a single light that only served to bathe the rest of the room in a dense darkness except for a single band of light that fell upon the bed. The scratches were all over me now. They were tracing their nails across my forehead—circling my brain. That was when I flung myself down onto the bed. And I fell, and fell, and I fell until I noticed myself falling and jolted upright in my own bed at home.

"That was when I realized that my fingers were clutched to my body, the nails digging deep into my flesh. One of my hands was clutching my head with my palm on my nose. The other was clutching into the side of my abdomen. I couldn't move the hands for a little bit after I woke up: they were still in the dream. I had to wait a few agonizing seconds as the rest of my body woke up. During that time, I was conscious of how my fingers still seemed to move: how they circled my flesh with their nails."

The shadow gets up and leaves. Dan did not hear a word of what he had to say: his hands had found their way over his ears.

6. Daily routine.

Dan wakes up in a blue bed below gray skies. His window rests above him; the window a gaping, gasping mouth.

It is not that warm outside. He gets up and goes through his mourning routine.

He leaves. He drives to school; this drive is the happiest part of his day. The path is smooth and channels him to the world of school. He is still waking up during the drive.

At school, they stand in groups. They all turn to watch him walk up to the group. They are

Sophomores. They are standing outside their classroom, waiting to be forced into the rough plastic chairs. They are all awake; stimulated on something that isn't caffeine. Sometime that makes their eyes grow wide and warm, as if they were anticipating something in their future.

They are all talking, some of their heads do not move from their phones. They are not ignoring one another; there is no malice between them. But something inside is in the air. Something that sticks to the pale, off-white walls. The time winds down, and the bulk of them find their way to their rough plastic chairs that are blue. Some wait until the big hand on the clock forces them down.

In class, the talking continues. The talking happens constantly. So constantly that there is no silence. So constant that Dan barely has time to think about anything other than what the school forces him to do. Dan does not notice.

That day is a Friday. There is a football game that night, a home game. It seems that the entire school has been lifted up and placed on the freezing metal bleachers. They all watch. Some of them are quite good. The home-team wins. Touchdowns receive cheers. Not everyone is watching, but the presence of the game can not be escaped.

Dan has friends over that night. They play video games through the night. TV screens illuminate sleeping dogs.

They try to stay up the entire night, fixated on their games. The night surprises them and throws its cloak over their eyes one by one. Dan is the last one to fall asleep. He turns the volume on the tv down out of respect. It is him alone playing video games in a silent house in the middle of the night. The house is dark except for the blue-light of the tv screen. Outside it is dark.

The next day is one of rest. That night there are parties. Dan stays home and relaxes.

One party happens on a college campus not far from Dan. People have a good time; drinks are consumed and passions are inflamed. A girl with long blond hair and warm skin looks at herself in a bathroom mirror behind a locked door. The mirror is coated around the corners with sticky discolored spots. She stares at the messy sink and then at herself and then she cries. She cries and her cries cannot be heard outside of the bathroom because of the music playing outside. Her cries do not get past the glossed window. Outside of the window, the tears cannot be heard under the orange light of street lamps and the dying leaves drained of color. It is dark outside.

The next day is a Sunday, Dan spends it doing work.

He wakes up in a blue bed with a gray world around him. He wants to toss himself back into the pillow and let his bed absorb him with it's soft blankets. But he cannot toss himself back into sleep. He forces himself to get up and go through his routine. He sighs into the towel he wraps himself in after his shower. He listens to loud music on the ride to school and tell himself not to be so sad. He yells the lyrics to the songs.

At school, they stand in groups around desks. Their desks seem bare and grey like they sky. Their eyes are bright and tired. They listen and slouch when the teacher begins to talk. Dan raises his hand to respond to questions sometimes.

He wakes up in a blue bed against a grey sky. They watch him walk up with sad eyes. They stand in groups. Dan has thought about his conversation with his crush. He wants her. He watches her with concrete eyes. The walls are almost as grey as the clouds outside that block the sun.

At lunch, they escape from the the thing that sticks to the walls and eat food and make each other laugh. They drive in cars to places not too far away. Some girls go off and drive to a coffee place to get brightly-colored drinks, they yell out the lyrics to their music on the drive back. Others stay inside where the thing sticks to the wall and do their work.

Dan returns from lunch and feels the concrete walls wrap around him. The walls have no windows. His friends are there. Something else is there that he can not see. But it slowly seeps down his throat like the colorful drinks his crush is sipping.

Dan wakes up in a blue bed with his open backpack next to the bed. The sky is gray. He hugs his dogs before leaving. He finds himself on these drives to school. It is barely light out. The stand in groups and watch him walk towards them with their dulled eyes.

He talks to his crush. They joke about a tv show they both watch. Dan thinks about the tv show in class. He thinks of the girls on the show and then thinks of his crush. He looks at his crush with soft, defeated eyes. The thing that sticks to wall begins to whisper to him. It comes from some place behind his ears.

He wakes up in a blue bed. The sky is grey. They exit the school mindlessly once the bell rings. He drives away from the concrete. He cannot escape.

He wakes up in a blue bed. The sky is grey. They stand in groups; their eyes are hungry.

About the Author:

Jimmy Christon is a student at Vassar College where he studies English and Religion Studies. He was born in Pocatello, Idaho but was raised in Eugene, Oregon. He writes to explore his experiences of growing up, and how these experiences get to more universal realities imbedded in the American experience. Both of these pieces are just such explorations.

STAY

by Mariana Sabino

As I stood outside the house, a bottled-down stillness came over me. I caught a strong whiff of mold – sweetened somehow. Soon enough, the door swung open and out came my aunt in a silky red dress which sausaged her into shape.

The tint of that dress looked like blood that had been sitting there, coagulating. Before I could defend myself, I was impaled against those lumps of meat, soft and hot and flaccid. From inside the darkness that enveloped me, I heard a muffled, "Let me take a look at you!"

I felt my face yanked away from her breasts by her veiny hands as she did just that, she inspected my face, lifted up by the chin, then going for the cheek, pinched and shook it repeatedly, "Look at that, so adorable!"

There was no flow to her movements, they went from thing to thing in rapid jolts, breaking at random points. Like lightning, a new torrent of sentiment burst from her body and I received another clamoring round of kisses. Her tongue and mouth were soft and pliable like those of a dead fish. I closed my eyes for an instant, to swallow the nausea that rose with the murky cake I'd eaten earlier - it tasted of detergent and bugs - sending shivers up and around my whole body. I was also beginning to sweat profusely.

My aunt took out a crumpled handkerchief, flower-patterned over anemic pastels, and blew her nose – hard. When she was done, the bulb was livid and raw. In seeing the little wet beads on my face, she moved to bring that same cloth to it, but I caught her hand in time. She snickered at that, "Sorry, darling, I didn't realize." My aunt's house was a refuge where light didn't enter. Between heavy, ornate furniture gleamed the smiles of framed people, "important people," they said.

My mother just sat there, looking at the pictures, her eyes languishing in one detail or another, totally content and oblivious to the torment I was having to endure for her sake. The woman's breasts were deep, two full sacks one could sink a hand in and pull out a gift, a jack-in-the-box of horrors. In blowing her nose, yet again, those sacks puffed further outwards, their sides bobbing up against me. I thought of native Indian women who slung their breasts back and over their shoulder so they wouldn't get in the way.

I wanted to recommend the method to her. I then smelled garlic coming from the kitchen, garlic and something else, I didn't know what, and that bothered me, as the two mingled, the garlic and the unknown ingredient, which together joined forces against me. Those big, fat, liquid eyes of my aunt were fixed on me too, they were laughing. They were amused! "So cuuute, and shy..." she said.

"Don't touch me!" I heard myself say.

"Laura..." my mother chirped, warningly.

"Please don't touch me. Please," I implored.

Waving her hands up in the air with an " I give up" gesture, she went towards my mother, who now sat before the piano, ready to dazzle with one of her five numbers routine.

"Ah, leave her. She's tired," and as I'd predicted, the first notes of Liszt's Sonata in B minor invaded the room. It meshed with the garlic and the murky cake from earlier and my aunt's sacks which bounced in triumphant abandon as they spread on the couch, prostrate and ready to listen. My eyes sought for something to reassure me, to calm or at least distract me.

I felt a little dizzy by then. My aunt's breasts had done that, I wanted to scream "See what they've done to me!" I saw my face against the cupboard glass as the music, which I loved on certain days but not that day, conducted the room. I looked orange, ugly and greasy. The important people in the pictures grinned stupidly at me – every one of them.

Of course they did, they were friendly with my aunt. I had to leave this place! I had to go! I had to escape my murky doom! That it would be murky was certain, I had no doubt. The door, heavy, was not that hard to open. A tiny wave of wind and dust came in, lifting the curtains slightly, so I got out and thanks to the sonata, they didn't notice me. The music followed as if guiding my movements. But I still ran, I ran as fast as I could while gulping fresh batches of air, stopping just long enough to remove my slippers, and kept going towards the beach.

Behind me I envisioned that dust, the little that it was, breading my aunt thoroughly so that when she went into the kitchen, she'd be mistaken for an extra-extra large fillet and thrown into the skillet. Like bacon, she already came with the fat. At the hem of the beach, which

also reminded me of a skirt, I wiped my face off with the back of my hands. Finally! I sat with my feet skimming the water's surface, and cupped my hands to grab as much as I could from it.

I needed to extinguish the rest of what was left of that sickening aftertaste of my aunt's breasts and that warm saliva in the jar that was my mouth. Unable to contain myself, I vomited, my body away from the water, as all the repugnance resurged in me and from me. I could feel the wind bringing some of the vile bits up to my face as if to force me to register what I was doing. I opened my eyes. Below, the water looked strong and sure of itself. But its strength was just barely contained, one nudge away from an outpour.

My legs found their way to its cold, taut depths which pricked my body in a thousand points as I let myself in. It was then, and only then, that I began to feel better. I ducked my head in and swallowed a whole mouthful of salty, salty water. And in remembering I had been told not to do that, I did it again.

The murky taste was now effectively gone. The water was now calmly accepting me, and I aligned my eyes to its line, which was now and then furrowed by the wind. I saw the multicolored line clearly, clasping my gaze.

The sun slipped through the clouds and fell like electric gold. The water had no breasts; it had wings instead. And suddenly, I felt something blowing against me.

It was something intangible and certain coming from the water, from the water and from the taste of it on my tongue. I felt calm, strong in a way I hadn't been before. Ever, in fact.

I recalled what mother had said yesterday. That I was a strange, strange girl.

I brought my hands to the surface, and saw that the skin was now puckered – pruning, isn't that what they said? More like raisins, I corrected. With a little jump, I lay back on the water, letting it catch me and prop me up as I floated in place. I was still happy in that odd way. And it was then that it came to me and I understood that she was going to leave me to the ocean, to trust it to care for me. Officially, it would be that woman, that aunt, who would be doing it. But it was really the ocean.

Boundless. And it just might swallow me whole.

About the Author:

Mariana Sabino has been published in Rue Scribe, The Humanist, Seven Circle Press, Mediterranean Poetry, Up the Staircase Quarterly, Dogmatika, Culture Unplugged, and Taste of Cinema, among other publications. She has lived in many countries, imbuing her fiction with the atmosphere and experiences of navigating through different cultures.

THREAT OF RAIN

by Brian Stumbaugh

"Pass the scrubber?"

He slides her the yellow nylon scrubber, a soapy mesh lemon in his hands, slick in the luke warm water. Their fingers entwine for just a second, then disengage. He pivots his hips behind her and squeezes her with his upper arms, his hands covered in bubbles. "Thanks," she mutters, exposing her tanned neck as he nestles against her.

"Reminds me of Martha's Vineyard."

"Mmm," she smiles, scrubbing the non-stick skillet, pieces of chicken dropping into the sudsy mass.

"The hot tub?"

"The hot tub," she giggles, "was twenty years ago, Romeo."

"We should go now."

"It's May."

"Why not? I've got the time coming. You can get off. The kids are old enough to stay here." He pushes his hips against her. She giggles.

" I don't know."

"Why?" He pulls back a bit, but her head is still on his shoulder, her neck stretched in front of his stubbled jaw.

"Hey, guys, what's going on here?" Virginia slips into the kitchen, her green backpack hoisted on one shoulder. Tom retracts his hands and wipes them on his shouldered dish-towel. He notices her white mini skirt and snaps the towel at her exposed thigh, eliciting a squeal from his daughter.

"Don't you worry about that, Gigi. Married people still do this romantic stuff, too."

"Oh, brother," Tammy says, attacking the skillet with renewed vigor.

"It's OK, Mom," Virginia says, popping open a Coke and leaning against the doorjamb. "I know you and Daddy still, you know..."

"Virginia Katherine!" Tammy says, reddening, unable to suppress a frown as her daughter scurries out of the room. Once upstairs, her bedroom door shuts, and Tammy turns to face Tom. The "Jeopardy" theme plays from the television. She whispers, "I don't think it's a good time, that's all."

"Why?" he repeats. Tammy hushes him with a quick hiss and leads him back to the sink. Shielded from the living room, the glow of the television bouncing off of the crystal vase on the breakfast bar, she pulls him close.

"It's Gigi," she whispers.

"What about her? School? She has all her tests made up, right?"

"Yes, Tom."

" She's not skipping anymore?"

"No. It's something else."

"What?"

"Hey, Dad!" cries Chris, their son, from the living room, "Final Jeopardy."

"Lay it on me!" Tom cranes his head to hear his son, but his eyes are still locked onto his wife, who has turned back to the dishes.

"Quarterback who led the New York Giants to the 1955 Football World Championship? "

"Hang on." He glances again at his wife's hair as she scrubs at a dinner plate. His eyes roam down to her shorts and he smiles. "Got it C-Man: Charlie Connerly!"

"Cool!"

"Tammy, what are you talking about?"

She turns, wiping her hands on her denim shorts, looking into her husband's face. "Two things: First, Erika Thompson called me last week. She said on her mid-day bus run for the kindergartners she saw Gigi running up the hill from Main to McCullough."

"Midday? What was Gigi doing here?"

"She said that she had to run home to get her English paper. She said that Carrie Wilkes gave her a ride home."

"OK, so? The kid goofed, but she didn't get caught, right?"

"No, she didn't get caught, but..."

"But what?"

"I checked her room. It was a mess. There were muddy footprints up the hall, and her bed was a mess. It looked like someone tried to straighten it, but it was still messy. Jesus, Tom, she doesn't need to get caught to be guilty."

"Fine. Did you ask her?"

"Yes. She said she wasn't upstairs."

"Shit, Tammy. Did Erika see anyone with her that day?"

"No." She drains the sink. It makes a loud sucking noise that drowns out the Jeopardy theme music. She shakes her head.

"What's the matter, then?"

"I don't know. She's not telling me the whole story. I can feel it. You know I hate that."

Tom pauses and listens to Alix Trebeck belt out the answer to Final Jeopardy: Y.A. Tittle. Chris throws himself back in the armchair and shouts a sharp, "Dad!"

Tammy has started drying and stacking the dinner plates neatly in the cupboard. The silence sits between them like an ocean.

"Shit," he says, so low only she can hear it. He has, unbelievably, not seen this coming. "This isn't about Gigi, is it?"

She pauses and looks at him with a sidelong glance.

"Come on, Tammy, give me a break. Let it go."

"I don't want to do this, Tom."

"Sure. I don't, either. You were wrong, anyway. It never got that far.""

"Whatever you say, Tom." She pauses, looking out the window. "Your daughter claims she hasn't been lying, but I don't believe her."

"Did you believe me?"

"Of course I did. That's different."

"Really? How?"

"You're my husband, Tom. She's our eighteen-year-old daughter." And then she says, as an afterthought, as if it were obvious, "Teenagers lie."

"You want me to talk to her?"

"No," she says, finishing the drying and moving on to the next day's lunches. She is spreading peanut butter on neat rows of slices of wheat bread, her back turned to him.

"OK," he says, shaking his head and heading for the garage. He has to mow the lawn, which has become weedy. So much rain lately. He hopes that he can finish before the storm that has been threatening all day moves in. Behind him, kitchen noises blend with the "Wheel of Fortune" theme. Upstairs, unreachable, his daughter has turned on her stereo and block-aded herself. He is on the front porch thinking of hot tubs when he is pelted with thick drops of rain. Thunder rumbles like a distant warn-ing, driving him under the eaves and out of the rain. The storms had been bad lately, one after the other. At this rate, wonders if he'll ever be able to escape the rain.

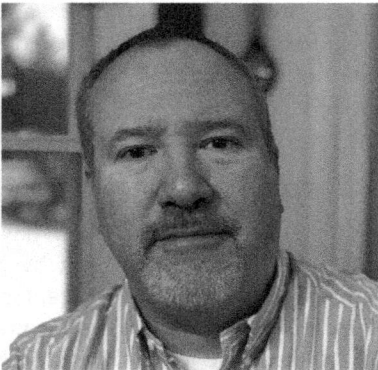

About the Author:

Brian Stumbaugh is a writer and English teach-er in upstate New York where he has lived, in various configurations, with his wife, four daughters, three dogs, and two cats. His work has appeared in Arbutus, the Square Table, Antithesis Common, Stirring: A Literary Collec-tion, Black Denim Lit, Flash Fiction magazine, and Dime Show Review.

THE RETURN OF THE TUNNEL RATS

by Michael S. Walker

It was in Great Vale Park that I last saw George Oliver.

He was a drummer. He had been the drummer in a punk band I had once played lead guitar for, wrote songs for. We were called The Tunnel Rats. I had come up with the name myself. It was the nickname for the volunteer infantrymen in Vietnam whose job it was to go down into the elaborate tunnel complexes dug out by the Viet Cong, kill any enemy soldiers hiding down there in those dirt mazes, and plant explosives to destroy the tunnels. What had always amazed me was that those kids routinely went down into those burrows, burrows that were booby-trapped to the hilt, armed with almost NOTHING. A 45-caliber pistol. A bayonet. A flashlight. That was it. To me it seemed almost like sending someone to the moon, clad in a T shirt and Bermuda shorts.

So I really admired them.

"Non Gratus Rodentum." That was their sullen motto.

Not.Worth.A.Rat.

I had felt that way my entire life…

I was in Great Vale Park on the last day that I saw George Oliver, for a three-day music fest they held there every year. It was called Tribe Quest.

My hippie Christmas really…

I guess that during the Civil War the park had been a staging area for Union troops going off to fight the Rebels. You would never have known, walking along its winding gravel paths, sheltered by oh so many flowering trees. In the very center of Great Vale there was a yellow gazebo. And a long, narrow concrete pond where Canadian geese swam and strutted.

And at the tail end of June, they held Tribe Quest there. A non-corporate music and arts festival. Like Woodstock on 37 acres. The yellow gazebo would be taken over then by banjoes and Stratocasters. The gravel walkways that wound through the park would become a gauntlet of white tents. People selling their tie-dyed shirts and spin art. Buddhists asking you to chant and sign petitions.

Black bean, corn and saffron rice tacos…

So there I was, on the second day of Tribe Quest, sitting on the hard, patchy ground in front of that yellow gazebo, listening to some prog-rock band that was really beginning to get on my nerves. (NOT my favorite music.) They were called Pearls Before Swine or something like that. Even had the initials PBS tattooed on their bass drum head. That might have struck me as funny, but their grandiose music was really boring into my skull. (Like an acoustical trephine.) They were a three-piece ensemble, and I guess that they fancied themselves to be the successors to Rush or something. Every song that they did was long, dull, intricate, and pretentious. There was one that they played, sweating up there in that yellow gazebo--I think it was called "The Flight of Daedalus and Icarus"—that seemed to last as long as an eternity in hell. All cadences and key changes and mathematics. I would have wandered off, went to see what the Canadian geese were up to in the concrete pond behind them, if it had not been for two essential things. 1) I was halfway into my third mug of Tribe Quest beer. (That was what the organizers actually made their money off of—selling plastic mugs of Molson and Rolling Rock to addled hippies.) And 2) About three feet to my right, a young brunette girl wearing ripped, tight blue jeans and absolutely nothing else was dancing to the monster noise of the Public Broadcasting System. I mean, ahem, Pearls Before Swine.

Did I say dancing? That wasn't really what she was doing. At all. It was almost as if she had been practicing some solitary tai-chi ritual in the park and, much to her irritation, Tribe Quest had happened while she was doing her movements. I watched her with intense fascination, pausing only to sip my acrid beer, as she very slowly and deliberately snaked her arms around, as if she were actually trying to sculpt the heavy, humid air. She would bend her knees and take a few troubled steps forward, then backwards. As if she were a half-naked astronaut testing the gravity of a planet thats mass was way more than our own. She had a yellow flower painted on one gaunt cheek, and her tiny breasts were painted also. A rough, purple peace sign encompassed one, and a blue tulip (or maybe it was a heart?) masked the other.

I watched her do this little "dance" for quite a while, fascinated, a tiny shiver of electricity

running up and down my spine each time her naked feet deigned to touch the dusty ground. I wondered what good Tribe Quest drugs she was on. I wondered how such a spirit could exist in the real world, away from the rarified air of Great Vale. Come Monday would those little breasts, that cheek, be showered clean? No flower? No peace sign? No heart? Would she don business-appropriate attire, climb into a Prius or something, and drive to some fiber-board cubicle in a downtown office? It seemed so unlikely.

Really, I probably could have sat there in front of that yellow gazebo, watching that brunette for an eternity, draining my plastic mug of beer. But in the middle of it all, with PBS still sending out their fugues of boredom, an old guy with a sandy goatee and an oil-smudged t-shirt that read "Vote For Pedro," sat down right next to me. He was very very drunk. Way drunker than me.

And THAT had to be pretty drunk...

He was armed with a plastic mug of the Tribe Quest beer, and he proceeded to water himself (and the ground) between sullen mutterings in some unknown language. He was sitting waaay too close to me. One gaunt naked knee in ripped blue jeans was almost touching my own knee. And to continue staring at my beautiful priestess of dance, I also had to meet his hillbilly face in profile.

Something told me it was time to move on. See for real what those geese were up to in that lily-pad covered pond. Stock up on one more Tribe Quest beer.

Maybe get one of those black bean, corn, and saffron rice tacos.

So I stood up, dusted my jeans and got ready to leave. Fare thee well to Drunk Goatee. Fare thee well to PBS, still hammering out their mythical, mathematical doldrums.

Fare thee well to my half-naked nymph, still sculpting the air with her bronze arms and hands...

That was when I felt someone tugging the leg of my jeans. Hard.

I looked down. It was Mr. Drunk Goatee, of course, staring up at me with unalloyed amazement, his blue eyes made much bluer by a deepening sunburn.

"You're HIM, ain't you?" he slurred.

I knew immediately what Mr. Goatee was on about, of course. A very very famous rock guitarist lived in our little city. He was originally from England but about five years ago (supposedly) he had met some girl from here. The daughter of a man who had bought into a small chain of sexy lingerie stores in the mid-60s and parlayed them into a billion-dollar enterprise. I guess the rock star liked our flat little town well enough. He and his bride (again, supposedly) kept a stone mansion on the west side of the city, close to the municipal zoo. At least that is what I had heard. I had never had it confirmed on the Interwebz, or actually seen this fabled mansion. Maybe it was all bullshit and the fabled guitarist was single and lived in an ivy-covered bungalow in the Outer Hebrides.

Anyway, people kept mistaking me for this famous shite. On the street. In bars. It was embarrassing, really. Every time, these would-be stalkers would get the same wondrous look on their faces. As if they were Archimedes and they had just solved the problem of the votive crown. I would have to actually convince them that no, even though I used to play guitar, I was not HIM.

Just some sap who washed dishes in a Mexican restaurant.

"You him, ain't you?" Mr. Goatee repeated, staring up at me, that wondrous look beginning to slowly suffuse his gaunt, red face. He exhaled heavily on the "you," sending a deadly salvo of Tribe Quest beer directly towards my face. I winced.

"No man. Sorry. I'm not him," I said, thrusting my hands toward him, palms up. As if that movement proved it beyond a shadow of a doubt.

"Hey...ya gonna get up there and PLAY?" he continued, as if he had not heard me. At all. "Damn, man. That would be super COOL."

He picked that opportune moment to accidentally knock over his plastic mug, nudging it with one knee. The lightweight cup toppled, and his brew flooded the sparse grass.

"Shit! Godamnit! Fuck!" Mr. Goatee shouted, as if he had just lost his last chip (and his life's fortune) at some Vegas roulette wheel.

I walked away from him. Toward the gazebo.

I glanced over toward where, earlier, the brunette had been dancing in tantalizing, excruciating slow motion. She was no longer there. (Of course) Either she had become finally acclimatized to our oppressive gravity, or the mother ship had come from her own planet and beamed her to safety.

Too bad...

PBS was still soldiering on, of course, their baroque noise booming out of two giant PA cabinets that dwarfed the gazebo stage like Stonehenge trilithons.

It was then that I caught the eye of their drummer. I hadn't really paid much attention to him at all during their set, save for noticing that he was a competent time keeper. Tell truth, I had ignored Pearls Before Swine almost entirely, focusing my addled attention on my little Tai-Chi master. On her tiny painted breasts and muscled biceps.

Pearls Before Swine's drummer was MY old drummer. In the Tunnel Rats.

George Oliver.

Holy shit...

I stood there, just watching my ex-drummer as he flailed away at his elaborate kit, my feet touching one side of a narrow, pebbled walkway that skirted past the gazebo's steps. I hadn't seen George Oliver in close to eight years, ever since the demise of the Tunnel Rats.

Non gratus rodentum.

George looked up from some elaborate para-diddles he was tapping out on his silver snare drum. He went to bring one of his big sticks down on his ride cymbal.

And then he saw me.

George smiled at me and nodded his head. In synch with his kick drum.

So I sat back on the grass, waiting for PBS to finish up their set. I really wanted to talk to George. He was the first familiar face I had seen in Great Vale, all the live long day. I glanced back quickly to see if Mr. Drunk Goatee was still in the vicinity, because I did not want to have to explain to him, yet again, that I wasn't HIM. I was not the fabled one he was seeking, who, in the mid-60s had been declared God by London graffiti writers. But Mr. Goatee, like the little hippie girl, had, thankfully, disappeared. Probably in search of more drink.

I could not believe that George was the drummer for this overblown, operatic bullshit, but then again, George had been the wrong drummer for The Tunnel Rats as well. He had hated punk rock. Known absolutely nothing about it. Could not tell you the difference between The Sex Pistols and The Saints. His whole tenure in the band had been peppered with bitter arguments. Mostly between him and me.

Now, all I wanted to do was embrace the man, hold him in a big bear hug and say: "Good show, man! Good show!."

So I sat there, waiting it out once again on the hard grass, as the band played up their last few numbers. The singer/lead guitarist for Pearls Before Swine was particularly annoying. He was a really really young guy, nineteen (maybe younger) and he strutted across the stage in a tight-fitting paisley shirt and even tighter jeans like Apollo down from Mt. Olympus, his bow

now a sunburst Strat. And his song intros were excruciating. The ghost of Sammy Davis Jr. would have probably told him to stop being so full of himself.

"This is our last people," he said, breathlessly, into his microphone. As if anyone in the park would be sad to see them exit. Well, maybe a few. Maybe a few girls. "We'd like to thank you for coming out today. Allowing us, in our little way, to bring the molecules to the light..."

Shit. Had he actually said that? Bring the molecules to the light? What the fuck?

"This song...this song is called Sisyphus, and it's about an ancient king who, because of his deceitful and evil ways, was punished by the gods. And you know how he was punished? He was forced, for all of eternity, to roll a bolder up a hill. Only to have it come crashing back down for all of eternity. For all of eternity," he added, dramatically, closing his eyes.

George counted in the number, clicking his bat-sized drumsticks together. It sounded, to me, like everything else they had played during their overlong set. Full of meaningless time changes. Guitar solos in which the only rule seemed to be: Play as many notes as you can in the space of a minute. A power trio of Stuarts, shouting "Look what I can do! Look what I can do! In the background, George kept the beat, stoically. You could not tell if he was having a good time, or if he was about to fall asleep behind his elaborate kit. Of course, that had been the case in The Tunnel Rats. When he was playing.

As Sisyphus went up and down and up and down his hill, definitely tearing past the five-minute mark, I thought of the last time The Tunnel Rats had played together and how disastrous of a gig that had been. It was at a house party that some drug dealer named Gut (certainly not his Christian name) was throwing and we were one of three bands scheduled to play in Gut's overgrown backyard during the course of a long, boozy afternoon/evening. (Oddly enough, two people at that party had mistaken me for the guitar god I supposedly resembled.) When we took the stage--well took the ground, actually—the other guitarist, Tom Lee, was already pretty shit-faced and incoherent. This had happened in the past. Sometimes the booze acted like a great demonic catalyst, and he would attack the strings and the whammy bar of his white Stratocaster like he was Jacob wrestling with some angel. Other times it would just send him down into a catatonic stupor, and he would stand there on stage swaying, his long black hair down in his eyes. I had learned then that it was best to signal our soundman, have him cut Tom out of the mix because, inevitably, the chords that he played would be wrong.

When we started playing, Tom seemed to be doing OK. George counted in our first number: "Sonic Reducer," by The Dead Boys. We had revamped it to include a long intro of feedback from Tom on the guitar. He wasn't the greatest guitarist in the world. As a a matter of fact, he couldn't even play minor barre chords. But when it came to getting other-worldly robotic death rattles out of his Strat, he was like Paganini.

It started out well. Tom held his guitar very close to his black Peavey amp, and the feedback began to build, as usual. I stood there watching, marveling as always, as Tom began to sculpt that siren song, using his whammy bar and the proximity of his guitar to the amp to build that feedback, tear it down, and then, slowly, build it back up once more.

And, suddenly, it all went south. I was poised to kick in, blast out the four-chord figure that drives most of the song's bitter verses, when guitarist Tom Lee broke his D string, with one violent wrench on his tremolo bar.

"Shit!" he yelled, looking down at that dangling string as if it were some weird snake he had never seen before in his life.

I stood there, clenching my teeth, suddenly aware of the thirty or forty people who were standing in that trashed yard, gawking at us between chugs of draft beer.

I guess if Tom Lee had been relatively sober then he would have just soldiered on, waited until the last thundering chord to notice that he had indeed broken a string. Changed it quickly. No problem. But no. He kept staring down at the guitar, as if he were waiting for the string to magically change itself.

"Free Bird!" someone in the crowd shouted. Someone laughed, and took up the slow chant. And then it snowballed, until everyone was shouting and laughing.

"Free Bird! Free Bird! Free Bird!"

Tom Lee continued to stare at his guitar, at the broken string, oblivious. He began to sway slightly. As if some strong sirocco had just descended on that white trash lot.

"Lee!" I shouted. "Change your fucking string!"

The bass player (whose name escapes me now) stood on the other side of Tom Lee, his large ponytailed head cocked at a quizzical angle, as if he were pondering some unsolvable mathematical problem, his pudgy fingers just resting on the strings of his black Ibanez. He was just another soldier for hire really, just another in a long line of bass recruits for The Tunnel Rats. He had only been with us for less than a month. He was a strange cat. He could hammer out these elaborate figures on the bass, like he was Jaco Pastorius's redneck twin. But something easy? Say like the root notes in "Louie Louie"? That seemed to trip him up like he was being asked to play Beethoven. So once again, not a good fit for the group. But, on the plus side, he had gotten us the gig. He and Gut were, supposedly, as thick as thieves.

Now I bet he was regretting the move...

"Lee!" I hissed. "Change your fuckin' string!"

"You SUCK!" someone in the crowd shouted, as if The Tunnel Rats were the source of all the world's woes and if we were to just exit the yard all would be again right in the universe.

It was then that I heard a sharp crash behind me. I really had forgotten that George Oliver was back there, sitting behind his kit, patiently waiting for his band members to get there shit together so he could do the one thing in life he lived to do.

Play.His.Drums.

I turned around to see what the HELL was going on. The crash even seemed to have roused Tom Lee from his sullen coma. He looked up, turned his head vaguely in the direction of Oliver's kit.

George had thrown his sticks in disgust. Hit one of his ride cymbals with them apparently.

"I can't take this any longer," he said, shaking his head, and standing up behind his kit. He said it matter-of-factly, really. As if he were just ordering some sandwich at a local deli. "I quit…"

Tom Lee, the bass player, and I, just stared at George Oliver. With varying degrees of comprehension.

"What do you mean QUIT?" I was very aware that my face, my ears, seemed to be on fire. All I wanted to do was slink away with my red Charvel guitar, crawl under the back porch of Gut's gray shingled house. Just die under there, like some old old hunting dog. Why the hell had this all gone south so so quickly? And in front of a bunch of drunks who found it hilarious? Thirty or forty people. People who could care less that, in the space of twenty seconds or so, my sole reason for living had now, apparently, dissolved….

Non Gratus Rodentum.

"I mean…I quit. All I ever wanted was to play my drums. I don't need this…drama."

With that he just walked off, toward his Ford Explorer, one of the two vehicles we had used to cart our equipment to the gig. I watched him walk out of that jungle of a yard and out of the band and out of my life.

For good.

I didn't even think about anything as all, as I watched him retreat. Didn't think about getting home. Didn't think about the drums he was just leaving there, like some evil father abandoning his child.

All I could think about was that Latin logo. The one we had so lovingly stenciled on his bass drum head six short months before. It seemed like an eternity now. It ran through my head like some kind of perverse tape loop. Playing over and over and over again…

"Non Gratus Rodentum…"

#

"How you been, man?" George Oliver asked, clutching my hand tightly and giving it a few rhythmic pumps.

We were standing together on one side of the gazebo, very close to one of the giant PA cabinets. Another anonymous band was getting ready to storm the gazebo. They were busy now, setting up their gear, swarming the concrete stage like efficient little worker ants. Guitar amps. Drums. Once they started blasting away, George and I would probably have to move somewhere else. That is, if we valued our remaining ear drums.

"Good man. Good…good," I replied, nodding. It was a lie. I hadn't been good for a very long time. Just treading water. Working like a waterlogged dog at Los Gauchos Taqueria, five, sometimes six days a week, sometimes double shifts. Just to pay the rent and keep all the creature discomforts coming. Writing sporadically and joylessly. Depressing little stories about my shitty lot in life. Stories that would inevitably come back to me with rejection slips. Like some heavy boulder raining down on St. Sisyphus.

"You still playin'?" he asked.

"Some…" I replied. Another lie. I hadn't picked up a guitar in over two years, probably. My red Charvel, the one I had played in The Tunnel Rats, that had been sold a long time ago. When I had been quite desperate to scrounge up the deposit money for the studio apartment I lived in. I had a shitty little acoustic, but the strings were badly in need of changing. It just sat in the utility room of my apartment. Gathering dust.

"Awesome," George said. "I always thought you were a really really good guitarist. That's why I stayed in The Rats as long as I did."

"WHAT.THE.HELL?" I thought, as George and I continued to grin at each other uncomfortably. "Why didn't you tell me that when we were together?"

"Yeah. And I really liked your songs, man," he added.

Again, WTF? Was he just being polite, or did he truly mean it? I thought back to all the acrimonious rehearsals we had had together when we were Tunnel Rats. George hot to play some dodgy old Kiss song, maybe "Lick It Up," or something. (Kiss being his favorite band of all time.) And me being more receptive actually to the idea of jumping down into a booby-laden tunnel, armed with only a 45-caliber pistol.

"Thanks...thanks. That means a lot to me," I replied, numbly.

About twenty yards away from where we were standing, in the shade of a giant white oak, the singer for PBS was busy chatting up some girl, leaning in close to her, his blue eyes fixed on hers like twin tractor beams. I realized, with a start, that it was the slow-motion dancer I had been hypnotized by earlier. He was really pouring it on. Touching her bare arm every ten seconds or so to underline, I guess, some dumb point he was trying to make. Maybe he was relating to her the myth of Theseus and Ariadne? Or some other drivel. Anyway, she looked more than willing to hear the tale. More than willing...

"You ever talk to Tom Lee?" George asked. "Or Donny?"

Holy shit. THAT was the name of that bass player. The one with the ponytail and the selective ability. Donny Lumm. How could I have forgotten that?

"Not...not in a long time," I said. "You?"

It was amazing really. I had spent every day of my life, for more than half a year, with this man. With George Oliver. With Tom Lee. Rehearsing. Drinking. Planning out how the Tunnel Rats were going to, inevitably, take over the callous uncaring world. Become the "toppermost of the poppermost" as John Lennon used to say to The Beatles. Back before they were famous. "Where are we going fellas? To the toppermost of the poppermost..."

The singer for PBS now had his arm firmly around my little, half-naked goddess. And he was whispering in her delicate ear.

It all had collapsed with one broken D string...

A memory suddenly came to my mind of the three of us—George Oliver, Tom Lee, and myself—eating breakfast together in a little hole-in-the-wall bar and grill, across the street from my apartment, after an all-night rehearsal where everything just seemed to come together magically, and the windows rattled with the awesome unstoppable noise we made. With our western omelets we had longneck Buds on the side, and we smiled at each other, and clicked those dark brown bottles together, toasting the sound still ringing in our ears. Our bright future.

"The Tunnel Rats!" Clink Clink Clink...

Non gratus Rodentum...

#

Later that night I sat alone in my shitty apartment, listening to music. I was very drunk, very sunburned, and more than a little depressed. George and I had stood there talking to each other for about fifteen minutes or so until the next band, some unlikely combination of punk and calypso (?)started blasting out their first number: a speeded-up version of Blue Oyster Cult's "Godzilla" replete with steel drums.

"Hey man, you wanna get a beer? I'm buying!" I shouted in his ear.

George begged off. He had to get his drums

loaded up, see where his bandmates had gotten to. The last time I had seen his preening singer, he was wandering off toward the concrete pond behind the gazebo, his arm still around the lithe body of that dancing girl. As if she were his possession now. The spoils of war or something.

George got my number though, put it in his phone. Told me he would call me soon about some up-coming gig Pearls (he called them Pearls) were playing at some dive bar on the west side of the city. I got the feeling though that he probably wouldn't call me about it. That if I ever saw George Oliver again, it would only be through another incredible twist of fate.

"Really nice to see you man," he said, giving me a big bear hug. "Keep on rockin' in the free world."

"You too man, you too…" I said.

And with that, he was gone.

As I sat there listening to music at top volume, I suddenly had a desire to pick up my guitar and play it. Like I said, I probably hadn't touched the damn thing for two years or so. Now I flew to the utility room in my apartment, got the acoustic out of its flimsy cardboard case. The blond wood was very dusty and the instrument was horribly, horribly out of tune. It took me about a half-hour or so to get it sounding approximately right.

I started singing and playing. The verses to one of my old songs. One that, a thousand years in the past, I had believed would fly to the toppermost of the poppermost. Make me a millionaire. Bring me a stone mansion by the municipal zoo. And a blond, debutante wife…

"Well I've been working for seven years

Down here scraping on my knees

Well they say there ain't no spices in those woods

Still I'll be free if I just believe

If I can hang on…If I can hang on…

If I can hang on…"

As I played, I thought of George Oliver, tapping out elaborate paradiddles behind his kit. Being the rhythmic engine for PBS. Was he free? He got to play his drums in front of people, certainly, show off his deft ability for an hour or so. But where was the vision? What was the risk? After The Tunnel Rats I had stopped because the music the music the music just seemed to take a second seat to so many other trivial things. How much are we getting paid? Where are the girls? Why is the wiring in this shitty club making my guitar buzz? Why can't Tom Lee keep his drinking in check? Why do I have to learn the chords to "Cold Gin" when all I wanna do is fly on my own songs? Stand on my own? Not compromise?

Jump down in that tunnel…

Who was better off? George Oliver was still up there. Still making music. Still fighting in his own way…

And me?

I just kept thinking these things, playing that one song over and over, trying to make the dirty widows in my apartment rattle (and failing) until there were tears streaming down my face…

The End.

About the Author:

Michael Walker is a writer living in Columbus Ohio. He is the author of two published novels: 7-22, a YA fantasy book, and The Vampire Henry, a "literary" horror novel. He has seen his fiction and poetry published in PIF and Fiiction Southeast among others.

WHAT THINGS, THESE THINGS, STIR THE HEART
by Joe De Quattro

In voicing his uncertainty Martin Colliver felt he was making a declaration.

"I have no idea how to do this!" He understood that admissions such as these, especially in the 21st century, were mostly unheard of (perhaps simply unnecessary), and had there been anyone within earshot he might have felt embarrassed by the strength of his voice. But the small, yet airy house he'd come to rent in a buggy, florid part of Massachusetts, an hour or so from the Cape, was set back a good distance from the road. And the Coverly's, his nearest neighbors, whom Martin had met in the spring when the town had distributed solid waste and recycling barrels, were away for the summer.

"Really no idea how to do it," he howled again. The "this" or the "it" of his distress was, generally speaking, philosophical, overwhelming, and ambitious. Less generally it was about getting on now in that giant, consuming baler that was the sexy, swift, plastic technology age. In other words, utterly out of Martin's grasp. He was out of step, out of place, even before he'd split with Clare the previous winter. What *was* he fighting, after all? Who had time for it? It was best to allow oneself to be placed into that baler and be sorted out, go with it. Everyone, everyone to Martin appeared to have it together. Even as much had continued to go off the rails in the country, everyone seemed to be scurrying to their place. What was worse, every *thing* seemed to have its place. Intellectually he knew this was untrue, knew there would always be need, work to be done, much left unresolved. But emotionally, wildly, he believed it, believed he'd come awake with a sudden dawn nausea in a time that wouldn't wait for him, couldn't wait for him, that quite simply had no space for him, as he went on breaking forward through the blandness of his middle-age.

The girl in the other room he had met four nights ago at a laundromat not far from the house. At first it had concerned Martin that the house came without laundry. But he was a schlepping pro, had spent much of his adult life living in apartments without laundry facilities (item six on Clare's list of grievances), and saw himself as an aging grad student, forever lugging his soiled things out into public (he didn't ever drop-off).

The situation with the girl had begun with a meeting of eyes. At first he'd assumed she was looking at him merely out of curiosity as people often do when coming upon a car crash.. Needing to see the failure. One's own possible end. Martin had gone on sorting and separating his clothes until after a while there were the eyes, this girl's eyes, meeting his, curious but not gawking, unflinchingly direct, blinkingly sand expectant. Were they trying to ignite something within him, Martin dared to wonder. Not lust. No. Far greater, and certainly more complex. As he'd increasingly come to see it, eyes were the biggest problem in the 21st century, buried as they often were in a downward tipped skull so as to never *really* see other eyes, least of which his. This tool of observation, of love and hate, thought and peace, wonder and discrimination, of acceptance, deterrence, reason, rage, lust and smoke, of digestion, discourse, sadness, purity, happiness and toxicity, the eyes had miraculously become little more than a product of self-promotion. Of navel gazing. The few times, especially in the last six months, when strange female eyes locked on his, it was never for more than a nanosecond. A flash and away. A bounding rapidly away as if the woman would turn to stone if she held Martin's gaze a moment longer. It wasn't due to a lack of attraction, for on paper Martin had a level of attractiveness. Rather, what those looking eyes in their momentary appraisal saw: a man out of step and out of time with his time.

These eyes, though, the eyes of the girl...

Perhaps, Martin thought, as he folded his last t-shirt, placed it into his laundry bag and made his way over to where she sat, perhaps they understood something. He was just about to speak, not altogether sure what he was going to open with, when to his surprise she spoke first.

"I haven't seen you here before."

Martin, though he understood this statement to be directed at him, looked around.

"Yeah," the girl said matter-of-factly, "you're new." She was seated with what appeared to be a celebrity gossip magazine (from the look of the photos), spread idly in her lap, and without any of the usual laundry day accompaniments: bag, soap, dryer sheets, an overall unshowered countenance. She was wearing brown lace-up boots into which her jeans had been neatly tucked, a wide leather belt, and a tan blouse open at the throat. The overall demeanor was that of someone on a layover between flights.

"Most people hide it better," she continued with no urgency.

"Hide what," Martin said.

"A trans—" she started then stopped. "Moving from one place to the next." There was an artificial brightness to the way she said this.

"I didn't realize I was that obvious." Martin's tone was flat, though really he was ecstatic over what he'd just heard. Startled and overjoyed.

"Not obvious," the girl said, "just a little transparent. It's nice."

She had turned up at dusk the following day. From the window of the kitchen and without a beat of concern or trepidation, Martin had watched her moving among the blue bell dahlia's, asters, violets and crocuses. The evening sprinklers were going, *fwick fwick fwick,* though she didn't appear to notice even as a forceful spray of water shot a dotted line across the front of her peach colored t-shirt.

Feeling instinctively that he couldn't instruct her, Martin went and stood at the back door until she made her way around. With little verbal formality, he showed her inside, the great room (great here used as a classification rather than as an adjective), above which was the loft area where Martin had been retreating more and more often, the bathroom, the kitchen, the two bedrooms. The girl dropped her bag, which in its size suggested nothing temporary or permanent, in the large back bedroom.

"So I can go whenever I want?"

"I won't keep you," Martin said.

"What if you get sick of me?"

"Whenever you want."

"Do you work?"

Martin was hesitant. "I do a lot of work," he said, "but if you mean do I have a job, at the moment, no."

"A while, then," the girl said.

Martin considered her. "You don't have a Massachusetts accent."

"No," the girl said, but as if the observation bored her. "I'm from the South."

She didn't have a southern accent either, though Martin didn't press. He watched her as she unpacked, and as she pulled items from the bag, items for neither a long or short stay, she would intermittently look in his direction.

"Expecting something?"

Martin didn't say anything. The girl went on unloading her personal effects, a brush, a hair drier, a cosmetics bag (though it didn't appear she wore make up), her cell phone. Martin looked away. How could he be disappointed? The girl was only twenty-one, maybe twenty-two. He couldn't expect her, even in her laconic understanding of him, to be part of his declaration and so be without a phone. Besides, he had one. He wasn't a Luddite. Wasn't against technology. That was too simple. His phone was off, though. Twenty-seven days.

Martin left the girl and then disappeared up into the loft space above the great room. This he accessed by way of an oak staircase he'd had installed after much configuring and expense, like an airstair brought out on a tarmac for the President or the Pope. The space was furnished sparsely: a chair, a small white table with a lamp. It was sufficient, even if since gaining access his intentions were unclear. When he first saw it, though, standing on the carpet of the great room, he felt deeply stirred by something, and after going up by ladder to test his weight, sweeping out the chipmunk droppings and the spiders, he understood the spot to be something necessary. Necessary to go to.

"Hello?"

Martin looked down and saw the scalp of the girl's head where her hair was parted. Her hair wasn't particularly clean, he thought, but the scalp was a healthy whitish red like the breast bone of a chicken. She began to climb. Martin lost sight of her then, listening to her feet, which were bare now, on the oak steps, listening and waiting, breathing silently, waiting for her to appear.

"Hiding?"

"No," Martin said, "the opposite." He leaned back in his chair, trying to appear casual. At ease. There was nothing on the white table. "Hey, let's go out."

But they didn't. In fact, well-stocked as the house was, each time they gathered themselves to go there was something to prevent them: beer; salami and cheese; cans of beans; bread. Together, innocently enough, they proceeded to remain there. And while often they were on opposite ends, even on opposite floors seeing that Martin was spending a good deal of time in the loft looking for its intention, an undeniable connection grew.

"Adultery," the girl said late one night. She was watching the news in her room. This was the third or fourth night. Martin often heard her talking to herself in her room with the television going. Mainly it seemed she watched the news.

"Look at this," she said. Martin, standing in the doorway, hands in pockets, looked. It was a story about a forty-two year old Afghan woman who'd been executed by the Taliban for cheating on her husband. "Incredible," the girl said. She was wearing men's pajamas (not his), powder blue, and sitting in a plaid oversized chair that had been left behind by another tenant. "For adultery. For adultery they kill you. Right there for everyone to see. Bullets. Sick how men think."

"In some regions," Martin said.

At first the girl looked at him reproachfully, but then she nodded.

"Men," she said.

"Men," Martin said and nodded.

The girl muted the television and considered him now for a few long moments.

"What don't you know how to do?"

The question, though it shouldn't have, disarmed him.

"I hear you," the girl continued. "Often at night. Sometimes in the morning. What is it?"

"It's a small house," Martin said, flushing heavily in the face. "I'm not keeping you here, I told you that."

The girl offered a barely perceptible nod. "What don't you know how to do? Really? You seem a little broken, but otherwise entirely capable."

Martin didn't say anything. It was his house and he felt no obligation to explain his declaration. He wasn't bothering her, forcing her to stay. She was there of her own will.

"Tell me," she said again.

Overwhelming as her insistence here was, the girl's voice was soft, and when Martin looked at her, looked her dead in the eyes, he saw what he'd seen nights earlier at the laundromat. Not curiosity, not a need for facts or information, but genuine interest.

"Be in the current," he said finally. He meant this, it explained a great deal, but because he'd never said it aloud it only sounded silly and pretentious.

"What does that mean? The current?"

"It's what I don't know how to do," Martin said, trying to reassert some sanctity over his plight. "Like I was—look, I just wanted to be. Okay? Want to be, I should say. But as things were, in day to day existence, I began to feel more and more like I was in junior high school and everyone else was at the cool table. But

it's life! I mean, it's *not* school. I was a man and I felt that way." He was aware that he was using past tense. "Was unable to see my place, and so couldn't be in it any longer."

To this the girl offered no response, though the lift of her brow suggested he'd hit upon something of shared value.

"So you're a rebel, then, is that it?"

Martin laughed, one quick snort. "Do rebels even exist now with all the advertisers chiseling away at individuality for years? We have monsters, sure, but rebels? Rebels often have heart. Are heroes." He paused in thought. "There must still be some, I suppose."

The girl appeared about to say something, but Martin stopped her gently. "I'm not a rebel, no. I want to exist in the current, in life, as it is now, in the face of its shining, sleek, plastic sexistence." He paused imperceptibly to see how the girl might like this invented word. "I know it won't change, in other words, that I'm outnumbered."

"But cutting yourself off isn't going to help."

"That's just it," Martin said, "I'm not cut off, per se."

"Not per se," the girl said, "just overall." She smiled. "At least you let me in."

"I see it as stepping away in order to regroup."

"Transition," the girl said.

Martin ignored this. "I'm figuring out how to be in the current, *back* in it, and be myself. Myself. Does that make sense?"

The girl gave no indication either way.

"As it was I just felt horribly alone, more and more alone," Martin said. "There's other stuff, too, things I haven't told you, about my marriage, and I'm not sure I want to get into it to be honest. It has its place but it wasn't driving everything. I felt more and more alone. Despite the—connections. My God, all these freaking connections, socializing and not seeing anybody, words, talking with words and saying what, really? I couldn't stand how alone I felt."

Martin understood that he didn't know the girl well, that while she was here with him, sharing this house now for however many days, he didn't fully know how she viewed things. But perhaps this was best. Knowing too much might be painful.

Wanting to change the tone, he ventured further into her room and sat down just on the edge of the love seat which like the big plaid chair had also been abandoned by a previous tenant.

"When I was a kid, around fourteen or so," he said, "I delivered papers." At the word papers, he could tell that the girl became at once more curious yet confused. Given their age difference, more than two decades, and the look on her face now, he understood that there was a distinct possibility that she'd grown up in a household without actual newspapers around.

"I had a newspaper route," he explained. "Over the back wheel of my bike I had these two metal baskets, like saddle bags, specifically for the job. The route. One day, as I was loading up the papers, a small bird, a finch or a thrush, I never knew which, I don't know birds, landed on one of the little metal bars of the baskets. I waited a few moments for it to fly away. I mean, it's a bird, they speed off when you blink at them, right? But this one didn't. Just sat there like it was completely normal. Where it should have been."

"It was hurt?"

"That's the thing, it looked fine. There was no evident distress. Gingerly as hell I finished loading up the papers, I mean I had to get them delivered by a certain time or I caught hell from customers, then got myself onto the bike and started to pedal. Slowly. As I made my way down the street, I kept looking over my shoulder and there the thing was, black glass-like eyes looking around, looking back at me as if to make sure *I* was there. I'd park the bike, gently

pull out a paper, drop it on the doorstep, come back, bird still there. Must have taken me two hours that day to do a route that normally took me forty or forty-five minutes."

"You didn't try to shoo it away?"

Martin made a face as if this were the most ridiculous thing he'd ever heard.

"Never."

"So you kept it," the girl said. There was assumption in her voice.

"No," he said, "eventually it flew away. I don't know when exactly. It was there until I nearly finished but then at some point it was gone."

The girl blinked all this in.

"Nothing happened," Martin said more urgently than he'd wanted. "It was just an occurrence. Nothing beyond that. But it was out of control, if you get what I'm saying. Out of the normal pattern of things. Now—" but Martin stopped.

"Now," the girl said softly, "what?"

"Now everything has a designated place. Stuff, I mean. Things. Garbage. Plastics."

"But isn't that a good thing?" She half-laughed these words.

"Yes," Martin said, "of course." He hadn't ever spoken about this to anyone before, but his tone was exasperated, as if he'd said it a million times already. "With a person, though, with people, I don't know, it can't be the same. It can't all be compartmentalization, can it?"

The girl didn't say anything.

"I knew I'd never forget the damned bird," Martin said angrily. "I guess that's the point."

The girl nodded. "It's a sentimental point."

"Yes," Martin said. "I suppose it is. So?"

"So is that what you're looking for? Another bird-type situation?"

"How do you mean?"

"The look on your face. That look I noticed the other night at the laundromat. Do the two things connect?"

"Are you asking if I'm looking for sentimentality?"

"Sure," the girl said, "whatever."

"I don't know," Martin said. Then, almost laughing, "would it be so terrible if I were?"

"No," the girl said. "Only unfortunate."

"The bird affected me unlike anything before or since, really. Something I can only tell about and never unravel. Grand uncertainty. Mysterious. Opposite of compartmentalization, opposite of that current. Nothing sorted out."

"So you are looking for a kind of adult version of that, then."

"I'm not sure if that's what I'm looking for," he said. "I can say that that couple of hours with the bird, especially in light of the last year of my life, it feels unparalleled by any adult human relationship I've experienced." Here, when the girl frowned, Martin, perhaps misinterpreting her expression, added, "I guess you think that's pretty sick or sad."

She shrugged and got to her feet. "Hey, should we go out?"

The question took Martin by surprise. "Yes," he said, "sure. I mean, yes, we really should."

But neither of them moved.

Nights they spent in their rooms, although more and more often Martin retreated to his loft space. In the mornings, sometimes in the evenings, he could be heard crying out, "I have no idea how to do this!" It began to comfort the girl, really, which was saying a great deal. Another might easily become annoyed. Days, many, began to pass. The weather turned. It rained, cooled, became humid, buggy. Smoky clouds drifting like ominous dirigibles over the house rolled into dark and monstrous cliffs, then dispersed.

"I know why you like it up there so much," the girl said suddenly one afternoon. Weeks had gone by. Martin had only been able to keep track of time by way of his phone, off now forty-four consecutive days. They were lying side by side on the carpet of the great room, staring up at the cathedral ceiling.

"It forces people to look in order to find you," she continued.

"People," Martin said, "what people?"

"Fine," the girl said, "me. In that one moment, looking for you, you've eliminated the possibility of distraction. I can't just bump into you in here. Isn't that it?"

This embarrassed him. "No," he said. "That's not it at all." But then he wondered if it weren't true.

"Sure," the girl said, "come on. I'm always looking *up* there to find you. It's actually kind of arrogant, really."

As he'd been unable to determine various other things about her, if she was ever putting herself forward to him sexually; if, for example, she had felt contempt for his sentimental bird story, Martin was unable to see how she meant this.

"That was never my thought," he said. "And again, there hasn't been anyone here but you. What relevance can your point have then?"

Martin hadn't said this with any vehemence, not even defensively, but suddenly the girl rolled into a sitting position and stared straight ahead a few moments.

"You understand what I'm saying," Martin said, getting himself up on an elbow.

The girl didn't say anything. She only got to her feet, looked straight ahead a moment or two more in that same way as if a phantom palm had just slapped her face, then went to her bedroom and closed the door.

That night Martin was far more demonstrative in his proclamation, "No idea how to do it!," than he'd been since he'd started. Not shouting, but annunciating each word with a fervent depth and urgency unfamiliar to him thus far. He felt at once anxious but tremendously moved. He wanted, he supposed in some blind, blank area of himself, to send a message to the girl, an all consuming message, pull her forward and up to him once and for all. But she never emerged.

In the morning, the forty-fifth day, he expected to find her room empty, but there she was, on the day bed, asleep. Martin went about his business up in the loft, albeit more quietly now, "I have no idea how to do this," until he heard the girl stirring below. When he came down, he saw that she had her things together. They stood in the opaque light of the kitchen.

"Coffee?"

"I'm fine," she said.

"Are you?" Martin said.

"Are you?"

"It's a process," he told her both as a way of explanation and apology. Despite the apparent friction, the packed bag, he felt lifted. As if they were finally getting somewhere.

"By the way," the girl said with her hand on the doorknob and looking directly at him now. "Your bird story is sentimental. You have to know that at least."

Martin nodded even though he was unsure how she meant this, and a moment later she left, pulling the door closed behind her. From the window over the kitchen sink he watched her exit the property just as she'd entered it, past the dahlias, asters, violets and crocuses, that same deliberate yet meandering quality evident in her stride. Martin remained where he was, unmoving, listening. He had no idea how long. He only remained there, still, without stirring, listening to the *fwick fwick fwick* of the morning sprinklers, and the sound of her footfalls as they took her away over earth laden with dead leaves.

About the Author:

Joe De Quattro is a Pushcart Prize nominated American Fiction writer. A finalist for the Curt Johnson Fiction Award, his stories have appeared most recently in Mystery Tribune and The Los Angeles Review.

PICKIN' UP THE PIECES
by Larry L. Hamilton

When Uncle Luke called him "Your Honor" in his best big round revival voice and rolled out words about satisfying the court and serving the needs of justice, Judge Brown just beamed. Uncle Luke hoped to get us to our next performance on schedule; we had folks to feed back home. That old sinner of a southern country magistrate said that we at least looked

like a band of sorts. "They don't have anything much to serve us Vets down here and the money we get for recreation don't go far. There's some visitors comin' to see how we're treating our Vets, and it's nearly Veterans Day." He didn't have to paint in more numbers for Uncle Luke. It was settled that we'd do two shows to cover the sham of an outrageous fine for speeding, resisting arrest and other charges.

VA buildings are pretty much the same inside with endless corridors paved with green or brown linoleum and marked every half-mile or so with yellow signs warning about wet floors. According to a marker out front, this one began as a state insane asylum in 1898. We'd played these places before and we knew those veterans' home faces well – some old, some younger. Each resident was missing some parts: some physical, some mental, some both. Plus, some of us had lived this life. Me and another of us couldn't walk naked through an airport metal detector without it going off because of the bits and pieces of metal junk some Viet Cong boy had packed into his homemade mine. Those simple mines shredded bodies the same

way a lumber mill's chipping machine turns loblolly into gondola loads for 3-M.

The staff seemed happy seeing us. The first show would be in their cafeteria and they helped Latrell hook up our smallest system. By now we were certain that the Deputy and the Judge were in cahoots and it was them instead of Justice that we were serving.

If we had a secret weapon to help us make a getaway with no serious damage done it was Uncle Luke. Back home some folks thought he was something of a conjuring man. There were more tales about him than could possibly be true. But as a first cousin, I knew that he had been raised up to live honorable and to use his considerable wits to make his way with whatever was available. I figured he already had the makings of a plan but that judge had us over a good-sized barrel.

The evening show was just for the hospital workers, the vets and a few special friends the Judge was busy rounding up. While we were setting up, a young woman from the Judge's office fixed up flyers for the next day's afternoon show. Uncle Luke assigned me to help her. When he left, I told her he picked me because I was the only one he trusted to tell the truth.

The first things she wanted to know was the name of the band, where we had played and were we famous. I told her we were so unfamous we didn't have a name, but when needed we were Uncle Luke's Band. I told her we did a lot of studio work for small labels, played clubs, fairs and sometimes revivals because we all had done a lot of gospel growing up. And some of us were still doing that - growing up.

She laughed at that one. Since she just asked about the music I didn't volunteer about carpentry, painting, and occasional body-guarding. That part of the music business is sort of assumed unless you really are famous.

I noticed she had put down a ten-dollar price tag, five for youngsters and twelve and under free. I guess Uncle Luke already had figured that Judge Brown would find a way to work a little extra dividend from our predicament. Maybe we were wrong but we figured the Judge wasn't planning to share any of the gate money with us and most likely the Vets' recreation fund wouldn't see any of it either.

Her name was Patti Sue. She worked for the Judge but she weren't kin. Her Daddy was minister of the biggest of the three churches in the city limits and she was engaged to a minister's son from the next county. She was right pretty, smiled and blushed a lot; said she had been a volunteer for the vets since junior high.

She introduced me to the oldest resident when a man she called "Chief" came up and asked what was going on. He was called "Chief" because he'd been a very senior Chief Petty Officer in the Navy when he got a medical retirement in the late innings of the Viet Nam war. 'Nam was the third battle star on his flag. Another resident told me Chief was just a year out of high school and most all of it spent on the USS Arizona except for that first Sunday in December 1941, when he had forty-eight hour liberty ashore in Pearl Harbor.

Chief was a tough old salt, even though he carried his teeth in his shirt pocket and his eyes were weak. He didn't have family left but he was cheerful and full of history. What female nurses there were kept their eye on him because he was full of mischief they said. True or not, he liked to hear it. You could tell because

he'd look around and catch somebody's eye and give a wink and a toothless grin - unless he had his teeth in. Sad, thinking that the bathtub was about the most water he likely would ever see again.

As Patti Sue finished the flyers, the Recreation Director, Mr. Gabriel Hubbard, came by to talk private about one of the local boys named Ruel Lee Jeter, who was a part time resident. He played guitar pretty fair and had a special thing with Hank Williams' music. According to Mr. Hubbard, he did some of old Hank's songs like it was him reincarnated.

Local folks who liked country blues style loved to hear him do it. Some others just liked the excitement. He would play some then stop, look real sad for a bit and then smash the guitar into splinters like he was Sampson with that jawbone working on the Philistines. He didn't ever try to hit any people, but, whenever it happened, he would later claim he didn't remember anything about it. When Ruel Lee was living outside, Mr. Hubbard said local pranksters were always trying to set up some unsuspecting stranger so he would hand over his guitar to hear that boy play Hank.

Mr. Hubbard didn't want to see us get stuck with a busted guitar nor misunderstand about this haunted man. "It must be something about them Hank Williams songs that puts him into some kind of torment. I've seen it happen and there ain't no doubt that boy's fightin' for his life wherever it is he goes in his head."

He also told me the boy had been awarded a Silver Star for gallantry in 'Nam after his unit had been over run. There was some bickering about it 'cause he was a Medic and technically a non-combatant and not supposed to be shooting at people. But he got it anyway along with another cluster for his Purple Heart.

After I told Uncle Luke about Ruel Lee we had a little meeting before the rehearsal. Then Uncle Luke sent me to fetch him and Mr. Hubbard. We each introduced ourselves and them that had been there told him what unit they'd been with in 'Nam and when.

Odell was the last one - our standup bass, rhythm guitar and keyboards man. I thought he was staring kind of strange at Ruel Lee, but he did that a lot. Finally, he said, "Look at me real close Ruel Lee. You used to call me Boojee. You remember that?"

Uncle Luke got his "Now what next weird is going to happen?" expression for a second and then he looked hard one at a time at both of them.

Ruel Lee blinked a couple of times and smiled real polite. He looked close at Odell's face. You could tell he was trying hard.

"I don't think so," he said real soft.

"Look at this." Odell bent over and pulled up his pants leg to show the artificial leg attached at his left knee.

"You used to see me at the Rat Shack in Nha Trang. You called me Boojee 'cause I played boojee-woojee on that beatup old piano they had."

Something seemed to register. He squinched his eyes up tight looking way back hard. When he opened them he said, "Beard."

Odell's beard was thick, dark and curly. His hair hung past his shoulders and matched his beard.

"Yeah, man. I was a grunt back then. No beard, no hair either. Skinnier too."

He gestured downward again, "Look at this tin leg man." He grinned.

"You fixed that. I know it ain't the only one you did, but it's the only one of mine you did. And maybe it was your last one. My platoon was at your base camp when it got overrun."

"You were showin' me and my buddy TJ some licks on your guitar outside the medic hooch when the mortars and rockets started droppin' in and me and TJ went out on the fire line."

"After I got hit TJ hauled me back there and you had put a tourniquet on my leg when the VC finally broke through and started hosin' the

medic hooch. There musta been twenty or thirty of us dead and wounded stacked up around there. Damndest thing I ever seen, man. You bashed your guitar on the first one that came inside before you got hold of TJ's M-60. He'd a-been proud of what you did with his chopper man. I heard later you got the star but was messed up worse than me."

Ruel Lee blinked a couple of times, looked at Odell for a bit and then, like he was just waking up, said, "Boojee."

"Yeah, that's me man - Boojee." He went over to the old upright in the corner and standing up began some left hand work that started in New Orleans and worked its way up to Chicago before his right hand joined up. When he stopped Ruel Lee was looking happier than he probably had in awhile.

"Yeah, Boojee. We did some jamming at the Rat Shack a couple of times, a bunch of times."

He paused. "Your buddy, TJ, he was a big black dude?"

Odell nodded yes.

"He didn't make it did he?"

"Naw, man. He already had some holes in him when he drug me to the tent. You had just put the tourniquet on my leg when Charlie came in there. TJ took most of the first burst. I guess Charlie could see he still had that M-60."

"I reckon you and me took some of that burst, too. But he got too close and that's when you took after him with your guitar. The last I remember was a crowd of Charlies rushing the hooch and you workin' out with TJ's M-60. You saved some lives, man. Thanks."

Then it was still like a thick quilt on a cold night. I thought I could hear Ruel Lee's eyes blink it was that quiet. He had a way of looking at you that made you stare at him because you could see his face working like he was fixing to say something. It took a few minutes to realize that what he was seeing from his side of those blinking eyes was far far away.

But he answered when you spoke to him. He answered again like he just woke up when Odell asked if he'd like to sit in while we rehearsed a little.

"Don't have a guitar, Boojee."

"Man, I got one you can play. It's real special."

His face worked like he was struggling real hard inside.

"Boojee I break guitars. I don't know it when I do it, but the people here have seen me do it and I've seen a couple I busted. One was a really nice old Martin. I felt awful bad about it when they told me I had done it."

"Maybe this time it'll be different. Like I said this guitar is special."

Odell brought out a battered hard shell case and set it down between them. Ruel Lee looked at it then looked up at Odell who nodded his head, "Do it man, it's OK."

He slowly opened the case and pulled out an electric that had been re-worked some but would be a treasure to any guitar player. He caressed it like an infant child and whispered, "Man, this is a Les Paul."

We were all impressed. As long as I'd known Odell he'd been a bass and keyboard man and good at it. It had just never registered with any of us that he was carrying a Les Paul guitar in that old case because all we ever saw him play was his bass guitars, keyboards or his standup.

"Yeah, well maybe it's a Les Paul. It's been re-worked and it came from Saigon. I think it's mostly a Les Paul original, but what makes it extra special is who it belonged to."

"Its not yours?"

"TJ willed it to me. Just like I willed him my Fender bass. He wanted somebody to have it that would appreciate it and make sure it got into good hands. I been carryin' it around near twenty years now Ruel Lee, and I think you got the right hands."

"Aw man, I ain't all that good and I don't hardly ever play anymore. God, what if I broke it?"

"It don't matter Ruel Lee. I don't know if TJ was still alive when you busted your guitar on that first Charlie that hosed us, but I know he would have wanted you to have it. He liked pickin' blues. I'm sorry ya'll never got to jam together."

"But man, what if I break it?"

"It don't matter Ruel Lee, it's yours. Me and TJ are givin' it to you. You do what you want to with it. If you play it and break it that's OK. If you want to play it and not break it I'll do my best to stop you if you want me to. But it's yours man. Now, you gonna' hook up and set in or what?"

"I don't want to break it Boojee."

His face was beading with sweat. His left foot was heel-tapping at high speed, but the rest of him was still.

We waited. Nobody was sure if what Odell was doing was the best thing but it was real personal and he was doing what he felt was right, no question.

"Will you help me not break it?"

Odell lit up. "We'll sit on you man."

He hadn't let that Les Paul run down a bit. Ruel Lee tuned it slow and careful and worked some chords and he looked like a man having the best dream of his life.

He played "Red River Valley" like the slow country waltz it was in its first life and everybody smiled. When Toby our pedal steel player gave him some old time support, it sounded like the Porter Wagoner show on TV in the fifties. Then Ruel Lee changed tempo and style and took it to country rock, R and B, and then did a little jazz progression. He was a little rusty, but he was a man come alive and happy.

It was kind of strange him feeling so good. He was surrounded by the rest of us and we were picking and grinning. Although Mr. Hubbard had told us that he'd never hit a person when he had a guitar smashin' spell, we all were tensed to jump him if he tried to whack somebody with that Les Paul.

Must of been that a lot of VA folks knew about Ruel Lee's guitar picking and smashing because they started drifting into the cafeteria. We were working through some old Jimmy Reed and people were smiling and shaking around like they were ready to dance. The head nurse who came into the cafeteria was the biggest black woman I think I'd ever seen. She had to go at least two thirty and she towered over just about everybody there except Toby and Uncle Luke and a couple of others in the crowd.

Chief went right over to her and pulled her out to do a little jitterbug. I thought he might've gone too far and be getting himself into trouble. But fool me, she grinned at that scrawny old man and took him two laps around the dance floor that suddenly opened up. In spite of the differences in their size, color, and age they looked for a minute or two like a team in an old movie dancing the 1940s.

When Chief and the nurse stopped dancing the music stopped too. The crowd was looking at Ruel Lee like something might be going to happen. But nothing did. Mr. Hubbard and the head nurse shooed people out so we could get ready.

Ruel Lee smiled and listened while Odell and Uncle Luke set him up for rehearsal, which wasn't much. Everybody made a little cheat sheet, then we went through the first few chords and talked about solos. We'd just do our best and make room for some audience requests and some sing-a-longs if they were in the right mood.

We went at it for nearly an hour. Odell stayed close to Ruel Lee, but he did fine.

The VA cafeteria offered to feed us and while we were eating Uncle Luke talked serious with Patti Sue. Then she bustled out with her notebook held high like a woman on a mission. Uncle Luke went back to eating his bowl of corn muffins and buttermilk.

We started at sundown. The first two rows were mostly people in wheelchairs and a few beds. There were about a hundred or so vets and a bunch more hospital people. I saw the Judge at the beginning but I guess he left before the end.

That kind of free show don't feed your belly, but it does feed your soul some. If he could have figured a way to do it, Judge Brown probably would have fined us for having a good time while we were working for him for free. One of the best things was that Ruel Lee played and played and nothing bad happened. He even played a couple of his favorite Hank Williams songs that Mr. Hubbard had warned us about, and when he was done he bowed to the applause. He was real shy about it, but I think he understood that everybody was pulling for him.

When it was all over, Uncle Luke told us to sleep all we could and keep our gear together. We would depart the Judge's jurisdiction as soon as we loaded our equipment after tomorrow's afternoon show for the town folks.

Next morning we were setting up in the combination gym and auditorium when Patti Sue appeared with four boys in tow from the local high school. They carried heavy green canvas bags with ARMY ROTC in gold letters. They left the bags on the stage and Uncle Luke asked Mr. Hubbard to close down the gym because we had some new material and special effects. He was happy to oblige.

When Uncle Luke explained to us what he had in mind, there was considerable chuckling and grinning. He finished up saying, "As long as they're willin' to feed us free in the VA messhall you better fill up 'cause we'll likely have a couple of days of slim rations before we get paid next."

Latrell blushed and grinned when somebody said we'd maybe better put a governor on the bus engine so he couldn't race any more deputies. Of course this was why we knew that we'd been sort of set up by the Judge and his deputy. It was a miracle that Latrell could keep that bus above the required minimum speed on the Interstate.

It was kind of surprising how many people the Judge turned out on such short notice. Ticket sales were just inside the auditorium door and I heard Patti Sue tell Uncle Luke they'd taken in over four thousand dollars and the vets got in free. The staff people paid half price. She said the Judge sprang for twenty tickets to cover admission for the VIPs he was trying to impress.

Maybe I was misjudging the man, but I figured he could afford to spring for twenty tickets because, if I suspected right, his plan was to pocket the gate receipts anyway. The ticket buyers probably figured they were paying for the band, if they thought about it at all. Except for us, the Judge and his deputy, nobody knew this show was a part of Latrell's sentence.

Uncle Luke came out and started explaining how we were glad to be helping provide recreation for the vets. He told them, "We're all Christians and we're all veterans. We may not be the best of either that you've ever seen, but that's what we are."

Then he said, "We're going to give y'all a chance to fatten the kitty for the recreation fund. We're gonna pass collection plates just like it was church. Since ya'll don't know us, I'll ask Judge Brown and his deputy if they'll help out supervisin' the collection. We've got some collection plates we thought were just right for this special place."

The Judge got a handful of upstanding people in front of the stage and introduced them to the audience. Then Uncle Luke produced six steel helmets that were part of the stuff he'd borrowed from the high school Army ROTC. Seeing those steel pots sobered people a little but it sure got their attention. It was a nice touch.

Uncle Luke then asked Mr. Hubbard, the VA Chaplain, and the Head Nurse, that huge woman whose name I had learned was Annabelle Darden, to be the receivers of the offering. When they got up in front with the group holding the steel pots he asked the Chaplain to say a prayer thanking veterans and the people here who supported them.

Then he said, "Now there's one more thing. Ms. Patti Sue tells me there's a good chunk of change, a bit over four thousand dollars in that box she's guardin'. I'd be real surprised and disappointed if there's anyone here who would object to that box of cash bein' the first toss in the collection plate."

We were all watching the Judge out of the corners of our eyes, but were disappointed if we had expected him to have a conniption or something. His smile maybe looked a little forced and he didn't jump out to make a speech like he'd been doing earlier. But Deputy Brown was turning red, gritting his teeth and in general looking like a man who'd just found half a worm in his apple and was struggling with whether to throw up his last bite or ignore the whole thing. It never occurred to me that he might be stifling laughter.

Patti Sue, with tears streaming, trotted right over to the Chaplain, Nurse Darden and Mr. Hubbard and plunked that box down in front of them and then led off a big round of applause. In a heartbeat, Uncle Luke had the ushers moving those steel pots across the rows of metal folding chairs that were now passing for pews.

When it was done, the whole collection was presided over by what were probably three of the most honest people in the county. Uncle Luke had just neatly bypassed the Judge and put the gate directly into the hands of the VA folks.

The audience was ripe for the musical tour of American history we had ready. "Wabash Cannonball" had them singing the chorus before it was over.

Uncle Luke did some narrating and we did a few bars into "Yankee Doodle," "Dixie," "Battle Hymn" and then enough of the "Yellow Rose of Texas" so the audience got in on two choruses.

I don't know where it came from but I thought Uncle Luke would likely have been a sorcerer if he had lived in some ancient time. The way he handled that crowd was magical.

We did a history of the Opry and Ruel Lee got a standing ovation when he did a Hank Williams solo. Since most of the town folks knew him I guess they were cheering as much for him not smashing his guitar as they were for his singing and playing. In the middle of the applause he held that Les Paul over his head and then gave it a big kiss. That gave everybody a big dose of feeling good.

Soon Uncle Luke said, "This is grass roots gospel South," and that cued our quintet to form up. We did some of "I'll Fly Away" and "When The Home Gates Swing Open For Me."

Then Uncle Luke and Eddy Blair, who was one of the three black members of our band, joined us and we did parts of two spirituals that would have passed us all for black on any southern Sunday radio program. It was hard to tell who was more astonished, the black folks or the white folks in the audience. They all laughed and some just howled.

Now it was time to bring the house down. Uncle Luke said, "Folks, ya'll are a real fine audience and we're gonna do somethin' special to say thanks for this VA hospital and you folks who live in and around it. One thing that's already been special for us is findin' Ruel Lee Jeter. I guess most of ya'll know about him. Anyway, we invited him to join up and him and his doctor agreed that he'll leave the hospital and go with us at least to our next show. And he's welcome to stay with us until he can't stand us anymore."

That caused more applause and lots of smiles.

"A fact about what the military is all about is that not everyone comes home. And some of them that come back don't come back whole. And sometimes when the battles are over, the rest of us forget. We forget the price and we don't much want to be reminded."

Then Uncle Luke put on his black Johnny Cash hat and coat. The lights dimmed to one spot-

light. He strummed a low chord that matched his voice. With a little snare in the background he started singing low and deep, "Call him drunken Ira Hayes he won't answer anymore, not the whiskey-drinkin' Indian nor the Marine who went to war."

The timing made "The Ballad of Ira Hayes" just the right song for that group. You could hear the tension set in almost like a whip crack and then it was dead quiet while they listened.

When he got to the part about Ira and the others "raisin' Old Glory on that Iwo Jima Hill," the back-lights on the stage came up and there were our boys in silhouette wearing those steel pots, rifles slung over their shoulders, and raising the flag in a pretty fair imitation of the original. When they got it up they stood back and saluted it one at a time, about faced, and walked off into the dark. The back-lights kept the flag in profile and a fan came on to give it a little movement while Uncle Luke finished.

The applause was loud and sincere but not as wild as earlier because so many people were fooling with handkerchiefs and feeling a little sheepish about their wet eyes. We closed out with a medley from the Outlaws includin' Merle Haggard's "Fightin' Side of Me."

Mr. Hubbard got on the microphone and said the VA Rec bus was going to convoy with the band's vehicles to the county line as kind of a celebration parade for Ruel Lee and anybody who wanted to join the parade was welcome. He then asked the Judge if his Deputy could escort the whole shebang and he of course agreed.

We set a record for loading. It was some parade. With Latrell straining to keep the bus up to 55 mph, the Deputy led us all the way to the county line with blue lights flashing and a little siren wail. When he pulled over to let us by at the county line he was blowing his nose and didn't wave but we blew our horns and waved thanks anyway. We didn't think then we'd ever have a return engagement, but we knew it don't pay to burn bridges you might have to cross again.

I moved back to where Ruel Lee was sittin' and asked him about that deputy. I just didn't know what to think about him, or the Judge.

He smiled big at me and said, in the happiest voice I'd heard him use yet, "He's my Daddy. He started me on guitar and he said he was glad to finally have me back. He never gave up on it. Here's his card. He said if I have any problems, ya'll should call him and he'll fetch me home. He said to tell ya'll thanks, and he'll be prayin' for us all.

"What about Judge Brown?"

Another broad smile, "He's my grandaddy."

About the Author:

Larry L. Hamilton, native Georgian, now 75 and living in Asheville, NC, grew up as an Army Brat, traveling from school to school, state to state, 2 tours in Germany. He then spent a few years on active duty himself in Explosive Ordnance Disposal. He earned three degrees in Government and International Studies from the University of South Carolina many years ago and spent most of his career in SC state government while also running over 50 marathons and coaching his sons' soccer and chess teams. He has been trying his best for years to write some publishable fiction and is thrilled this is it!

A YEAR OF SUNDAYS

by Neal Storrs

Adelle Shipley squints through a mesh of tight black wire and pine branches. She is disappointed to see that the curtains in her sister's living room are still unopened. She'd hoped Odelle would be up before noon for a change, in time to have Sunday dinner with her and Gram. She backs away from the porch screen and into the cool, dark breezeway, shooing a fly off the light brown housedress she always changes into when she gets home from church. From the breezeway she turns into the kitchen, where she sees her grandmother leaning over the sink, framed by billows of steam, like a cherub midst heavenly clouds.

"Your sister up yet?"

"It was hard to tell, Gram. I didn't see anybody through the trees."

"You didn't expect you would, did you? What about her curtains? Were they open or were they closed?"

"They were closed."

"Well somebody better tell me whether your sister is coming over to have Sunday dinner with us and I don't mean next year, I mean *right now*. What'd you see out in front of her house? How many cars were there?"

"Just hers was all I saw, but that doesn't mean – "

"I reckon I have to set out another place, don't I? Don't see as you give me any other choice."

"Sometimes she has them park around in back."

"Say what? Speak up, girl. Stop fidgeting with them durn buttons like a twelve-year old."

"I said sometimes she has them park behind her house, even though she doesn't care what anybody thinks. What have you got I can help you with?"

"You can tell me whether your sister's coming over for Sunday dinner, that would be a big help. Get your daddy's plate out of the oven and take it up to him. Watch you don't burn yourself."

Adelle reaches up and slips a quilted hot pad over the upside-down question mark end of a magnet hook. She bends over, opens the oven door and pinches the rim of a plate containing four carrot slices, a tiny serving of mashed potatoes, and five bites of meatloaf. She lifts the plate out of the oven and places it on a second hot pad on the counter.

"After you take him up his food you can come back down and get him his iced tea. Lord, give me strength."

"I can get that for him now, too," says Adelle, opening the refrigerator door. "I have two hands." She stoops to lift a ribbed plastic pitcher and pours half a glass of tea. She opens a cabinet door and takes out a mahogany tray decorated with gold filigree depicting a landscape of flowers, birds, and a mountain lake.

"I want you to call Odelle right now, before you take your father his dinner. You know how much time your sister takes to pretty herself up."

"I don't think Odelle's coming, Gram."

"Oh, you don't, do you? Who was it kept saying all the way back from church that if ever there was a day your sister would have Sunday dinner with us, this would be it? Wasn't me, as I recall."

This was true, sort of. Somewhere between Dalton County First Baptist and Shipley Manor, Adelle had given voice to the hope that her sister might get up early enough to have Sunday dinner in the main house, though certainly she hadn't said it more than once, certainly not all the way back from church.

During the sermon, off and on, a thought had popped into Adelle's head: Today could be the day Odelle forewent one of her most cherished rituals, one of many which, in and of itself, gave her more pleasure than Adelle was capable of experiencing in a year of Sundays. Today could be the day her younger, prettier (everyone always said) sister rose up out of bed before noon, walked through the woods to their grandmother's house and, with dinner eaten and the dishes washed, dried and put away (by Adelle and her grandmother), settled herself in the old embroidered armchair next to Gram's upright and listened to the conclusion of the story Adelle had begun telling last Wednesday night. Something exciting had happened to Adelle, something romantic, even, but just as she was getting to the good part Odelle had bounced up out of the chair, flicked a strand of reddish-gold hair out of her face and said, "Gotta run. I feel my hotline heating up." And just like that she was gone, disappeared into one of the trails running back and forth between the three houses, Adelle's, her grandmother's, and Odelle's. Shipley Manor, the people of the county called them, as if the three separate but barely distinguishable structures constituted one big, happy home.

"She's probably still sleeping, Gram."

"Well aren't you the considerate one? She'd wake you up in a heartbeat if the shoe was on the other foot, I hope you know."

"I know she would."

"All I know is if somebody don't tell me what's going on before much longer there's gonna be somebody in one of these three houses that gets their fanny tanned."

Adelle sets the glass of iced tea on the mahogany tray and places a folded napkin next to it. She removes a fork from the silverware drawer and places it on the napkin. She picks up the tray and carries it out of the kitchen, into the breezeway, then into the stairwell that leads to her grandmother's three second-story bedrooms.

Over the last five months she has visited one of those three rooms dozens, maybe hundreds of times, sometimes to bring John Shipley food he rarely ate, sometimes just to sit next to his bed and talk. Her words, for all she knew, weren't heard, or understood if they were heard, or cared about if they were understood, but she has visited him at least once every day anyway, wanting desperately to delete the past, thwart the present, distract from the future.

She pauses on the landing of the stairwell and rubs the skin near her waist where last Tuesday night Mr. Cantwell's hand had touched her, a place where no man's hand had ever touched her before.

It had been near quitting time when Adelle was given the word she was wanted in the boss's office. A large framed photograph, centered high on the wall behind his desk, showed him in a football uniform, without a helmet, posing on bended knee. He told Adelle he'd heard about Shipley Manor, the three nearly identical houses buried deep in the woods west of town. He wanted to see them with his own eyes,

Southern rural residential architecture being one of his many interests.

Adelle had waited in the employee parking lot for him to pull up behind her in his little red convertible. With a honk and a wave, he signaled her to lead the way. She drove out of town into the country, regularly checking her rearview to make sure he was still behind her, that he hadn't lost his way, or his interest. Fifty yards short of a convenience store with two gas pumps in front she'd pulled off the two-lane state road onto a gravel road that skirted a wall of pine for almost a mile before turning into an unpaved trail that ran through a quarter mile of scrub woods and came out onto Gram's east yard. At the corner of her grandmother's screen porch she'd veered left, following tire tracks through two acres of pine and palmetto before emerging onto another lawn, where she stopped.

Mr. Cantwell pulled up next to her, climbed out of his little red car and asked, "Who lives in the house we just drove past, your sister or your grandmother?"

"My grandmother. My father lives there, too."

"Your father? Nobody told me about him."

"He's been sick."

"Sorry to hear it. I didn't get a good look, but I'd say the latticework on the veranda of your grandmother's house exhibits extraordinary craftsmanship."

"My father did it. He practically built all three houses all by himself."

"Is that so?" Adelle's boss backed into a palmetto bush to get a wide-angle view of her house. "I see he didn't invest as much time in your lattice as he did in your grandmother's."

"That's because that's the one he and Mama were moving into."

"Is that your phone I hear?"

It was. Adelle went inside and sat down at the end of her sofa. Her body sank as Mr. Cantwell sat down on the cushion next to hers. She picked up the phone, held it to her ear and waited. She knew what she was about to hear.

"You'd best tell me right now who that man is you brought home with you."

Adelle pictured her sister in her living room, which was identical to hers except that the furniture was more expensive and stylish. Sprawled like a magazine model across her sofa, Odelle would have flicked a strand of reddish-gold hair from her eyes before aiming them through three acres of scrub pine and palmetto at Adelle's living room window.

"It's my boss. He followed me home. We're finishing up some work we didn't have time to do in town."

"Work? Yeah, I bet work. You haven't offered him anything to drink, I see. Don't you remember anything I taught you?"

"We're going over to Gram's after we're done."

"What the hell are you taking him over *there* for?"

"Mr. Cantwell wants to look at the trim Daddy did on Gram's veranda."

"Now you listen to me, sister. You need to let me come over there and arrange things so that you and your Mr. Cantwell don't get off on the wrong foot. The man has still got his jacket on, for Christ's sake. First thing you do, *always,* is you take a man's coat. Have I got to teach you *everything*?"

"I told you. All we're doing is finishing up some work."

"Okay, have it your way. I'll just tell you one thing. Don't screw this up, like you screw up everything else."

"That was my sister," Adelle said, hanging up. "She lives over there through the woods."

Mr. Cantwell's eyes drifted into a maze of green and brown. "And has *her* house a veranda as exquisitely latticed as your grandmother's?"

You don't need to see my sister's house, it's exactly the same as mine, Adelle thought, but did not say.

"No. Daddy put something extra into the house he and Mama were moving into. Some people I know resented him for doing that. Not me. I would never resent Daddy for anything."

Adelle emerges from the stairwell into the second-floor hall and places the mahogany tray on the frayed carpet in front of the first door to her left. She opens the door of the facing room, the room in which her mother had died of breast cancer three years ago, and walks around the bed to the window.

From here the view of her sister's house is less obstructed than the view she'd had from her grandmother's porch. She still can't see Odelle's second-story bedroom window, which is around on the eastern wall. She does see that the curtains on the living room window are still closed. Odelle's car is still parked in front of her house, so she hasn't gone out for breakfast, as she often does in the early hours of Sunday afternoon, if she's alone. No other car is visible on the front lawn or on what Adelle can see of the side lawn. It is behind her house that her sister occasionally instructs her visitors to stow their rides.

Adelle leaves the room, crosses the hall, picks up the mahogany tray, opens the door of her father's room and enters.

John Shipley has managed to get himself out of bed and into a chair by the window. The chair is sturdy, straight-backed oak, sawed, sanded, painted and polished by her father's own hands over forty years ago. She avoids looking down at his unbuttoned pajamas. She wants to remember him as he was when he was younger and stronger, strong enough to horsey-back ride his daughter from one end of the park to the other. When it was only Adelle, her mother and her father, living in a two-bedroom house

on the lake in the center of town. When there was no Shipley Manor, no Odelle.

She places the tray on a wobbly TV dinner fold-up table and looks out the window. She doesn't see what is there − her own green-shingled house behind a maze of trunks and branches − instead, through the restorative eye of memory, she sees a black Ford pickup cruising down Main Street on a warm summer evening. A little girl's arm hanging out the window points at the buildings they pass. "Did you build *that one*, Daddy?" she asks, content that his answer has only three directions in which it can go, that deep inside her is about to flow, like a river of sweet, warm honey, the easeful country drawl that told her nothing in her life could ever be wrong, nothing bad could ever happen, nothing could ever hurt her. "That I did," her father says, or "No, my daddy built that one," or again, "No, it was my daddy's daddy built that one."

"Excuse me, but would you be my daughter Odelle?"

His drawl is cracked and feeble now, like his skin and muscles and bones. It is not unusual for him to mistake Adelle for her sister. He might just as likely have taken her for his late wife, or for one of the girls who worked at his construction company twenty, thirty, forty years ago. It wasn't even Adelle at whom he was looking; he was looking past her at her grandmother, who strides to the wobbly little folding table, scowls at the plate of untouched food, picks up the fork and stabs mashed potatoes at her son's pathetically half-open lips.

Adelle shrinks away to the door. "I'll go see about Odelle," she says. "I reckon we'll be having dinner soon."

"You reckon!" Gram explodes. "What have I been saying for the past half hour? You go on and see about Odelle. I got three places set, if you can manage to hogtie the hellcat."

Adelle descends the stairwell into the breezeway, walks down the breezeway onto the porch, then down four wooden steps onto a dry brown lawn. She follows a trail that winds through pine and palmetto to Odelle's front lawn. Halfway up the porch steps she looks up and sees her sister standing behind the black mesh of the porch screen. Odelle is wearing a T-shirt that falls just short of her knees. One hand scratches her hip, the other rubs sleep from her eyes while spinning a strand of golden hair.

"What you want to bet I can guess what brings you over here to my neck of the woods?"

"I bet you can," Adelle falls in behind her sister as they cross the porch, enter the breezeway, then turn into Odelle's living room.

"I imagine you're in a hurry to get back, with dinner waiting and Gram cackling at you to do this and do that, but I got something really, really important I need to talk to you about first." Odelle plops down on her couch. Adelle sees that her sister isn't wearing panties. "What you got planned for Saturday night? If it's nothing, like it always is, I got a *big* surprise for you."

Adelle sits down three feet to the left of her sister. "It's nothing," she says.

"Then don't you dare move a muscle."

Odelle springs up off the couch and flies up the stairwell. Adelle hears whispered voices before her sister returns, holding a photograph.

"Tell me if you ever in your life saw a more gorgeous male body."

Adelle sees three men on a beach, their arms draped over each other's shoulders. They are wearing tiny green, yellow and red bathing suits, striking muscle-man poses in front of a thatched cabana with a bamboo sign over the door: CERVEZA. One of the three men is Marco, Odelle's current boyfriend-of-the-month.

"Pretend you could make a wish and have any one of the three you wanted," Odelle says, "other than Marco. Which one would it be?"

"I don't believe either one of them is my type," says Adelle.

"Well you're sure one of their types." Odelle points to the man in the middle. "His name's Salvador de something or other. Marco calls him Sally. It's his cousin. He's from the Dominican Republic."

"I thought you said Marco was Mexican."

"So? Does that mean he can't have a cousin from the Dominican Republic? He's the only Dominican person in the whole of Dalton County and he's yours for the taking."

"How do you know I'm his type?"

"Let's just say it's possible he's seen a certain picture of you that shows you off to your best advantage, if you know what I mean."

"You better not have shown him that picture you took of me trying on your red dress. I'm half naked."

"Would you believe that's the first thing he noticed?"

"You showed that picture to a bunch of men I don't even know!"

"I only showed it to Sally."

"What about Marco? I bet you showed it to him."

"Maybe I did. What of it?"

"What about Mr. Cantwell?"

"What about him?"

"Don't you want to hear the rest of what happened between Mr. Cantwell and me Tuesday night?"

"Sure, as soon as you tell me where you'd like to go dancing Saturday night. After that we can talk about your Mr. Cantwell till you're blue in the face."

"How do you know Mr. Cantwell and I don't already have something planned for Saturday night?"

"Because you just told me you're not doing anything."

"Maybe he's coming out to my house. Maybe we have more work we have to do. Who's that you got up in your bedroom?"

"There's isn't anybody up there."

"You've never been bashful about any of your boyfriends before. What's so special about this one? How come you won't tell me who it is? Because it's not Marco?"

"I believe that falls into the category of none of your business."

"If I wanted to I could walk around back and see if there's a car parked behind your house."

"I don't see anybody stopping you."

Adelle crosses her sister's living room, then her screen porch, then descends four wooden steps and walks around the side of the house to the back yard, where she sees, parked in the shade of an oak tree planted by their father – a tree that for some inexplicable reason had grown to be twice as big as the one he'd planted behind Adelle's house – a little red convertible.

About the Author:

A wide variety of **Neal Storrs's** work is available on Amazon, including a novel (In Times of War), a memoir he co-wrote with the daughter of Johnny Mercer, and six stories in the 2018 issue of Spot Lit magazine. In 2006 he moved from Florida to Richmond to teach French at Virginia Commonwealth University.

EROSA

by Whitney Judd

"Damn you, Erosa, for ever coming into my life!"

"Shii, poor little boy." It was a crawling sneer and spoken slowly, and it ate up everything. "Pobrecito garcon, you be back. Always you be back."

"That's not French. You can't speak it, not French, not you." He turned back from the door, turned his head towards her and wanted to shout those words. They came out weary.

He pushed through the door, walked with his head hung, "Damn, damn, damn."

The steps in the path were white stone. There were brown weeds in the garden and thistles. The light of mid-morning was clear and in it the smooth skin of his face wrinkled around his eyes. The door was open, left that way, and he could hear the echo of her standing in it, knowing she smiled.

"Avi," Drawn out, high at first then low, almost to a whisper, rich and hot, of dancers held close.

Passed through the gate out into the dust of the street, he still muttered, "Fuck, Erosa, fuck, fuck," and it trailed off.

The muscles in his arms and legs strong and lithe but they were now too worn. They pulled back at him, and he was hungry almost as a

sickness that kept growing. And he couldn't look.

Erosa stood and watched and smiled. The olive cast of her skin was pale beneath. Her eyes were brown and bright. She touched the corner of an eye and went back into the rooms. In the rooms they were shadowed and brown, deeper for the light outside. The thick walls made the rooms cooler. She was a bit taller than he, and when she bent a leg and pushed a hip that much shorter. And that pleased her, the bending and the pushing, not that so much but what it did. Supple and she moved easily, move well among all the people of the town, among those who were ragged and with those whose clothes were silk on their skins, those that came off, always with those eyes and that smile. Perspiration had began under her clothes and arms, and as she move in those rooms the small swing of the arms beneath the gown was more fluid. She liked the smell of sweat; he, too. The gown was finely woven and white and when the breezes came they blew through it.

His shirt and pants were white and rough cut, with stains at the arms pits, around the waist and at the knees. The chord which held his pants up, and the shirt loose, was knotted and frayed. They smelled like her.

"Pobrecito, bebe."

In that brown light in the room she sat at the wooden table they had sat at, pushed a glass of wine away, licked her lips and laughed deep from her chest. It made the air flutter and her ripple.

"You be back like always, Nina."

When Avi worked he worked at anything, hauling in nets from the sea and mending them; in the fields cutting grain, leading the plow horse and kicking stones away. He painted some, drank wine at the Taverns with friends, but not so much lately. Now he worked as an apprentice to a stone mason. He lifted stones, cut them from larger blocks. Now his friends were Erosa only. He hadn't gone to the taverns to drink in months, and his hands had become hard and rough. There had been other girls, his age or nearly, but now there was Erosa. And he shivered, sitting at a table in front of the tavern, looking up through the light and the street to Erosa. He sat alone, no one else, now, was there, and the door always opened to the inside, opened black. No music played; no other clothes he had. He sang with no one here, anymore.

"Damn, damn, damn, fuck, Erosa."

The streets were empty. The doors from Mass hadn't opened; not even the widows dressed in black walked. The streets wound narrowly among the buildings, except up the hill where they were wide and where Erosa was. His hand thumped on the table. His nails were ragged. The other hand he held clenched in his lap.

"Oh, damn."

He sweated a bit under his arms, at his waist, and it was worse, feeling of it, how skin slides when it is moist, and the musk. His hand stuttered. He swore and got up.

"I'll work tomorrow. I won't do this .... not this, damn."

The rest of the day, slowly and awkwardly, he walked through the streets, along the shore line and over the hill to the quarry, staring down or before him. At night he lay on his bed. Nothing moved in him but a shallow breathing which he'd stop and hold. The mattress was stuffed with rags and grass, with anything that was soft, and held up on a wooden frame by leather straps. He lay clothed with his eyes opened. The breeze from the ocean came through the door, and he lay in it all night with his eyes wide, and it began to smell like Erosa. He twisted on the bed, and his clothes tied around like arms and legs holding him.

Once he got up, wandered in the breeze and outside and stared into the black ocean and came back into the one room and stared into the mirror hung on the wall; held his head in his palms, "Damn me, damn me." Only in the pale light from the stars and ocean could he see. Sleep was, after, no rest.

In the morning he got up. His face was lined and he was wrinkled. He was dirty and he hurt. The smell of Erosa was on him still, and he was hungry. He ate the bread and meat and drank and left, and the hunger was still there. The scrub of the bushes on the path to the quarry dragged at his pants. The sky was hot and white. The ocean faded and dust kicked up easily.

"Today, you come."

"I work today."

"You look like shit. Everyone knows. Go to work."

Before noon he had piled the stones he carried in the mason's shack. He cut bigger ones to smaller ones, beating them with an iron hammer and chisels. He lifted and stone dust covered his clothes and clung to the scruff of his face. He was hot and loose and sweated.

"Erosa," something like a whisper in him.

"You, what's wrong?"

"Ah, there is nothing."

"Her. Why? You have nothing now. Before . . .. You're a fool. Go back, get some better stones. These break."

Like a whisper in him, like a cascade, and from among the rocks in the quarry he looked up into the sun. On the ledge above him Erosa stood. The breeze came in from the ocean and he began to cool. Her hair rose up from her shoulders. Cheek bones cast shadow and caught the light, and the red dress blew loose.

"Fuck." It fell out mumbled. He could see her smile above him; see, as if they were close, her lips move.

"Avi."

And he watched the slow turn back, the glance back waiting, then the roll of her hips away, and the wind blew. He stood and watched with his palms over his ears; sting from the sweat in his eyes.

"Damn." He hung there amid the cut rocks, his hands moving like the rhythm at the tavern. "Damn." The stones he brought back he'd picked for the cracks in them.

"Put them there. Go get something. Go eat. You're too slow, walk like the dying."

It was the rolling away of her that made him hungry, again. And he cursed himself. He sat in the quarry with his back to the sun and ate, and stared before him to the sea. It looked dry, and his last bite stuck in his throat and he spat, stood up and his shoulders sagged. He took off his shirt to rinse clean. It was the burn of his skin in the heat, it held like hands, and the water stung. What had stayed and sloshed in his mouth he spat out. But there was still the roll of Erosa beneath; that drink of cool air in those walls.

The old man craved into the stone. "You know how many people die, widow's son?"

"No."

"Every week two, three maybe. I cut these stones for their graves. I never hunger. And you, always." He worked the stone as if it were nothing else. To Avi he looked like that sea, flat and barely moving. And there was the wind blowing eddies around his feet. He picked up the hammer and began to cut another.

"Always, boy, you hunger. She eats you, no other way. You go when she wants. She eats you, boy."

Avi stood up form the stone he cut, blankness like the gray flatness of sea on his face and the eyes, that realization, not from the sea or night, but looking at the stone cutter. "Wha ..."

"You know. You go from jobs, this to that; work here for me when she's done. Every body knows. Nothing, you have nothing, boy. A home, a home anymore, what was your mother's? No family, never. No, what you do, now. No friends, not a thing you have. Every week two, three people die. You die, what happens? You bury yourself."

Stone carver look at him. He hung in that air like the chisels and hammer from his hands.

"Go get more. You'll break these."

All afternoon he carried rocks. For every one broken he was sent for two, till his sight was black, and their weight stopped him, and the sun burned through his throat. All afternoon like the sun behind me, all blackening as that night sea and his hands over his face. Between each load he'd hesitant, look back to the ridge where Erosa had walked from. There, where he was, where the stone carver worked, among the fallen, broken and upright stones it was like looking up out of the earth. A ground hot and filling his breath. Everyday he would do this, here and sleep at night somewhere, soon in a place black and opened; wander with those ragged men only the widows gave food to. He looked up and it was looking out of a grave.

"No more, no more, no more, no more."

After those hesitations, when his sight was back, he bent hard over the stones and lifted them. The wind pushed him, and the flat sea.

"Will you pay me more?"

The hands of the carver, as veined and heavy as they were, lifted up lightly from the head stone.

"You work everyday, you make money."

Avi nodded and walked back for more stones. Every time he bent and lifted there was strain through his back, over his shoulders. *Who buries you.* Every time the stone carver's face and the white dust over his hands, and the widows hunched and walking. *Who buries you.* He bent and lifted more, intent and only seeing the grains in the stones, and the cracks. Night, every time, and the twisting of his clothes about him. It was all he saw, even with his eyes opened.

"Go home, there is enough here. Go on. Go home. Go sleep. You work tomorrow."

"Tomorrow, I'll work, and after that. I'll work."

He dragged his water skin over his shoulder. Beneath it was the only place cool. The slope up from the quarry was dustier and into the face of the sun. He stopped there, on it, closed his eyes and brought the water to his lips, breathed for the first time. *Who does?* He held his eyes closed. And there was that strain.

Erosa was at the crest, and the water ran down his chin.

"What?"

"Pobrecito, you come to me."

She waited at the top of the hill, pushed her hip, smiled and shifted and turned so the wind blew hair across her mouth. He, stuck on the slope up.

"I can't."

"You come to me, Pobrecito."

He was left standing at the top of the hill, where she had been, above the sea, staring, weak and drooped, "I can't."

Behind him the quarry, its dust and that black heat. "Who buries me? Who buries me . . .."

In the evening he walked into the ocean, naked, sunk into it and let it wash him, and he lay in the waves on the shore. It was rough as his hands. The sun reddened the sea, let it reach out to purple on the sand. He got up and dressed and walked up the hill.

"Pauvre, garcon, mi amour."

The shadows in the open robe, the sheen like oil on the skin in the fall of light: "Like always, bebe. Avi."

EL SEÑOR DE LOS MILAGROS

by Janet Barrow

Señor Arellano walked slowly along Jiron Junín, his cane tapping nervously against the ground. The streets, a hive of agitated activity less than an hour before, were now vacant. Red and white relics hung over every doorstep. A street dog dug through a pile of garbage, the colors of its country painted into its greasy fur. A block further, a schnauzer lay in the sun, a Peruvian flag tied around its neck. After years of grumbling about the ceaseless racket of car horns, drunken street-fights, and the crazy old Catholic women self-flagellating on the corner outside of his Chinatown apartment, Señor Arellano was surprised to find the silence of today more oppressive than the previous seventy-years spent enduring the sounds of chaos. The streets were too wide without the regular crowds. And with no need for constant vigilance against thieves, nor the careful calculation it takes an old man to weave his way through a swarm without being trampled, his thoughts took up too much space.

Why does she always have to be so stubborn, he wondered.

"I'm just not superstitious like you," she had said, her words hitting him like a slap in the face.

"It's not superstition, Erika. It's logic. These kinds of events attract chaos. And in this country, when chaos breaks loose, people end up dead."

He'd imagined her eyes rolling at the other end of the line.

"The police don't have any need to demonstrate their power anymore, papá. The war is over. No one's trying to show the commies who's boss."

"Erika," he had pleaded, his voice growing soft, "The National Stadium is not safe. You've never had a problem listening to me about this before, why are you starting now?"

She paused for a long moment.

"I've always listened to you because I'm sorry for what happened to you," she whispered into the phone, "But Perú is going to make history today. It's been thirty-six years since-"

"And in 1964," he cut her off, "It had been twenty-eight."

"I know, papá. But this is different. The world is watching us, and they don't want to see any more violence. They've seen enough in Venezuela. All they want is to see a clean, respectful game. And that's what they're going to get."

"Oh," he scoffed, "I'm sure that's why a couple hundred drunk hooligans spent all last night dancing around outside the New Zealand team's hotel. Kept them up all night paying their respects, no?"

"Come on, papá. The New Zealanders made up those rumors anyway. They just want some stories about rowdy Latinos to bring back home. Look, I've got to go now. Stop worrying. Call up aunt Vanessa and go watch with her in Magdalena. She told me she's making tequeños and inviting some friends over. I'll call you at half time. Te quiero, papá."

"Hijita, I really –" he insisted, but she had already hung up.

If his daughter was stubborn, she was nonetheless a watered-down version of her viejito. He would not call up his sister. He would not take a cab to Magdalena, nor would he eat tequeños on a crowded couch amongst wrinkled contemporaries. Instead, he would walk the eerie distance between his Chinatown apartment and the Sanctuary of Las Nazarenas. And once inside, he would sit and pray until it was all over.

****

Silvio Gensollen and Sofia Ortega, who normally sat back to back in the tiny control room at the Geophysical Institute of Peru, stood up and lifted their ancient wood-backed chairs, one over the other, so that they could sit side by side.

"Can't wait until the new assignment comes in and we can finally get out of this hole in the wall," Sofia murmured.

She propped her ten-year-old son's cracked iPad against her input panel and found a website live-broadcasting the game. *Somos libres, seámoslo....* The players were singing, hands crossed over their hearts.

"It's such bullshit that we have to be here, huevón," she sighed, pushing her feet against the wall and reclining back until her seat balanced in the shape of a 'V' over its back legs.

"Even on a national holiday," she continued, "They need us here making sure the *automated* system doesn't screw up."

"They're just worried about the problems they'll be in if this thing ever fails," said Silvio, "Like that government security app in France, did you see that? Delayed three hours getting a message out during a terrorist attack. Imagine how screwed we'd be if that ever happened here."

"But it's not the same, Silvio. If the system detects a tremor, the alert goes out. If it doesn't detect it, there's no way for us to see it either. The only plausible failure would be with the detection system, not with internal software connections."

Silvio let his hand brush against Sofia's thigh before answering.

"At least this way we get to watch the game together, no?" he asked.

"Luis and the kids are watching at the puto National Stadium," she said, pulling away from his touch, "They got there early and sold my ticket to some huevón outside."

****

Señor Arellano turned right onto Calle Capón. Though he'd never been to China, he liked to walk beneath the green and red pagoda-style roofs and imagine the pueblo where his great-great-grandfather had grown up, what his life had been like before he ever heard the word *guano*, before he decided to come to Perú and dedicate his twenties to collecting expensive bird shit on the beaches of Callao with the aim of selling it to rich gringos in Europe. The story had it that he'd landed himself in Perú on account of being a money-grubber, which he was until the day that he died, but that he had his dignity too. Eventually, the crowds of guano-fiends got to be too big, and the day he found himself punching a kid from Xi'an over a pile of bird shit, he decided he'd prefer to spend his days sweating over the stove of a Chifa restaurant in Pueblo Libre instead. Thus, he became the first in a line of Chiferos that stretched over four generations and at least a hundred thousand bowls of steaming fried rice before Erika decided she'd become a teacher.

Lost in the unfamiliar silence, the smell of his father's old restaurant, Chifa Xi, began to precipitate out of the still air. Señor Arellano fell back through the years, until he was scrambling between the legs of the cooks and waitresses in the kitchen, trying to throw a spoonful of chili powder into an order of Chaufa de pollo on a dare that his older brother had made. And then he could hear the roaring voices of the customer's out front, screaming at the television during a match between Alianza and la U. But when he looked left, he realized that the screams were coming from down the street. Chifa Wong and Chifa Amigo had stayed open, and they were packed full of all the television-less Peruvians of downtown Lima. The game had already begun.

His heart began to speed up then. He was late to the church. He was always late for everything, but this time, it was unacceptable. Erika needed him. He began to walk faster, but all at once, he tripped forward over a discarded sandal.

"Concha su madre," he cried out, and he veered left, barely avoiding a steaming pile of brown and coming to land on one of the red tiles that clustered into the shape of a rat, the first year of the twelve-year Zodiac Cycle.

"You have the abundant imagination of the horse," he remembered his father teasing him as a young boy, "be careful not to let it take advantage of you."

He felt a pang of resentment.

"If you were here," he grumbled under his breath, "you'd be just as worried about Erika being there as I am."

"If I were there," he imagined his father answering, "I'd have preferred locking her in a closet to letting her go. But she's an adult now- we don't get to make the decision for her."

"I just don't understand why she has to insist when she knows-"

"That's because you've forgotten how you felt during the first half of that game, before that day became a nightmare that neither of us would ever forget."

But Señor Arellano hadn't forgotten. In fact, he remembered it better than the day of his marriage, or even the morning of Erika's birth. It was fifteen days until his eleventh birthday, and his father had blown three-days wages on tickets to what would be Arellano's first game at the National Stadium. Perú was to play Argentina in the qualifying round for the Tokyo Olympics.

He remembered how cool his plastic red seat had felt against his legs when he sat down, and that he'd eaten his bag of canchita way too quickly, his whole body a bundle of nervous energy, waiting for the game to begin.

Just like for any other poor kid in Perú, for Arellano, fútbol had represented the shining medallion in the distance, the Peruvian dream. At age ten, he already knew that his future held few options. Chifa was option number one. Option number two involved earning hundreds of thousands a year for soaring a beautiful black and white sphere of hope across the wide field of the National Stadium while fifty-thousand people screamed at him in ecstasy.

And so he'd watched that game like a phantom – his body was in the stands with his father, but his soul was down on the field. The dreams he had for his country jockeyed with those that he had for himself, until he couldn't decide if victory was more important for the future of Perú or for his own future. Somehow, he'd felt certain that if Perú won, his fate would be sealed. A win at his first game, and a game as important as that one, would have been a sort of taking in, an ecstatic pronunciation that 'yes,' that was where he was meant to be.

****

Twenty minutes into the game, all of Lima was silent. Ten million people held their breath. Twenty million eyes moved across flickering screens streaming live-broadcasts. Perú had not been to the world cup in thirty-six years, meaning there had not been a victory since before the civil war, the death squads, the forced sterilizations, the floods that left seven-hundred thousand people homeless, nor the magnitude eight earthquake that leveled Pisco to the ground. In the first qualifying match against New Zealand, they had tied 0-0. Now, if they won, they would be the final team to qualify for the 2018 World Cup in Russia.

"Kuczynski says tomorrow will be a national holiday if we can pull this off," Silvio whispered, hunched forward so that his head was only a foot from the screen.

"Yeah, I'm sure he'll be excited about the twenty million dollar check we'll get for making it through. He can use it to make some accessory to the airport he's going to trade the Fujimori party for letting Alberto out of prison," she scoffed.

"He's not going to pardon Fujimori," Silvio countered, "It would be political suicide."

"There's not a politician in the history of this country who isn't crooked as the Pishtaco's smile, Silvio. Kuczynski doesn't care about Alberto's forced sterilization campaigns, nor all the innocents he had gunned down during the war. If he can get something out of it, I bet you a dime he'll pardon Alberto. He won't even bat an eye over it. He can't. There's no way for him to understand the terror this country went through under Fujimori. When we were, ay-" she shouted, jumping to her feet as Perú closed in on the New Zealand goal post. But New Zealand intercepted quickly and sent the ball soaring back to center field.

"When we were living through car bombs and daily assassinations," she continued, sitting back down and pushing her chair back up onto its hind legs, "Kuczynski had already run back to the US, already decided he'd rather spend those years getting rich managing private equity funds and leave it to Alberto to clean up the mess with the terrorists."

"You know something crazy?" Silvio said then, "My father's a Fujimorista. Puts up his fists whenever he hears a word thrown against Keiko. Says the femenistas should have rallied behind her. Says they should've been thrilled to see a woman get so far."

Sofia laughed so hard she started to tear up.

"Now that is one I have not heard before. What level of machist do you have to get to before you think that putting literally any person with a vagina in office would be a win for feminism? Keiko's not even a woman, for Christs sake! She's a puppet. If she took office, the first thing she's do is pardon her father, watch him skip merrily out of his prison cell, and then let him take the reins from behind the scenes, maybe even run a second sterilization campaign, just for kicks. All her puppet strings would be visible, but we wouldn't be able to touch Alberto. But really, how can any-"

"Vamooooos," Silvio yelled, jumping to his feet.

"Ay, vamos muchachos," Sofia echoed.

Christian Cueva was at left of field, close to the New Zealand goal. He passed to Jefferson Farfán, who was closing in at center field.

"Holy shit," Sofia yelled, jumping into Silvio's arms.

Farfán had made a clean kick, and the ball soared clear over the goalie's head, flying into the net with exhilarating grace.

"Concha su madre, we did it," screamed Silvio.

On the screen, Farfán ran with his arms outstretched. Somebody threw him a jersey from the stands and he draped it over his eyes before falling to the ground in tearful ecstasy.

"I can't believe it," Sofia shouted, her body suddenly stiff.

"Me neither, Sof-"

"No, Silvio, look-"

On the right side of her control board, a red light was flickering. The screen beside it showed the location of the imminent earthquake.

"Dios mio," she whispered, her breath hollow, "It'll be at the National Stadium in thirty seconds."

****

Señor Arellano looked down at his watch. It had been fifteen minutes since the game started, and at last, he was less than a block from the church. Every few steps, he reached into his pocket and took out his phone, punched in Erika's number, and then hung up before the first ring. She had promised to call at halftime. He would have to wait.

Besides, if something had happened, he reasoned, *I would know about it right away.* All of Lima had its eyes on the stadium. The persistence of the silence meant that there still hadn't been any goals, and, more importantly, no disasters either. Or did it? If catastrophe broke loose, would people begin to scream inside their houses? Or would the silence only grow stronger and thicker until it lay over the city like a heavy coat, muffling any sounds that tried to escape?

Suddenly, he felt panicked. *How had the people watching at home reacted in 1964? Surely, they'd cried out in indignation over that idiot ref's disallowance of our goal, the goal that had put us at one to one, with only six minutes to go. Surely, in their rage, they would have all stormed the field, like that kid up front did, like I would have done had I been sitting any closer. But when the strange violence began to drip over their screens in the moments that followed, when our own police put their bats against that kid's young body, and the whole front section pitched into the field to defend him, did they keep screaming then? Or did they fall silent? And if they were screaming, did their voices become hoarse, as more bats were put against more bodies, as Peruvians and Argentinians began to fight against each other, and the police against everyone? As everything turned into chaos, did they keep screaming the way I did, because even though I was way up high in the stands, I still felt like my soul was down there on the field? Or did their silence bloom outwards, so that even their chests refused to heave when the cameras cut off and the tears began to stream?*

"Are you going to come in?" came a sudden voice.

Señor Arellano had stopped short on the threshold of the Sanctuary of las Nazarenas.

"Huh? Yes, of course," he stuttered, rattled by the interruption.

He stepped over the threshold at last and walked slowly through the church, welcoming its familiar musty smell. He took a seat near the front of the pews, and then looked up at the venerated painting, "El Señor de Los Milagros," whose mysterious survival of two massive earthquakes and a variety of officiated attempts to destroy it were celebrated, each October, by the largest procession of Catholics in the world.

"We both understand what it's like to survive a catastrophe, Señor," he began, "how quickly a day that starts off full of hope can transform into a nightmare of agony and disbelief...After it all started, my father grabbed me firmly by the hand and pulled me to face him.

'Forget it, hijo,' he said, his eyes filling with tears, 'we've got to get out now.'

I was still shouting at the field, cursing out the ref and the police, calling them all 'pendejos,' and 'concha su madres.' I hadn't yet realized that what had just begun wasn't something that we could win. Even with fifty-thousand of us and just a couple hundred of them, a fist is nothing against a bullet. But then, I hadn't supposed it would come to bullets. Or that, instead of at a sporting event, we would find ourselves in a battle against the ideology of merciless suppression that had arisen long ago, with the first threat of a communist uprising.

When they started throwing the smoke bombs, I understood that there is no longer a fight at all when one side loses the ability to breathe.

We were in the thirty-ninth row. We ran the

same way that everybody around us was running - for the stairs. But as soon as we got in, we realized the mistake we'd made. There was no way out, and we'd just checked ourselves into hell. From the tenth floor, it didn't make any sense to us that we simply could not get moving. We could never have realized that the police had already locked the doors at the bottom, that for every step we forced ourselves down, for every person who squeezed into the stairwell after sputtering for too long in the poisoned air of the tear-gased arena, we were pushing those at the front harder against the locked doors, until their bodies were pressed so firmly together that children floated between chests and backs, their feet not even touching the ground, and those who fainted from lack of oxygen or the plastering of their organs were held upright by the crowd, which hadn't even felt them fall limp. We couldn't have known that our collective desperation to get out eventually began to transform the bodies at the front into corpses.

In the two hours it took for somebody to ply open the doors at the bottom of our stairwell, Señor, nearly three people died every minute. One person every twenty-two seconds, three-hundred and twenty-eight of them in all.

When the doors finally did open, the corpses spilled out like water from a breaking dam, and all the living just flowed right over them. I was looking down, trying to find my father's hand after somebody shoved between us, when I realized my right heel was pressed against the cheek of a teenage girl. I jerked it away and saw that her face was covered in footprints. Her mouth was open and her teeth had been knocked out.

I thought we would find relief when we finally reached the cool air of the street. Instead, there were shots. The chaos inside had transformed into a skirmish with the police in the streets surrounding the stadium. But they weren't shooting tear gas canisters anymore; they were shooting bullets. I found my father's hand and we ran until we couldn't hear the screams anymore. When we knew we were out of it, he sat down on a stoop and scooped me up like an infant. He rested my back against his legs and we both cried, his tears falling onto my face and into my mouth, coating the back of my dry throat, which ached with confusion and dehydration. And then I fell asleep, as if I were trying to turn the whole thing into a bad dream.

The next morning, I woke up covered in bruises from all the bodies that had marked their insistence to live upon me."

When he had finished, Señor Arellano looked up into the eyes of the sacred image.

"I hope you understand what it is I've come here to ask you for, Señor," he whispered.

Just then, he heard the screams begin to sound from all around. It was easy to tell a scream of glory, he noted then, from a scream of despair. Perú had scored. Señor Arellano tried, but he couldn't restrain the grin that began to spread over his lips. And then he felt his phone vibrate in his pocket.

"Disculpe, Señor," he smiled, "I wouldn't take it, but it could be Erika."

But it wasn't Erika. Instead, it was an automated alert from Sismos Perú, an application that Erika had downloaded onto his phone for him a few months before.

"Tremor of unknown magnitude detected in the northern part of Cercado de Lima. Seek safety immediately."

"Dios," Señor Arellano breathed, falling to his knees, "what have you done?"

****

*This story is based on the events of the qualifying match between Peru and New Zealand for the 2018 World Cup, which took place in Lima in November of 2017. The extreme celebratory commotion following Peru's first goal was so intense that it triggered a series of magnitude one tremors throughout the city. Ultimately, nobody was injured.

NOTES GOING UNDERGROUNG

by Joram Piatigorsky

Ladies and gentleman, thank you for inviting me – an ordinary man who, like most, thinks himself special but knows he isn't – to deliver my own eulogy at my funeral. It has taken much soul searching whether or not to accept your invitation. I asked myself, why should I, or anyone, deliver a eulogy at my funeral? Why not just say, "Good-bye," and let it go at that? Does a life need an explanation? I still am who I was. Dying hasn't changed my status or anything else. I had nothing to do with my birth, so I can't explain that. I came and now I'm leaving, just like any squirrel in the garden that was born and will die. There's always another squirrel. Anyway, who would believe a eulogy to myself? Praise would be taken as self-promotion and belittling myself would be considered false modesty. Isn't that what you thought when I called myself an ordinary man?

Death has always been considered an abrupt process, like crossing a line from living flesh to dead meat. A person was either alive or dead, never both at the same time, like I am now. Due to modern technology, the final stages of death can be digitized and captured in slow motion. This lets me talk to you during a suspended state of being partially alive and partially dead simultaneously, as my remaining life seeps into my corpse in the lovely coffin by my side. I have a grace period while leaking life but still breathing air to reminisce – size up my life – as my corpse receives my death in preparation for burial. It's not physically painful and I don't like it, but it is what it is: we're born slowly and die slowly. We have tapered ends, so to speak. Only when my entire life has passed – in today's lingo, has downloaded – into my corpse will I fade out and go underground.

I first was exposed to gradual death at college in a physiology course when I decapitated a turtle to study its heart. Not only did the heart continue beating for hours, but the headless body of the turtle continued walking for some time! It made me wonder whether the bodiless head was still seeing or thinking for a while, or whatever turtles did with their brains, and if so, for how long?

What a disturbing notion for us humans: a guillotined head still thinking in a basket!

I asked a friend for advice on what I might say at my eulogy. "Tell them about a few of your career contributions and recognitions, and the love and support you received from family and friends, like me," he advised. Then he suggested some nonsense that I talk about being a down-to-earth regular guy who roots for the local sports teams and likes to eat desserts before entrees. I have an incurable sweet tooth. He also added a stupid joke that I can't even remember. I guess he thought I should appear like a successful mensch, everybody's good guy. But, is that really me? A mensch who tried his best? That seems as lame as describing me as "nice." Yuk! Why not include that I rescued a puppy from the pound once?

Getting to the essence of a human being – of me in this case – giving a eulogy that's honest and worthwhile – is impossible due to the many contradictions, inconsistencies and conflicts in anyone's life. Moreover, we all, including me, have suppressed ghosts begging to get out of our skin, playing havoc with our psyches, and like it or not, are silent partners of our complex identity. I've pondered at length to understand who defines my identity: me or others ("us" or "them")? It's both, I think, which creates a conundrum. If I give my own eulogy, how others perceive me – my "them" identity – will be absent; if someone else gives my eulogy, my view – my "us" identity – will be lost.

So, here's my plan, even if imperfect. I will tell a story, a true story involving several sides of myself (cryptic perhaps), and let you draw your own conclusions. Keep in mind that we're more than one person, and you'll appreciate how slippery identity is and how incomplete eulogies really are.

A man of middle age and medium height, an average looking man, a life-long bachelor, was walking down the street in tattered clothes and a light green jacket in Chicago on a gray afternoon in January. The wind chill was in the teens and piles of dirty snow lined the street. This gentleman – and I call him a gentleman because of his gender, not style – lived in a poorly furnished, one room apartment in a shabby section of town. His prized possession was a rust colored ceramic vase, the only present he ever received from his alcoholic father. I know nothing about his mother. A broken piece resulting from an accident had been glued back carelessly on the vase in its original position. He had lost track of both of his divorced parents. He supported himself by doing odd jobs and holding temporary positions from which he was usually fired because of his inability to be punctual. He was a sorrowful case. This drab January was a low point because one of his employers who occasionally paid him to take the trash to the dump had just died.

As he was ambling down the street feeling sorry for himself his eyes struck gold! The corner of what appeared to be genuine U.S. currency was protruding from a small mound of icy snow surrounding a lamppost. He leaned over and pulled it out. Yes! $20! Christmas was over for the rest of the world, but it had just started for him. He rubbed the bill with his thumb and index finger as if to assure it was real, put it in his pocket, skipped a step or two, took it out and used it to wipe his forehead, a gesture that gave it a pleasurable physical presence. He had suddenly transformed to a larger, more important person, a man with sharp eyes able to grasp opportunity and could now afford a warm cup of hot chocolate with a doughnut and have change left over.

I know I'm rambling a bit, but I have always tended to drag things out. It's who I am, and it's not easy to give one's own eulogy.

Where was I?

Oh, yes, this pitiful, lonely person was cold and hungry, yet on top of the world; he had just changed from a pauper to a man with $20 in his pocket.

As he strolled, he noticed shops that he had previously ignored. A shiny $35 Timex wristwatch in a display window caught his attention. Well, that was for a king, not for him, but perhaps someday...who knows? If he could find $20, he might find $100 another time. He started kicking the snow heaps hoping that more money would tumble out.

What an optimist, driven by pipedreams.

But there was a problem. Alone the idea that $20 could grow to a larger sum made it feel lighter in his pocket. It suddenly became less money, and he was less happy. Apparently $20 was not even enough to keep track of time; that cost $35.

Poor man. He allowed a little success to balloon into greed.

The city streetlights clicked on as dusk descended. Darts of frigid air pierced his exposed face with each gust. He pulled his jacket tight around his neck and slid his frozen chest deeper into the garment when he heard a low-grade shuffling sound behind him. He turned and saw a man perilously thin – eyes bland, oversized ragged pants held up with a tattered rope, and filthy, bare toes protruding through holes in his shoes.

"Gotta a dime?" croaked this pathetic bag of bones as he extended a frail arm with palm upturned.

Our newly-rich gentleman stared at the miserable excuse for a man.

"Gotta dime, even a nickel?" the beggar repeated.

"I have no loose change," came the honest response. Despite his defects, he was impeccably honest.

Our gentleman with $20, now looking like a success story by comparison, noticed that the beggar's blue fingertips trembled, and that his ring finger was a useless amputated stub. The beggar produced a phlegm-rattling cough, and pink saliva dribbled from the corners of his mouth.

Now, here's the interesting part. Our hero, if that's what he could be called, reached into his pocket, pulled out the $20, kissed it and placed it into the beggar's outstretched hand.

"God bless you," said the beggar, without

looking at the amount, and he proceeded slowly down the street crunching the $20 bill in his hand.

Was this a noble act of charity? No. I knew the gentleman from high school. His name was Tim. Even as a teenager, Tim was always his own worst enemy. I remember when he ran for senior class president, craving the prestige, the power and the satisfaction of winning. What did he do? He voted for his opponent, and not because she was pretty or that he thought she was more qualified than he was. He felt voting for himself was self-indulgent, impolite, improper. He wanted it too much. Talk of a loser. That Tim gave away his $20 was entirely consistent for him.

By the way, he lost the election, by one vote!

I ran into Tim once not long ago when I was at a scientific conference in Chicago. I had gone for a walk, got lost and entered a cheap diner to ask directions. There he was, sitting with a some cruddy-looking guy. Imagine the scene. Two lowly flops in a God-forsaken dump having afternoon tea: one was destitute, no doubt a homeless, pathetic man who seemed too far gone to know that he was in such bad shape. The other, Tim, was struggling to stay afloat, no steady job, no family ties, no ambitions. The best thing one could say of Tim was that he didn't smell too bad. *That* one certainly couldn't say about the other guy.

It had been years since I had last seen Tim and so I focused on him trying to remember exactly what he looked like in high school to make sure that I was correct, that he was in fact Tim. The two men seemed oblivious to their surroundings and neither noticed me. Tim was doing all the talking, and the other guy occasionally responded with "uh-hum," or "yep," or "suren'uff."

In the middle of a sentence, Tim turned his head in my direction and barked, "Whadaya starin' at, buddy?"

I stammered, "Err, nothing...sorry, I mean... Tim...is that you?"

"Howd'ya know my name?" He looked startled.

"Yes, you are Tim, aren't you?" I said, amazed that I had remembered correctly.

"Yeah. Who r'you?"

After I told him that I recognized him from high school, he just gazed at me with his mouth gaping, advertising his brownish, crooked teeth, and didn't say a word. That's when I discovered how long a minute can be.

Tim blanched, developed a nervous tick in his right eyelid, which kept fluttering. He ran his fingers through his greasy hair and said, "My god, it's true. Yes, I recognize you. You're just a little more wrinkled and pudgier."

I didn't mind the wrinkles, but pudgier was another matter.

Tim's voice changed, became deeper, more self-conscious, the vernacular disappeared, his eyes darted here, there, everywhere. He avoided looking directly at me.

"I'm so ashamed," he said.

I didn't know how to answer, so I reached out and touched him on the shoulder. His head tilted a notch towards my hand, his face relaxed, as if a great battle was over.

"Reckon I'll be movin' on," said the other guy. He got up and left without another word.

An indifferent waiter drying beer mugs stood behind the seedy looking counter lined with empty stools fixed to the stained wooden floor. There were no pictures on the walls, no tablecloths, no flowers or decorations of any kind. The olive-green paint was peeling off the walls, which had numerous gashes. Floor lamps standing in the corners on either side of the front door accounted for the dim light. There were no windows and the stale air had an odor of burning grease.

It was a closed environment, secluded in its own way, as was a posh country club. You were a member or an outcast. Yet, I thought, even in this dismal scene lacking charm or purpose or any class whatsoever, Tim, downtrodden and pathetic, was as human and vulnerable as I or the King of England.

After a moment of silence, Tim put his arms around my neck, nestled his head on my left shoulder, and cried. I felt him tremble, and his grip tightened. The waiter looked at us with a peculiar expression and went into the kitchen, leaving us alone in this miserable, stinking hole.

Tim kept repeating over and over again, "It's *not* my fault, it's not *my* fault, it's not my *fault.*"

Tim had said he was ashamed, and he was, I'm sure, but it was I who should have been ashamed, but I wasn't.

Why should I have been ashamed?

Well, unfortunate, defeated Tim, a friend from high school, most certainly a good man in need of comforting, was crying on my shoulder, begging for sympathy and understanding, and what did I do? Nothing. What was going through my mind? I'm almost too ashamed to say, but, what the heck, I sense the download is nearing the end, so it's my last chance to confess. Fact is fact, and it's no different than a stone in the ground. I was thinking that Tim was dribbling snot on my new Alpaca wool sweater.

"Now, now, Tim, it's okay, really. We all have hard times now and then."

We don't all have hard times anything like that. I never did. What do I know? What right did I have to empathize? It may have been true in general, but it was dishonest coming from me. If anything, I blamed Tim for being such a loser.

"It's good to see you again, Tim," I said, another falsehood. I was thinking, "How can I get out of this?"

Just as suddenly as Tim broke down, he released his stronghold around my neck (he should have been a wrestler) and said, "Hey buddy, let's have a cup of something hot and catch up."

"S...ure," I answered, but I wanted out.

We ordered coffee (I paid) and I briefly re-capped my life – research scientist, married, a couple of kids, grandkids. I was sketchy. I didn't want him to feel bad, which was presumptuous because, apart from his appearance, I had no idea what his life had been like and, anyway, I was no hero.

Then I lied again, well, I distorted the truth is more like it. I told him that I did research on hearing in earthworms, which I never had done. I worked on eyes.

"Hearing in earthworms? Do they hear?" he asked, suddenly displaying curiosity,

"Maybe,' I answered. "I'm trying to figure that out. Who knows? If earthworms can hear, at least in an earthworm kind of way, my work may help deaf people someday. Big industry, deafness."

Why did I say that nonsense and fantasy and imply that I cared about industry, which I didn't? I had modified my image to appear differently than I am. Since I didn't know much about ears or earthworms or industry, I knew I wouldn't be able to say much (I tend to talk too much), and then I could get back to the hotel sooner. I wanted to see a basketball game on TV and work on my lecture for the meeting the next day.

Tim told me of his drab life, the disappearance of his parents, how his one and only girlfriend left him, how he had dropped out of community college, how he'd given away his $20, and so on. I was hardly listening and wondering how to get out of there. Finally, I told him that I had another appointment, still another lie. He sagged a bit, like a worn drape. I felt guilty not to spend more time with him, or maybe even take him to dinner. I was selfish.

"Will we get a chance to see each other again?" he asked.

That simple question has haunted me all these years.

"Will we see each other again?" he repeated, looking earnest.

So simple, so sad, so lonely. Tim gave away his prized $20 to a miserable beggar, and I lied to have some more time to myself.

"Sure," I said. "Let's keep in touch."

He gave me his phone number, but never asked for mine. I called him once a few months later and received a recorded message that his telephone was temporarily disconnected. Temporarily, that's important; yet, I never called again. I did think about him from time to time, even worried about him, as I did about other people and causes I neglected. I collected lists of things I never accomplished, humongous lists of lost opportunities, too focused on myself to follow up. I collected absences and lived in my own head. And now, it's too late to make amends...

Wait! Why should I apologize for what I didn't do? What I did do made sense from my perspective – that's another eulogy – so apologizing for past behavior would be denying who I was. That doesn't work. I was who I was.

Did I say another eulogy? Isn't that what I implied earlier? There's never one eulogy or one story or one interpretation. There's "us" and "them". We are many people wrapped together, and we are even present in part in other people. I trust you to understand the eulogy I chose to tell, the story I told, the person, or persons, I am, in part, and was, sometimes.

Excuse me, I must sit down. My back hurts, my legs ache, my feet are numb. I'm tired, very, very tired. This must be the end...yes, it's getting darker...the lid is closing...I'm sure you can't hear me anymore...I'm going underground, with my notes and everything I learned along the way.

There's always another squirrel.

About the Author:

During his 50-year career at the National Institutes of Health, **Joram Piatigorsky** has published some 300 scientific articles and a book, Gene Sharing and Evolution (Harvard University Press, 2007), lectured worldwide, received numerous research awards, including the prestigious Helen Keller Prize for vision research, served on scientific editorial boards, advisory boards and funding panels, and trained a generation of scientists. Presently an emeritus scientist, he collects Inuit art, is on the Board of Directors of The Writer's Center in Bethesda, blogs (JoramP.com), and has published a series of personal essays in the journal Lived Experience and a novel, Jellyfish Have Eyes (IPBooks, 2014). He has two sons, five grandchildren, and lives with his wife in Bethesda, Maryland. He can be contacted at joramp@verizon.net.

NOW, THAT'S EXTRAORDINARY

by Michele Sprague

Between taking the kids to soccer practice, hosting sleepovers for their friends, working, taking graduate courses...Whew! And that's only part of my to-do list. No wonder, my mind seems to work in overdrive, racing towards the next thing to do.

Then one day a surprise living in the now experience happened to me. A living in the now experience focuses your awareness on what's going on in front of you, at that moment—the sights, the sounds, the smells. It's putting aside to-do lists and worries, and putting your mind in neutral.

This living in the now experience was a first for me. Colors seemed brighter, a cool breeze carried the intoxicating scent of flowers, and high energy music played in the background. It was a beautiful, seemingly perfect world. And that happened in a local business' parking lot on one memorable Saturday night.

It started with a simple trip to the video store, which was located in a strip mall. I planned to checkout a video and return home. But I never made it to the store.

Once I left my car in the parking lot, I felt as if I entered another world. My senses heightened as I took in the sights, sounds and smells. My to-do lists slipped away until all that was left was peaceful, happy feelings. I was living in the now—a strange place for me. There was nothing to do but enjoy the simple things in life, which brought surprising happiness.

The moon shone brightly atop layers of dark clouds on that cool, July evening. Tree branches danced gracefully as their leaves whispered in the breeze.

The colorful, neon signs and letters appeared brighter than usual against the backdrop of the dark sky. The lights inside the businesses' windows exposed what appeared to be slide shows. People dined and gathered in groups; a waitress waited on a table; and a man stood behind a cash register while talking to an elderly woman.

Three teenage girls giggled as they left the video store. One of them had purple hair.

Another form of magic took place in front of the drug store as a teenage boy flirted with a teenage girl.

And high energy, rhythmic, Middle Eastern music poured out of a nearby subdivision, occasionally interrupted by what sounded like a disc jockey, cheers and applause.

For some reason, everything in my surroundings seemed charged with positive energy. Everything seemed harmonious. This was a slice of everyday life, and it felt good to be a quiet observer and have my head free of schedules, lists and assignments. So, instead of going to the video store, I sat on a bench and continued to watch life unfold.

A teenage boy, who wore a backpack, baggy shorts, and a baseball cap, skated by me while talking on a cell phone.

Couples, children and single folks walked in and out of the video and drug stores, as well as the restaurants. The chatter, the laughter, the conversations, and the stolen kiss I witnessed as a teenage boy kissed a girl, contributed to what turned out to be the evening's entertainment. These folks seemed oblivious to the life story taking place in which they shared starring roles.

Then, as if a movie director said, "Cut," the clouds overshadowed the moon and the sky grew darker. The magic that seemed to surround the evening vanished, and I my to-do list began crowding my mind. I remembered the birthday cake I need to bake for my daughter and the paper that was due Monday.

I still marvel at the sense of peace and joy I felt that evening. I don't know how or why the living in the now experience happened. After all, it was an ordinary Saturday night. Yet everything was extraordinary.

About the Author:

Michele Sprague is the author of the book, Single Again 101. She also wrote hundreds of stories for corporate magazines and newsletters, and other publications.

(portfolio.michelesprague.com)

MACHINE SHOP SUNDRESS
by Claudia Geagan

On an ozone drenched summer day in 1961, Mr. Stevenson gives me his black '54 T-bird and sends me to the loading dock at Lockheed with a shoebox-sized rush delivery.

I've never been to a loading dock so I don't realize in advance that it's built for semi-trailers and don't realize the kind of attention a seventeen year old blond in a 54 T-Bird will get when she arrives. I climb out of the car, lean in to retrieve my thirty-thousand dollar package from the backseat, and everything around me stops. The dock is higher than my head. I walk up the metal-edged steps and hand the box to the man with the clipboard, who, along with the truck drivers and Lockheed workers, is standing still, staring at me and waiting. I explain that it's a rush and he assures me it will find its destination. I get his signature on the shipper and walk back down to the car, trying not to feel the eyes on me, and wondering if I should have found some other entrance.

***

I have a job in an office. In fact, I am the office. I sit alone at a chic parabola of desk in the dramatically darkened reception area outside of George Stevenson's glassed-in confines. At George Stevenson Precision Machine I answer the phone, handle shipping and invoices, do payroll, file blueprints, type letters or wait to be needed for one of those tasks.

Between my desk and the shop is a dark walnut door that Mr. Stevenson likes to keep closed. If he finds it open, he'll kick the stopper, glare at me and shut it.

"I told you, keep this door closed." I don't understand why Mr. Stevenson insists that I sit alone in the semi-darkness, just like I don't understand why my father wants what he wants. I only know I should do what my father or my boss says. It is their world, not mine.

On the other side of that door, the spotless shop is filled with glittering lights that make the metal of the machines and the silver of the parts sparkle. The lathes whir and a radio belts out Elvis or Chubby Checker. Half a dozen machinists cut and drill and shape parts destined to put a man on the moon. When Mr. Stevenson (to this day it's tough to call him George) is out of the office I cheat and leave the door open to hear the machines and the radio. There are five machinists from the young guy who runs the drill press to the old guy who cuts the teeth for the tiny precision gears. The foreman, John, operates a lathe. Only Mr. Stevenson runs the ultra-precision jig borer.

I had been the Stevenson's babysitter, three sweaty little kids and one female German Shepherd. I don't remember the name of the dog but she and I shooed the kids to bed unwashed and then climbed in a recliner together and fell asleep in front of the television. If the dog hadn't awakened when the Stevenson's got home, I wouldn't have. Anybody could have walked in and stolen the children. I couldn't imagine who would want three sticky kids, but I did think the Stevenson's should have paid their pooch instead of me. Therefore, I was astounded when Mr. Stevenson offered me a job in his shop.

On the groggy ride home in the spring of my junior year in high school, Mr. Stevenson asked what classes I was taking.

I tried to sound awake. "Latin, social studies, chemistry, English literature, journalism, gym."

"Can you type?"

"Yes."

"What are you doing this summer?"

"Mom says I should find a summer job, save up for college." Wherever and whatever that was. I'd applied to four of them but never made a campus visit.

"Would you like to have a job in my office, help earn a little college money?"

"I have to ask my parents."

"Ask them and call me."

Mom is giddy. "Call him back. Call him back or I will."

I walk the mile and a half from our pink stucco bungalow on Las Lunas down to Mr. Stevenson's Jetsons-like shop on Foothill Boulevard. I'd like to say I trudged back and forth in the snow, diligently saving for education, but it is Pasadena and I walk on sunbaked sidewalks under a smog-clouded sky. At noon I walk a block to a diner and order the cheapest item on the menu, a seventy-five-cent grilled cheese. I forgo the Coke because I can't afford it. Minimum wage is a dollar an hour, and I save almost every penny I earn. My mother is a sales girl at Bullocks Pasadena and my dad negotiates union contracts for Safeway Stores, but I feel poor. Dad instructs Mom to spend her earnings for groceries. My little sister pretty much lives at her friend's house. I

shouldn't feel that poor. I come home from school and toss myself in a pool surrounded by lemon trees and bougainvillea. The house and the pool squat on a square of dichondra and though it is small, everybody's house is small, and only my dad's thick anger makes it feel crowded.

In the interest of economy Mother makes some of my clothes—gathered skirts in tiny prints, topped with starched white blouses, on-sale cotton remnants shaped into sleeveless dresses with Puritan collars. Dad gets stylish clothes from Bullocks with Mom's discount. Mom does without.

My work at Stevenson Machine is reasonably interesting. I'd known nothing about FICA or shippers or invoices or blue prints, or Apollo projects, but there isn't enough of it to fill my day. If Mr. Stevenson isn't around, I toe kick the rubber wedge under the shop door to keep it open in case the phone rings, and wander into the shop, drawn by its mysterious activity. The machinists all wear white cotton coats that overlap in the front and tie in the back. They wear steel-toed, rubber- soled black shoes and stand on mats. I stand on the concrete floor, in a bare shouldered sundress and summer sandals, observing, but unaware of being observed.

I am engrossed by the spinning lathe and watch John adjust the chuck, angle the cutting tool, then palm the spinning wheel, check the size of the part with a micrometer, fuzz another millionth off. The sweet smell of chartreuse coolant intoxicates me. As John is short and I am tall, I stand behind him and watch him work the lathe, looking down at the bald spot that shows through his backcombed poof of black hair. The man is wiry with a huge misshapen nose and an air of trashiness about him, but he is magic with the lathe. When I wander into the shop all the men glance then return to their work, except John, who looks over his shoulder and grins.

"You really interested in this stuff, ain't cha, Peaches?"

"Why do you call me that?"
"Cause you look like a bowl of peaches and cream."

At home Dad inspects his family of women as if our hips and breasts nauseate him.

He watches my size eight Mom sway as she walks away and says to me, "Don't get so fat your ass looks like that." Mom is self-conscious about her looks. She's generally athletic and pleasant looking, but she has a crudely carved cap on one of her front teeth and she's self-conscious about her legs because maternity girdles left bulging varicose veins. Moreover, Dad has convinced her that her 'ass' is 'fat'. His cruelty amuses him, and she tells me "sticks and stones can break my bones, but names can never hurt me." Nonsense. Names kill a soul, and even then I knew it.

He spends dinner time criticizing what we eat. "Lay off the potatoes. No self-respecting man wants a fatty." He looks through his bifocals at my cheek, on the prowl for a blackhead so he can accuse me of not washing. Being compared to a bowl of peaches and cream is as consoling as Linus' blanket.

I was not quite five years old. I wore a starched white organdy pinafore that my grandmother had sewn, lacy socks and new black patent leather shoes. My curly blonde hair was pulled back with a big flower print bow. My parents and grandparents were taking me to a fancy supper club, adorable daughter used as an accessory. While Mother dressed I followed my dad around. He walked through our one car garage and out into the fresh air, tapped the tobacco tighter in his Chesterfield and flicked his Zippo.

"Daddy?"

"Stay in the house."

I heard the big brotherly voice of a boy in the park across the street. "You can do it, Sport. Come on. You can do it." I imagined an older boy running astride the bike of a younger boy, and I wanted that big brother.

I took off toward that voice. On the oil slick garage floor, my feet flew out from under me, and I splayed on my belly in the dirt and grime, screaming, blood running down my shin.

"Damn it, I said stay inside." Daddy flicked his cigarette into the yard, grabbed me up with one hand and swatted my bottom with his other. "Look at your dress. You're ruined."

I did not go to the supper club.

That summer of 1961 passes. Senior year arrives and school starts, and Mr. Stevenson asks me to work two hours a day after school.

At school I wear white Keds and "hose" before the "panty" part is attached to them. The school forbids sandals and requires either socks or stockings. Like most the girls, I choose stockings. Stockings are held up by a garter belt, a garment currently reserved for porn videos, but in the early 1960s a garter belt is white cotton with heavy white elastic and "supporters," soft rubber nubs that fit inside a metal hook. On top of the garter belt my sister and I wore white cotton full coverage panties.

Mr. Stevenson complains about the looks of my white tennies. He wants heels. So I keep a pair of hot pink spike heels under the desk and dutifully switch into them for work and feel guilty when I realize I have pocked the elegant cork floors of my office.

I wonder now what Mr. Stevenson was thinking, because he had to notice the floor. No, I don't wonder. I looked older and sexier in those pointy toed, high heeled shoes. No one ever came through the front door. Those shoes and the look they produced were for him.

I remain fascinated with the shop and continue to wander out there in my pink heels. I still love the sweet smell of coolant. In the fall of my senior year, the school gives us some type of skills testing and along with being able to recite numbers backward and spell *accommodate,* I can recognize a micrometer and differentiate between an Allen wrench and a drill bit so the results indicate mechanical aptitude. It doesn't matter for girls though. What matters for us is marrying and having babies.

I was fourteen when Mom took me to see a gynecologist because I was becoming a woman. I slipped into a hospital gown with nothing under it and lay on my back, feet up in stirrups. My mother stood by my head assuring me everything would be all right. No one, including me, had ever put fingers between my legs much less inside my body. The aging doctor put what looked like clear Vasoline on the tips of his gloved fingers and forced them inside of me. Then he pressed those fingers upward toward my belly button and pushed down with his free hand. My discomfort was enough to make me jump off the table if Mom had not been pressing down on my shoulders. "Don't move, Claudia, it's going to be all right." Then the discomfort turned to pain. I shrieked and he quickly pulled his fingers out. The rubber glove had fresh red blood on it. Mother looked pale and her mouth hung open. The doctor offered me help up with his dry hand; "You can get dressed young lady." At home that evening I watched out my bedroom window as Mom sat on the terrace sobbing to Dad about how my future husband will never know I'm a virgin. She twisted her Kleenex. It wasn't her fault. She didn't know he would do that. I thought, "What future husband?" From where I sat marriage did not look appealing.

In the fall of 1961, teenage ennui, senioritis, a sense of purposelessness permeates me. I apply to four colleges, UCLA, Cal Berkeley, USC and William and Mary. William and Mary is my first choice because it is so far away, but I am not accepted as an out of state student. The others want me, but I select USC because my best friend is going there. No one in my family has been to college.

Later I make a campus visit by myself. I park on the street near my soon-to-be dorm home, across from a car with a middle-aged white man whose pants are open. I walk on by. The group leaders give a campus tour. They explain what to do in case someone tries to rape us. "Don't resist, because that way he won't hurt you." The indication is clear that this threat is thought to come from black males who live in nearby neighborhoods.

When I was sixteen, at the beginning of my junior year before I'd ever heard of George Stevenson Machine, my boyfriend du jour came to the house to study. My parents went out. When they returned I was sitting on his lap kissing. I wore a new yellow angora sweater and a dyed-to-match pleated skirt. There was no groping. The obligatory ceiling light glared down on us. I jumped off his lap. He stood up. My father yelled and insisted on taking the boy home right then. The boy sat in the passenger seat and I jumped in the back as though my presence would protect him from whatever was about to happen.

"I don't expect you'd be responsible if you got her pregnant," my father yelled.

The boy was only fifteen. "We weren't doing anything to get me pregnant," I defended. The boy stared at his hands. At home, Dad said to Mother, "that boy had an erection when she jumped off her lap." I wonder now why that surprised him. At the time I barely knew that men desired women, never considered the mechanics of sex. I'd never seen my father be even mildly sexual with my mother.

"No one marries an easy girl." Dad snarled and wagged his finger. As soon as I could, I headed for my room.

I graduate from Pasadena High School in June of 1962. At work that summer I wear heels and stockings with the summer frocks Mom sews and I spend a lot of time telling the phone lies to John's ex-wife that John has asked me to tell because his ex isn't getting the money he owes her. I say he isn't there and anyway the pay checks don't get handed out till 5:00. This annoys me. Other than that, I am by now good with blueprints and invoices and payroll and am occasionally permitted to put tiny screws in English muffin-sized gear boxes, which allows me to spend time in the shop. John F. Kennedy is president and as a nation, which includes me, we are excited about space exploration.

My family life is as weird as ever. Mother is making a mess in the master bedroom sewing me a white pique sundress. On a mid-July day covered in a cotton duster that she wears around the house she kneels in the middle of pique lint and short loose white threads. I stand in heels while she pins the waist and the zipper. The dress is cut low in the back and high in the front. It's her best work to date. Dad is objecting to the detritus of dressmaking. "Helen, get this shit vacuumed up before you go to bed. I don't want to look at it in the morning." She's pretending not to listen, focused on giving me a prettiness she has been denied. For once, I think the dress is stylish and flattering. The stiff pique has never been washed, and the belled skirt looks like an inverted tulip. Mom touches my hip to turn me and I seem slimmer, curvier than ever before. Her hand feels gentle. As soon as the dress is finished and hung on the back of my bedroom door, I slip into it and head to work, feeling pert and pretty instead of clownish. Mr. Stevenson is on vacation. John loiters around my desk all morning. At lunchtime, he says "Want'a go get a hamburger, Peachy?" His attention seems positive. I please John, amuse him. Dad I only aggravate.

"Sure," I say. Bob's Big Boy on Colorado Boulevard isn't that far away, and the boys who cruise it with me in their cars hardly ever have money to stop and buy a hamburger. I assume that's where we were going.

I know he would not have asked if Mr. Stevenson had been there, but I am glad he did. My curiosity and sense of adventure kick right in. John drives a metallic green Pontiac muscle car that I've seen parked behind the building, one with black bucket seats. Maybe for once there will be a little excitement.

"I'll pick you up out front in a minute." John closes the shop door behind him. To me John seems old. I know from payroll that he is almost 40, and his grammar is atrocious, but he smiles and I like that. Mr. Stevenson has taken me flying to Catalina in his Cessna with olive upholstery and red piping. He is 36, also old, but fun. The flight was exhilarating. I imagine the rumble of John's car beneath my seat. This too will be exciting.

My own dad doesn't have toys, doesn't do fun things, would never have trusted me to take his car to Lockheed. He is like a tarp, thrown down to smother laughter and joy and excitement. His women should look some unattainable way and be perfectly still like tiny china figurines. The whole idea of Cessnas and Pontiacs is out of the question. Noise and power enthrall me.

John pulls up outside, and I let myself into his passenger seat, check out my white skirt and hot pink heels against the black-leather-jacket vibe of the car. But John is not smiling. He doesn't rev the engine or even speak to me.

We don't head down toward Colorado but out toward Sierra Madre, the wrong direction. "Where are we going?"

"I've gotta get something from my house."

"Oh." Girls do not question what men do.

The house is only a few minutes out of the way, tiny and painted canary yellow. The garage juts forward and its doors are perpendicular to the house itself. "I would never buy a house with garage doors facing the street," he brags. "Big deal," I think. "This isn't exactly the Huntington Mansion." But I say nothing.

We pull into the parking apron, and John withdraws a heavy set of keys from his pocket. "I just finished redecorating. Wanna see?"

"That's okay."

"Oh, come on. It'll only take a minute."

I don't want to be rude. I step over the threshold from the bright hot driveway into the dim cool house. Black and white shag carpet covers the miniscule living room floor and two ergonomically designed chaises take up most the space, one black plush and one a funhouse shade of purple. I stop, repulsed by imagining John and some woman, any woman, whose hair is died as black as his, reclined on the furniture.

"Look at the master bath, Peachy. I just remodeled it myself." I am very uncomfortable without knowing exactly why, but I peek around the corner of the bedroom door and can see part of the bathroom. The side of the bed is two feet, maybe three from the door. John grabs my waist and plops me down on the bed. He throws himself down on top of me and I try to scoot back, away from him. My dress is being pulled down underneath me and I worry that the lovely dress Mom has just sewed will be ripped at the waist. I remember all that hard work she did and all the flak she took from Dad for the mess, all that she did for me to make me look pretty. So I lift my weight and when I do he yanks down my panties. Three or four thrusts and a loud grunt, and he collapses, full weight on me. It doesn't hurt. It doesn't feel good. "Is this sex," I wonder. "Really?" Is this what all the fuss is about? I never get the hamburger. He drives us back to work.

I sit down in my office feeling no more violated than by my father's outrageous condemnation or the gynecologist's exam. I feel that I let John have sex with me with the same passivity that I exhibited when my father swatted me or I was told to lie down on a table and let a doctor put his fingers in me or when I was harangued and threatened because a boy had an erection when I barely knew what that was, all the while being told how important for me it was to attract a man. I feel angry that John is such a jerk. My virginity is gone, if I still had it after the

gynecologist. But my dress is in one piece, only a little wrinkled. I stare at the empty typewriter.

I am home from work and have hung up my sundress and thrown on khaki shorts and a tee shirt. I look at my body in the mirror. I've heard that once you have sex you walk differently. I walk in front of the mirror. I don't look different. I feel different, empty, a bit depressed. I don't wear the dress to work again. I have my eighteenth birthday a few weeks later. I push the event with John out of my mind. I tell the people at work it is my birthday. "How old are you?" the guy who cuts gear teeth asks.

"Eighteen." Out of the corner of my eye I see John blanche. I have not been thinking of myself as jail bait. I don't yet know the word.

My period is late which it always is but I get worried and tell my mother that I had sex.

"Did you scream? Try to hit him?"

"No." I don't know what else to say. I am wholly responsible because I wanted to ride in his car and have a hamburger, and I walked to the door of the bedroom and I didn't fight. I cry. She doesn't like crying and doesn't know how to hold or console. She has never been consoled. I think she wants to stand with me but hasn't the courage. I want to curse about everything. About the unimportance of virginity. About why some man was supposed to be thrilled to get it. But I can't. I am a fallen woman. Mom swears she won't tell Dad. Within minutes she is whispering to him.

"Your Daddy wants to see you in the living room," in her most efficient voice.

I understand that she hasbetrayed me. She didn't have the strength not to.

Dad orders me to, "Have a seat," and he yanks out the piano bench out for me to sit down on. He sits in the wingback chair nearby, leans forward, glares at me, starts to shake with rage.

"Your life is ruined.' He's low, snarling, menacing. 'No decent man will ever have you." I sit sickened and mute. "How'd that asshole feel about having a virgin?" First of all, I want to scream, "he didn't 'have' me. I'm not dinner. And believe it or not we didn't 'have' that conversation." But I say nothing. I begin to sob. Mom has retreated to a far corner. She's over there so he can't yell into her face and mine at the same time. "Helen," he says, "go find Nancy." Mom paddles away to retrieve my younger sister who I feel sure is hiding behind her bed, hoping to avoid the conflagration. In a few minutes Nancy trails Mom into the living room and sits in a chair behind me, but I catch her in my peripheral vision. Mom has returned to her corner.

"Sit on the couch where I can see you." "I'm sorry to tell you your sister has disgraced the family name, and no decent man will have either of you." His face is smug and oozing with vitriol, like a vicious little boy killing bugs. My mother looks down and with her craven lack of courage, she says nothing. I think "what family name?" Dad never even knew his father.

Dad's disgusted gaze fixes on me. "I want you out of my house," He juts his thumb toward the front door behind him. I have ruined myself and deserve to be destroyed but I can't leave. I have no job, no money.

In that moment, I understand that, from Dad's perspective, this is a crime against him. Not me. Now he possesses a daughter who can't control her impulse to run through a garage at age five, who has the urge to kiss boys at sixteen, who has pimples as a teen, and now can't even be married off to the son of one of his non-existent important friends because she is damaged merchandise. I have embarrassed him and he doesn't think I deserve the shelter he provides.

I don't go back to work. I am not pregnant. Dad gets John fired. I'm not thrilled about the firing because I am ashamed for Mr. Stevenson to know what I let happen, and because I can imagine the histrionics Dad exhibited in Mr. Stevenson's office, the name calling, the finger jabbing, the foul language, the spitting anger. Better, I think, to have let sleeping dogs lie.

Half a century later I am glad that John got fired, but I consider him a forgettable asshole. The unforgettable asshole is my father. John didn't hurt me physically, and I didn't care if he lived till the next day. I already didn't think virginity was an achievement and didn't believe I was to be "had." People can't be "had."

I leave for USC. The freshman year is paid for by me and by my maternal grandparents' contributions. I rush a sorority because somebody says to. I know nothing about legacies and social connections. I know nothing about how connected USC alumni are in the social hierarchy of Los Angeles. I'm not invited back to either house I want, so I think they must know I am damaged goods. I remember standing on the sidewalk on 28th Street in the heat of a late summer afternoon, realizing that my clothes were wrong, and that I'd known no one prior to moving to school. I'm sweating in a black watch plaid wool suit which my parents thought would be appropriate. I am melting in the sun. To my parents, college is something they've seen in a movie. Reality is up to me.

The young heal quickly. I find other friends. A cute boy tries to force me into sex in his car after a date. I fight like I'm fighting for my life. Just when I think he's got me, he gives up. I do not fight because I am worried about my reputation or my missing virginity. I simply don't want to have sex with him and I think I get to say no, so I have learned that much. He turns the key, presses the starter button and heads back to the dorm.

"Why do you want to have sex with someone who doesn't want to have sex with you?" I ask. "You'd be surprised at how much I get that way." He barely slows down to let me out of the car. I do not understand this, not then, not now.

During finals week the end of my freshman

year my new boyfriend and I fall chastely asleep in his car in the fraternity parking lot after a movie. We've each been up for three days cramming for exams. His roommate wakes us at 2 a.m. I miss lockout. The pink-curlered housemother is grabbing at the smelling salts. I must appear before "girls court," a board of prim sorority girls. The sentence is handed across the conference table by a pale red-haired Theta. I am campused (grounded) for five weeks during my sophomore year for "disgracing the reputation of the USC woman."

"What reputation is that?" I think. She is smug and important, the queen of Girl's Court. But with nothing to do except read I make the Dean's List.

The explosion at home subsides. I don't speak of this for a long, long time. When I do I am an old woman and I say I was raped and tell the story, and my contemporaries say, "Why write about that now? People don't need to know that about you." But I think, "Yes, yes they do need to know, because they are all complicit in this story somewhere."

About the Author:

Claudia Geagan spent most of her life in big cities and big corporations, using her now aging degrees in English and Finance. These days she lives and writes on a leafy mountainside near the Piedmont of the Blue Ridge. She enjoys yoga and golf. Her work has appeared in The Lindenwood Review, The Louisville Review, Hippocampus Magazine, River Teeth's Beautiful Things, Persimmon Tree and others. She has been nominated for a Pushcart Prize.

MY DESERT

by Myla Grier Aidou

Moses and the Israelites wandered for 40 years in the desert. Every time I have heard this, I have said to myself, "Damn." Why did they have to do it their way? Why didn't the Israelites just listen to what 'thus saith The Lord'? As I mature and self-reflect, there are some deserts in my own life I could have avoided had I listened to what "thus saith The Lord." Today I give you one.

I was a teacher. Technically, I still am, but if I have my way, I will not teach in a K-12 school setting again. Having begun my teaching career in the state of New York, when my provisional certification expired, I had a dickens of a time obtaining funding to attend graduate school. In some states, a graduate degree is a necessary component for certification beyond provisional status. I was given an extension, not once, but twice and it was about this time that I was on a sabbatical and had written a novel. Well that's not quite accurate. I had begun a novel years prior; during the sabbatical I had chunks of time to finish the novel, which I gladly did.

Although the sabbatical was for health reasons, it was one of the best years of my life. I was getting an income (full then partial salary) and I was able to write FULL-TIME! Something I dreamed about from the time I could remember. Yes, I also imagined myself a teacher when I was younger, but it wasn't a career that hovered in my fantasies the way being an author did.

So my novel went to many agents and then a publisher after a query letter invited a "look-see." My novel went back and forth—twice, which is a huge step in the publishing industry. Super excited, I had already begun novel number two when the editorial team changed hands. The editor of initial contact wrote me a note of apology, breaking it to me that the new editor was uninterested in my novel. I imagine her intent to minimize the weight I felt, sledge-hammer of rejection, crushing my dreams. Damn. Damn. And Double-damn.

That one rejection put me (back) into the desert, the land of safety where I knew what to expect on a weekly basis. To say I was discouraged is understated. My hopes and dreams of being a writer (of fiction) were sucked out of me. But if you know anything about gifts they are like air pockets; even if unseen, they are there waiting for a chance to surface. Thus it was with my gift of writing. Poetry began to ooze out of me and the idea of being a novelist kept me out of the literary world and into the desert of teaching.

Masters degree, $35,000 in tuition later (plus books and all the other college related fees) and professional certification, I stayed a teacher full-time, wrote part-time and trudged along in a world of stability: bi-weekly income, health insurance and a pension at age 62, 65 or 67. You may think this is a great deal. If you do, you have not been a teacher more than three years, if at all. Teaching these days is not our mothers' and grandmothers' fantasies. No, My Dears, teaching these days is emotionally and physically exhausting, and if you happen to work in a Title I school, it can also be demeaning as you bear the brunt of all student failings.

So if you make it to 62, 65 or 67 as a teacher, congratulations. I hope it was the career of your dreams. Otherwise, you had better dig deep and give those air pockets some room to grow into fruitfulness in the form of other gifts, talents and abilities God has placed within you.

Many people, well-known in the world of arts and science were formerly classroom teachers. Gospel artist Yolanda Adams, writer Stephen King, Kiss guitarist Gene Simmons, Grey's Anatomy actor Jesse Williams, and inventor Alexander Graham Bell, are a few who come to mind. Even former president Lyndon B. Johnson taught public speaking in Texas before going on to become the 36th president who signed the nation's groundbreaking Civil Rights Act of 1964.

So I left a land of perceived comfort to step into another dream. As Langston Hughes would say, "Chile, life ain't been no crystal stair," but I am climbing. Each day brings with it a chance to write, submit, and hone my craft. Sometimes I get published. More often I do not. But it does not stop me. Words are life to me.

Some wise person once said, one will know what their life work is when their passion for the work is such that he/she would do it without being paid. That person must have been a yet-to-be published writer.

About the Author:

Myla has participated in (and won!) "Slam" competitions, sharing verses along the east coast, as well as overseas in the United Arab Emirates. Her writing can be found in Teach Middle East, The Torch, Molloy Literary Journal, Resist Much Obey Little: Inaugural Poems to the Resistance, SalonZine, and Yes, Poetry!). The author of God's Daughter (www.amazon.com as Myla Jones), an inspiring text covering issues such as abuse and addiction, Myla resides in New York, where she maintains her blog

(www.empeejayblog.wordpress.com).

NOVEMBER SURPRISE
by Gabrielle Rivard

November 7

I took Harry to nursery school on Monday morning. He was happy to leave me and ran into the living room of the old house in Southeast Portland to the arms of Miss Monica, his teacher. He joined a group of a half-dozen toddler children, the offspring of the city's working parents, who left the school on bikes equipped with baby seats and orange safety flags, or in Subarus weighed down with multiple car seats.

In the picture from his first day, Harry's wearing a green patterned bandana to help mitigate his runny nose and chambray Toms slip-ons. I took the photo with my iPhone, full of excitement — not for his day, but for mine. After dropping him off, his baby sister would hopefully take a good nap, and I would have three hours to myself: a novelty, a sensation unknown to me for months. I returned home and lay sprawled the rug with my phone and my coffee, watching the news on TV and scrolling mindlessly through social media, alone; the guilty sensation of having committed a criminal act nipping at the sides of my tentative enjoyment.

Enrolling Harry in school for two half-days a week had given me a three-and-a-half-hour break in the procession of hours that make up the life of a mother of young children: a sea of hours, a mountain of hours to be gotten through, like a penance, and simultaneously treasured, rolled over in one's palm like precious jewels.

As I nursed four-month-old Frances I tried to focus on her little face, her baby sounds; to commit to memory the gentle feeling of her soft body nestled sideways on my lap as I sat on the floor; her blue eyes half-shut, hand clamped crablike to my index finger. I knew even in the moment that this time would slip away — that I couldn't hold onto it in the way I wanted, and my eyes welled up with emotion, as if to acknowledge and formalize this fact. The instant, punctuated by tears and properly recognized, rolled away and joined the million others I noted every day and uselessly tried to collect into some palpable thing I could pick up and take with me. I looked away from her face, back to my phone to scroll through the fusillade of dispatches from the campaign.

When you're a star, they let you do it. You can do anything — grab 'em by the pussy.

Already behaving erratically since his debate on Monday, Trump imitated Clinton's pneumonia-induced collapse from last month and fired off the most grotesque, personal, and fact-free attack at the nominee yet.

Such a nasty woman.

We had long since broken the unspoken national pact that expected our leaders to behave in a certain way. We were, as a country, lost in a no-man's-land, where presidential candidates were accused of peeping on girls in beauty-pageant changing rooms, and nobody blinked. Where presidential candidates were associated with judging beauty pageants, period. The stories coming from Washington dripped through the papier-mâché crust of my sleep-deprived mind like water torture, each more enraging than the last. I slogged through the daily barrage of news in a fugue state, humming with a whine of anxiety.

To say that I was having some difficulty with the precious jewels of parental life was an understatement.

Rather than carrying the moments with my daughter in a safe place, too many of the hours were saturated with a dry, helpless anger that seemed to well up from a spring of despair and frustration I recognized from other times in my life but didn't expect in the context of motherhood. It was the frustration of having to ignore catcalls on the street. Of being ignored in meetings. Of listening to a boyfriend dismiss my feelings with a cruelly timed word. It was the helpless rage of womanhood, writ large. The trappings of being female. How was I supposed to know it was a real trap? Steely teeth, sprung tight onto my leg, or maybe my breasts: it had looked shiny and real. They don't tell you about the rage.

Here was the thing I wanted — a baby — and in place of the dreamy-eyed joy I'd been promised I was greeted with sleeplessness, an odd sense of loss, a misplaced feeling of finality and loneliness. Nothing in my previous postpartum experience had brought forth this kind of furious sadness.

Anger crept in around the edges of everyday interactions until it became a constant, simmering fury that burst out through clenched teeth, directed at anyone in my vicinity, most often the children. I usually managed to remove myself from their presence before I hurled the Tupperware across the kitchen or used too many four-letter words, but not always.

At the end of the day, softly touching their sleeping faces in the dark, I was horrified and full of regret, certain that I'd inflicted irreparable damage to my two-year-old's psyche that all the soothing apologies I made couldn't fix.

* * * *

Frances was born in June. In four months the world had morphed from a mostly tolerable, sometimes enjoyable place into a grim landscape of hunched shoulders and bleary eyes. I'd had visions of waking in the dreamy haze of predawn and sitting with her on the outside porch, sipping coffee, savoring moments: Harry's babyhood had been this way, a sweet period of new tenderness and awe. I'd expected the same of my daughter's first summer.

She was born one day after what would have been my grandmother's 89th birthday. My mom had started hoping for a June 25 labor as soon as she learned my due date — June 29. "Well, maybe she'll have Mormor's birthday. Wouldn't that be sweet," she said, wistful.

As if I had any control over it. I would have been fine with June 25; I'd been counting down the days since March. At 32 weeks: the baby would probably be OK if she was born now. At 35 weeks 5 days: I'm as pregnant as I've ever been. At 37 weeks, full-term: I'll take it.

I loathed being pregnant; it felt so alien. I looked enviously at women on Instagram in tight-fitting maternity dresses, their hands curved along the radius of distended bellies, backs arched, luxuriating in gestational bliss. I thought they were full of shit. I was also jealous: not for one second did I feel attractive, or sexy, or "womanly," that catchall descriptor for everything round and feminine, during those long months. I wanted the baby, and I did feel excited. But any anticipatory tenderness was eclipsed by the feeling of being invaded; conquered by biology and the hormonal directives of the placenta, which I learned was programmed to override a woman's body — even going so far as to force her blood pressure up to dangerous levels, all in service of the fetus.

I ran my hands over the distended plane of my abdomen and gingerly checked for stretch marks, hoping I could emerge from this ordeal unscarred, as if from a fire.

It wasn't just the discomfort: I felt vulnerable in a way I never did while not-pregnant. The extra weight and the awkward slowness rendered me helpless and clumsy. At five feet ten and nearing two hundred pounds toward the end, I was a bloated distortion of myself: caged in a sweaty costume of extra flesh, short of breath, slow to stand up, unable to tie my shoes, lumbering through Target. I couldn't run if someone were to lunge at me out of the bushes; I couldn't conceal my bulky form if I needed to hide. I couldn't even sit for longer than it took to eat dinner, a heavy pressure building up in my pelvis, pushing on my cervix. Every minute I spent upright, my mouth flattened into a straight line of anxiety, certain that the force of the baby's head and the weight of the amniotic fluid would finally break through my mucous plug in a wet *pop* — a decisive and potentially disastrous end to what had been a normal pregnancy.

I knew what came next, if that were to happen. That story was the tale of the premature baby: wires and oxygen masks, an antiseptic smell hovering around the hard, clear plastic of a NICU crib. I'd read enough first-person accounts from mothers on BabyCenter that the scenario was familiar. I tried to stay away from the internet for a while, but it didn't take long to get sucked in to the stories of women in my

"Birth Club." I bookmarked several particularly tragic posts and followed these unlucky women as they endured the worst time of their lives: stillbirths; 26-weekers who almost made it; the woman who learned of her fetus's anencephaly early on but insisted on following through with the pregnancy to its inevitable end. In the photos, the doomed baby sat cradled in his mother's arms, dressed in a tiny blue doll's hat, his family gathered around him, smiling for the camera at his birthday-slash-funeral.

* * * *

Frances stayed with me for thirty-nine weeks, five days, twenty hours. She was born June 26, 2016, at 8:16 p.m.: 20:16, 06/26/2016. A full-term baby. I was glad she was healthy, but when they passed her to me through my bloody legs and up to my chest, crouched backward on the hospital bed, I could have been crying with happiness, or it might have been with relief. My only thought upon holding her body — waxy, white and gigantic though she weighed only seven pounds — was joy that it was over. And that I would never do it again.

I don't remember whether I said this aloud, if it alarmed the nurses. The baby felt ancillary to having my body all to myself; to never again feeling that kind of anguish, and not just the wretched pain of birth: the months of being cocooned in a dull sheath of worry and fat, unable to feel anything beyond a baseline of nauseous or not nauseous, exhausted or slightly less exhausted.

"It's over, it's over!" I repeated, lulling myself into a kind of anticlimactic stupor as they wrapped Frances in a blanket and pressed her to my chest.

There is no applause at the end of the grandest, most gruesome performance of your life.

* * * *

November 8

Driving home along Division Street, the oranges and browns of the autumn leaves pixelated into crunchy, heavy swirls, stark against a thin blue sky. The neighborhood was a forest of Craftsmans, yard signs planted in evergreen gardens out front.

I'm with Her
Black Lives Matter
Big Money Out of Politics!

I nodded in solidarity from my Volvo wagon, Beyoncé's Halo turned up to full volume — a rare treat, to be able to listen to music loudly, with no children in the car, only my own eardrums to worry about. It tamped down the hum of anxiety, a nagging presence that in recent months had reached a heady crescendo of barely contained panic.

Everywhere I'm looking now
I'm surrounded by your embrace
Baby, I can see your halo
You know you're my saving grace

My personal election anthem: a rallying cry to Hillary Clinton — this omnipresent woman I had been taught to despise growing up, but who became a savior for me, for women, for rational people who looked on in horror at the rise of the loathsome caricature of Donald Trump.

Halo played over and over that week, the last days of the campaign. I sang along in the car, in the kitchen. It was my wooden stake, a talisman against the sickness that had seeped into the air over the past year, when Trump had become a fixture of our everyday lives, glowing repulsively orange on TV, spewing his disgusting rhetoric; a bloviating clown.

It's like I've been awakened
Every rule I had, you break it
It's the risk that I'm taking
I ain't never gonna shut you out

The election took on a shape of its own; it became a real and controlling force in my life. I thought about the election as much as I thought about food, or friends, or, sometimes, the children. The Election.

As the weeks limped toward the day we could exhale and watch Trump slither back to the rubbish bin of quasi-celebrity, I rode the roller coaster onto which the country was unwillingly strapped.

In the group text called, among other titles, "Benghazi Architects," "beta cucks," "don't get too close to my libtard fantasie," we exchanged memes and news all day:

It couldn't happen. Look what he said!
Look at this email thing. What a load of shit.
He's disgusting, he makes me sick.
God, what if he won?

"Bring back Mitt Romney. I'd vote for him," my husband says, not joking. My stomach took on a fluttery nervousness that usually only showed up for things like international travel or surgery.

By early November, turning off NPR or being away from the television for a few hours — to say, sleep — was problematic. Every morning I groped on the floor for my iPhone to scan the alerts that had piled up overnight.

Whenever Something Happened we'd lob texts back and forth, trying to one-up each other on how ridiculous everything sounded:

"That's it, I'm voting for Trump, I love grabbing pussies."

"His supporters are so smart. MAGA!"
"You cucks just aren't patriots like me, get on
the TrUmP TrAiN"
"Lock her up!"

The absurdity of a Trump win made it unthinkable; we joked, but beneath the sarcasm there
was a cold dread. Unthinkable, but millions of
Americans actually supported this classless
man, and the Republican Party was willing to
abandon any pretense they had of caring about
"family values" and throw their support behind
a reality TV douche who called Mexicans mur-
derers and rapists, bragged about sexual assault, and clearly hadn't the faintest knowledge
of policy or history. The man had been married
three times and had five children with three
different women. He called Barack Obama an
illegitimate president. His campaign rallies
attracted the repulsive underbelly of America:
the racist, putrid mess that had been stewing
and festering in its own dark hatred for forty
years, as the GOP strung them along, promising
them they'd be allowed to carry assault weap-
ons into grocery stores to "defend themselves"
against the coming tide of brown-skinned for-
eigners who were coming to take their jobs
and fuck their women. The rich man — who
literally lived in a gilded tower and had probably paid for half a dozen abortions — was
somehow their beacon of hope: a voice for the
coal miners and the religious zealots, the evan-
gelicals and the billionaire hedge-funders; the
gun freaks and the closeted racists, all of them
emboldened, screaming their lunacy on Twitter
and town squares.

How could this be? I was shocked into a numb
resignation.

That we'd reached this point as a nation left
me breathless, indignant, and full of rage: I
could not wait to watch him lose and then banish him from my life forever, an idiot TV person
I never had to lay eyes on again.

* * * *

That August, I'd taken Frances to Powell's on
the bus. It was one of the only times I took her
out alone; her sleep schedule had become so
arduous that we'd given up on dinners out or
excursions in the car. Harry had often slept in
his car seat under the tables of San Francisco
restaurants, but Frances required silence and a
strict routine that quashed any thought of ven-
turing out. That afternoon I was alone with the
baby and climbing the walls, desperate to grab
some tiny slice of summer before it disappeared. I made sure she was fed, and figured I
had an hour and a half, tops, before she started to lose it.

At the bookstore, she gifted me with a nap as I
browsed the aisles. Doris Lessing's 1973 novel
The Summer Before the Dark is the story of a
woman in her forties coming to terms with her
children no longer needing her during the
course of a summer in which she reflects on
her life. I liked the title; I brought it home.

It sat on my dresser, and I'd consider it while
nursing the baby or preparing for bed: What if
this is the summer before the dark? The summer before Trump is elected — the last summer before the darkness?

I shook off these hallucinations, reassuring myself with poll numbers.

It's not going to happen. We're safe.

I didn't know that unwelcome visualizations of
grisly potential events is a common symptom
of postpartum mood disorder. Grisly imagin-
ings came to me in vivid scenes: the plane going down; the dresser as it tips and pins the
toddler beneath, squirming. In an instant, a
fully formed narrative played through my mind
like a movie reel, complete with narration: I'd
bought the apple at Whole Foods and picked it

out especially because of its perfect coloring. As I put it in the basket I had no idea it would be the thing that killed the baby. My training as a copy editor kicked in, and I'd see the headlines in front of me as the airplane left the ground: Two Hundred Killed in Horrific Air Accident.

I watched the soft spot on the top of the baby's head pulse gently in time with her tiny heartbeat: What if someone put two thumbs on it and pressed? I shut my eyes, shook my head to drive the thoughts away.

A morbid retrospective attached to everyday objects; the nightstand, the stairs. Kitchen knives. They tangled around my mind like choking vines, leaving me unable to complete basic tasks unencumbered. The Summer Before the Dark sat mutely on my black Ikea dresser.

After the election, she couldn't believe it had been true: the book had foretold what was to come. Donald Trump had won, and that summer truly had been the last one before the darkness set in.

* * * *

November 8

A rush of solidarity with my fellow Portlanders: We won't let him win. Hillary is going to show Trump and all of his disgusting supporters just what women are made of. We're going to blow him out of the water. We've got to. Instagram was full of photos of Susan B. Anthony's headstone, decorated with "I Voted" stickers. I posted a photo of Hillary from the 1970s: #imwithher.

I made breakfast, tried to clean up the house, played with Frances. She had to be nursed to sleep for her three naps, had to be carried and held close, could not sit up on her own. I tiptoed out of her room after putting her down;

any creak of the floorboards would send her into a wailing frenzy. A few days earlier I'd ventured out with friends to dinner, and spent ten minutes in a bar bathroom sucking out my own milk, my breasts uncomfortably full and leaking through my shirt: the secret rituals of motherhood.

2:00 p.m.

When the first returns from the East Coast started to come in, a cold tingle crept down my spine. It was still early, but the results were not in line with the latest polls.

"She's not going to win." I said aloud, surprising myself in the empty kitchen. I stood up sharply, trying to shake the thought out of my head like it was just another scene from the disaster reel: Impossible.

Signing my name to my mail-in ballot the week before, I'd felt a surge of pride. I couldn't fathom anyone willingly voting for Trump. I knew I lived in a bubble, but the televised Trump rallies, the police shootings, the horrific slaughter of innocent civilians at the hands of men with guns that should be banned during that hot, chaotic summer had shown what was outside of it, and I wanted no part of that America.

5:00 p.m.

I did my best to ignore the dull fear in my chest, to will it out of existence: a tightening in the abdomen, mouth pressed into a sharp frown of concentration; the same feeling as when the airplane wobbled mid-flight, not unlike the sinking feeling in the pit of my stomach when Harry threatened to come seven weeks early and I found myself lying stiffly on my left side in the hospital, sucking up an intravenous cocktail of anti-contraction drugs through my arm.

6:00 p.m.

I had the TV on, but I could barely bring myself to look at Steve Kornacki as he traced frantic circles and arrows across an electronic whiteboard, red and blue lines snaking through the flat image of America. There was too much red.

What would defeat look like?
A blackened hellscape.
The country unrecognizable.
A clown for president.

The anticipation, building for months, froze into a hard rock in my throat. The returns were not good. I ordered pizza and set the table in mute terror.

"Gabby's a little scared," Nate told our friends, who'd arrived to watch the TV coverage with us. They assured me that it was still early. I put the children to bed and opened a big can of beer, ate the pizza without tasting it, and sat tensely on the bottom stair, where I could hear the TV but couldn't see it. I refreshed Twitter on my phone.

It was starting to look bad.

7:00 p.m.

The others downed dark, sticky shots of Fernet. I couldn't bring myself to get drunk to dull the sensation of being sucked underwater, my face frozen in a stiff grimace. I went up to the baby's room; I didn't want any witnesses to my doomsday panic.

The plane is going to crash.

Someone had told me once to curl up my legs and stretch my arms out in front of me in a prayer pose to ease anxiety, and I dropped to the floor of Frances's room, despondent, and

tried to do something like praying. I stuffed my ears with earplugs so I couldn't hear the groans and swearing from downstairs.

On Twitter, people were freaking out.

It feels like someone has broken into my house.

Guys, there is no blue wall. It's gone.

The darkness has won.

9:00 p.m.

Walking past the grim silence of the living room, I went outside to the frigid porch, cowering under my hoodie. I drank another beer, something close to hysteria bubbling up in my gut. Where were the crashing airplanes? Missiles? Asteroids? The curtain had been ripped off of reality: I had no idea what lay underneath.

The street was quiet. No one else was outside, trying to escape the catastrophe that was happening to us all on the television. I rocked back and forth in some primal attempt to soothe myself as I cried.

"Don't even tell me. I can't look at it." I went upstairs without watching a single minute of the election coverage I'd anticipated for months, mourning the loss of the feeling I'd wanted so badly: to share in the exuberance and joy of millions of women; to watch Trump slink away into the shadows.

Nate came upstairs. We lay silently in the damp hum of the humidifier. I went down the list of possible ways out, grasping desperately at fraying ends of hope: the electoral college. Voter fraud. Recounts. "Maybe they haven't counted everything in Wisconsin. Maybe —"

"It's over," he said unceremoniously. "It's done. There's nothing we can do." We shook our heads dumbly, blinking in disbelief. I suggested we have sex, to stave off the sad panic building in my chest.

The next day felt like a purgatory. A horrible thing had happened, yet it hadn't really begun in earnest, and we were suspended in a dark place between two worlds. A dull stupor throbbed in my head. I couldn't bring myself to turn on the television and switched on the 1970s clock radio I'd bought Nate for Christmas. Frances and I sat on the floor, letting the calm voices on NPR soothe the room, an audible balm. There was a call-in show, everyone shocked and terrified. The host at one point outright called Trump an idiot, and I got a little glimpse of what the next months and years would bring: it was a sudden pivot from feeling confident and protected, of respecting the person charged with representing us to the world, to all-out disgust with half the country — a division that played out every day online and on TV and in living rooms where people sat, dejected, worn out, utterly spent.

We had to go to a teacher conference at the Treehouse School. I pulled on my Hillary sweatshirt again, red-faced and angry. As my mother arrived to watch Harry I brushed past her rudely on the porch, not speaking. That she could smile on a morning like this made me acutely aware of the ocean of difference between us.

We stopped for coffee on the way to school. I sat with my sunglasses on in the café, everyone around us discussing what happened. I looked miserably at my daughter in her baby carrier and pulled out my breast to feed her, in some kind of personal demonstration against the evil that had been let loose, released into the air and spread out over the country like smallpox. A woman at a table across from us wept openly into her arms as her friend patted her back.

"I'm sorry about that," I said to my mom, stiffly, as we returned home. She left looking sad. What did she expect?

Months ago, I'd set up a recurring donation to the Clinton campaign and they sent me a little sticker. I put it up in the front window, too late.

On Facebook people who hadn't posted anything in years were sharing horrified disbelief. Camaraderie surged up through the bitter anger and sadness: we were all in this together. Whatever it was.

Rachel Maddow came on the air at 6 p.m. as usual. I looked to her for something; solace or hope. She had clearly been up all night, her eyes red and bloodshot, fatigue that makeup couldn't conceal. She was as horrified and upset as the rest of us. I switched off the television and didn't turn it on for a month.

I did not watch Hillary's concession speech. Twenty months later, as I write this, I still haven't.

A couple of days passed. I read everything that was coming out, people trying desperately to organize and stop him from being inaugurated with the electoral college, people trying to get a recount, trying every avenue to stave off this absurd thing from becoming real. My Republican parents sent an email saying they thought it was better that we cancel Thanksgiving this year.

When Kate McKinnon as Hillary opened Saturday Night Live singing Hallelujah by Leonard Cohen, who had died that terrible week, I wept. It felt like a wound.

November 12

I booked two Airbnbs at the coast, four days away from the city and our daily lives, which had been hijacked by the news. I continued my television moratorium but listened to NPR in the car as I drove Harry to and from school. As the media tried to figure out what they'd missed, where they'd gone wrong in pre-election reporting and analysis, Portland mourned. There were protests and clashes with the police. I found myself breaking down into tears spontaneously during the day, my daughter staring up at me from the floor.

We drove to the Pacific for a few days and I declared a news blackout. I turned the radio off and put on Hail to the Thief. "I never thought I'd be listening to this and crying again."

I will
Lay me down
In a bunker
Underground

Everything was imbued with new meaning in the post-election world. Things I had always taken for granted had fallen apart or come into question: the stability of the United States government. The legitimacy of our elections. The idea that despite its flaws, America was still inherently a force for good in the world. The feeling of shock and exposure seeped into everything: if this could happen, anything could happen. I waited for the other shoe to drop, tight with nervous tension.

I won't let this happen to my children
Meet the real world coming out of your shell
With white elephants
Sitting ducks
I will
Rise up

At the coast we put the children to bed as early as possible and drank wine in the hot tub of our rental. We watched Twilight. We drove to a lighthouse and tried to look at the tidepools, but the wind was strong and cold, and I returned to the car with Frances, nursing her in the front seat as I watched the ocean churn. There is a photo of me on the balcony of the condo at Nye Beach, holding a glass of wine, eyes closed against the glare of the setting sun. I was worn out: with the collapse of democracy, with the betrayal of so many of my fellow Americans, with Frances' waking up five times a night. We made a little bed on the floor for Harry and he got up and fussed several times, confused or scared, and I yelled at him more than once for waking me, overflowing with anger and regret at the same time.

I am so tired. I just need to sleep. Please go to bed. Please go to bed. Goddamn it, Harry.

November 24

We spent Thanksgiving at home, just the four of us with too much food. Nate cooked all day, and the air in the house grew hot and close with all the windows closed. At four o'clock we set a plastic plate of mashed potatoes with gravy, cut-up green beans, and pumpkin pie in front Harry and settled Frances in her swing next to my chair, halfheartedly filling our own plates and topping off our wine glasses. The sense of giddy, carefree merriment I usually felt on national holidays had evaporated, leaving a bland feeling of detached cynicism. Harry ate the pie and the rolls and started to get restless after ten minutes; Frances squirmed and fussed, and I begrudgingly put the Sauvignon blanc back in the fridge to nurse her. We put them to bed and set about cleaning up the colossal mess in the kitchen, the day turned back into every other: full of chores and the vague, constant sense of loss and disbelief that had begun to darken the edges of existence.

November 25

My mother gave me a coffee mug for my birthday: "I Am Not Arguing, I'm Just Explaining Why I'm Right."

Every morning the dull fact of the election took a few minutes to settle in. What had been an absurd joke had become real. No one knew how to live here.

In Portland's bleak December light, I stared in dismay at the Lessing novel still atop my dresser, unmoved since summer, its prophetic title stabbing me with little pricks of irony. How was I supposed to know that was the last summer anything would feel all right? Ridiculous fantasies in which I discovered in October that the title was a clue flitted through my mind. I figured out Trump was on track to squeak through with enough votes and made a frantic call to Jennifer Palmieri, who thanked me for my incredible detective work and redoubled the Clinton campaign efforts in Michigan and Pennsylvania.

I turned the book to face the wall.

About the Author:

Gabrielle Rivard is a freelance copy editor and copywriter. She's worked as an editor and content manager at tech companies in Silicon Valley, as well as wire editor and copy editor at The San Francisco Examiner, and has a (mostly unused) master's degree in library and information science. She lives in Portland, Ore., with her software-developer husband and their two children, Harry and Frances.

BRILLIANT CORNERS: AN EXPERIMENT IN VISUAL PROSODY
by Michael Milburn

I was naked without my line end.
Robert Lowell, letter to Elizabeth Bishop

A few years ago I found myself adjusting the line lengths in my poems, replacing words and tinkering with punctuation and syntax to make the right margin appear flush on my computer screen. I didn't do this with every poem, just a few where two or three lines in the first typed draft lined up, which led me to see if the remainder could as well. I have always appreciated visual symmetry in poetry. When revising I try out stanzas with different numbers of lines, preferring but not insisting on the same number in each. After all, stanza length, whether fixed or variable, makes a big difference to a poem, affecting pace and therefore expression. Couldn't the same be true of lines?

Lately, my preoccupation with alignment has increased, as I have completed several poems where the lines, at least in my Helvetica typeface, all appear exactly the same length, and my quest for this look not only influenced word choice and syntax, but line breaks as well. Again, I don't insist on this, sometimes abandoning the effort if the poem resists it, some-times settling for a few matching lines here and there. I know this practice sounds pointless, counterproductive, maybe nuts—even if the end words line up on my screen and print-outs, they won't necessarily do so in a different font or word processing program. More than once a poem that I have labored to align has appeared in a literary magazine with slightly uneven right margins. This outcome no longer disappoints me—rather, I'm glad to have put those poems through whatever revision it took to get the margins straight, even as the published versions remind me that permanent alignment is impossible.

While I recognize the eccentricity of what I'm doing, I'm not sure that I want to stop. First, breaking a line so that it will look the exact same length as the ones above and below is not that different from doing so on the basis of syllable count, a respectable method of composing poetry. More importantly, trying to find the word, syntax, even punctuation to shorten or elongate a line requires more precise, sustained attention than my revision process used to involve. Even choosing between a colon and a dash (an em dash being equivalent in length to three colons on my computer), forces me to analyze ruthlessly what I want to say. Previously, the closest I came to this sort of sight-based scrutiny was deleting a line from the middle of a poem in uniform stanzas solely to avoid having a surplus line at the end.

I haven't heard of any other poets sharing my mania for alignment, or found evidence of it in published poems. But in this age of word processing and the poet's ability to experiment with how his or her poems look on the screen, I wonder if no one else has been tempted to try. When a few lines do line up in others' poems— inadvertently, I assume—the result is a sort of visual rhyme. Viewed both on my screen and on the pages of their respective books, the following lines please my eye through their identical lengths and their end words' vertical pairing.

Drove to this tumult in the clouds;
I balanced all, brought all to mind,

from "An Irish Airman Foresees His Death," by W.B. Yeats

He lifts his one great claw
And holds it over his head;

from "Lobsters in the Window," by W.D. Snodgrass

New ghost is that what you are
Standing on the stairs of water

from "Is That What You Are" by W.S. Merwin

be afraid. God does not leave us
comfortless, so let evening come.

from "Let Evening Come," by Jane Kenyon

When the end words rhyme, the payoff is even greater:

If lip-readers move their lips when
lip-reading, what do they say then?

from "From a Distance," by Bill Knott

don't quote me. This is all:
A rose is not a cannonball.

from "Prelude to a Glass City," by James Tate

Dying
Is an art, like everything else.
I do it exceptionally well.

I do it so it feels like hell.

Lady Lazarus," by Sylvia Plath

The visual rewards of alignment in these examples resemble those of two common poetic devices—assonance and alliteration. In addition to the appealing sound and sensation the following line produces when spoken, it also creates a visible pattern with its repeated vowels and consonants. What the eye sees reflects what the ear hears and vice versa.

The ploughman homeward plods his weary way.

from "Elegy Composed in a Country Churchyard," by Thomas Gray

Revising with an eye simultaneously on line length and expression reminds me of trying to write in meter, swapping words in the service of stress and syllable count. Often the metrical demands would lead the poem in new directions. This doesn't happen with free verse, which makes me wonder, as someone who no longer writes in meter, whether I miss having strict formal rules to work with and against— playing tennis with a net in Robert Frost's words. Alignment may not qualify as a legitimate prosodic practice, but it makes my writing of free verse less dauntingly free by providing me with a formal anchor. And even when I undo a length-driven revision, usually because it sounds wrong or a line break jars, the process has often led to other changes worth keeping. Sometimes that jarring line break, arrived at solely for alignment's sake, works, the kind of fortuitous discovery that must be familiar to poets who write in syllabics.

> You are so small, I
> am not even sure
> that you are at all.

from "Miss Cho Composes in the Cafeteria," by James Tate

As I said, not all of my poems bring out my compulsion. Typically, I'll write a first draft by hand and type it into the computer, paying little attention to line breaks or length. As I start to revise, cutting out unmusical parts and polishing promising ones, I'll start to notice whether any lines seem close to aligning and how they look or sound when I make them match. More often than not the pushing and pulling starts to feel forced, but if this process works for several consecutive lines, I'll go all in on it. Few poems—about one in ten—survive the treatment and are better for it. A few more contain two to five equal lines; any more and the contrast between aligned and unaligned distracts.

In most cases my length-based choices hold up as good choices for the poem. Recently I tried and rejected the phrases "by which I mean," "in other words," and "or rather," which made the line in question either jut out or fall short. They also sounded wrong, the first because it added another "I" to a poem that already contained too many, the second because it's a cliché, and the third because it sounded stilted. Finally, as I was doing sit-ups one afternoon, the phrase "which is to say" popped into my mind—impersonal, monosyllabic, succinct. Even before typing it, I knew that it would fit my length needs because it fit my poetic needs. To consider using a word on any grounds other

than sound and meaning might seem crazy, but I have learned that a formal fit often equals an expressive fit, even if the latter takes a while to reveal itself. One need only look at blank verse with its relatively even lines to see that length and rhythm are connected:

> Death closes all: but something ere the end,
> Some work of noble note, may yet be done,
> Not unbecoming men that strove with Gods.

from "Ulysses," by Alfred Lord Tennyson

> Now you and I would go to no such length.
> At the same time you can't deny it makes
> It not a mite worse, sitting here, we three...

from "Snow," by Robert Frost

Each of these lines contains the same number of syllables (ten) and stresses (five), so it's no surprise that they're similar in length as well. Conversely, my aligned lines tend to be consistent in stress count, suggesting that alignment dictates rhythm as much as iambic pentameter dictates the look of blank verse. Metrical demands can feel constricting, which is one reason that most contemporary poets decline to submit to them, but others find them liberating. For me, calibrating a line down to the width of a semi-colon requires discipline and invention in equal parts.

Other poets may not make such minute adjustments, but an attentiveness to line length is evident in much contemporary poetry. In the 2018 edition of the Pushcart Prize anthology, twenty of the thirty poems consist of lines roughly equal in length to the blank verse quoted above. Of these twenty, thirteen are uninterrupted by stanza breaks, resulting in a shape similar to that of an unjustified prose paragraph. If one outlined these poems in chalk like bodies at a crime scene, today's preferred visual style would be glaringly apparent. In some instances, the poets appear to break lines solely on the basis of length with no regard for craft, doggedly following the template rather than creating a specific pause or enjambment.

Poets have always played with the appearance of their poems, scattering words (e.e. cummings), laddering them down the page (William Carlos Williams), shaping them into pictures (George Herbert), or detaching them from sentence sense (Concrete poets). C.K. Williams creates one identity for his poetry when every line in his book *Tar* exceeds the page's width and needs indenting, and I remember "Stopping by Woods on a Snowy Evening" as much for its rectangular stanzas as for its clip-clop tetrameter.

In the modern era, before poetry readings proliferated, one's first impression of a poem was typically visual, established before one started reading. As I turn a page of *The New Yorker*, the sight of a two-page long-lined poem by Jorie Graham prepares me differently than two skinny quatrains by Charles Simic, the first promising discursiveness and the second pithiness. It seems likely that Elizabeth Bishop intended the wide lines of "The Man Moth" to mirror her creature's massiveness, and the jagged path of "The Moose" to trace the narrow provincial Canadian roads the speaker's bus follows.

The whole shadow of Man is only as big as his hat.
It lies at his feet like a circle for a doll to stand on,

from "The Man-Moth," by Elizabeth Bishop

down rows of sugar maples,
past clapboard farmhouses
and neat, clapboard churches,
bleached, ridged as clamshells,
past twin silver birches,

through late afternoon
a bus journeys west

from "The Moose," by Elizabeth Bishop

Even with prose poems I not only notice the right margin, I can't help reading it expressively. Three different settings from different publications of this prose poem from Claudia Rankine's *Citizen*, for example, cast the lines, line-ends, and, yes, line breaks in three differrent ways.

To live through the days sometimes you
moan like deer.
Sometimes you sigh. The world says stop
that. Another sigh.
Another stop that. Moaning elicits laughter,
sighing upsets.
Perhaps each sigh is drawn into existence to
pull in, pull under,
who knows; truth be told, you could no
more control those
sighs than that which brings the sighs
about.

Citizen IV, as formatted on poets.org

To live through the days sometimes you moan like deer. Sometimes you sigh. The world says stop that. Another sigh. Another stop that. Moaning elicits laughter, sighing upsets. Perhaps each sigh is drawn into existence to pull in, pull under, who knows; truth be told, you could no more control those sighs than that which brings the sighs about.

Citizen IV, as formatted on metaphor-formetaphor.tumblr.com

To live through the days sometimes you moan like deer. Sometimes you sigh. The world says stop that. Another sigh. Another stop that. Moaning elicits laughter, sighing upsets. Perhaps each sigh is drawn into existence to pull in, pull under, who knows; truth be told, you could no more control those sighs than that which brings the sighs about.

Citizen IV, as formatted in print in *Citizen, An American Lyric*

I prefer the last version, and assume that Rankine does too since that's how the poem appears in her book. The justified text makes the line ends and breaks meaningful, even if they're not intentional. Alignment heightens meaning, emphasizing the line as a unit, to some extent self-contained, and the line break as its provisional end. It gives the justified breaks an authority that makes the unjustified ones feel blander, weaker in comparison.

Version 1 Unjustified:

Another sigh.
Another stop that.

Version 2 Unjustified:

Another sigh. Another stop that.

Version 3 Justified:

Another
sigh. Another stop that.

If line length and equivalency matter this much in a prose poem, where technically they don't matter at all, it follows that they would affect verse, where a poet can make deliberate use of them.

My interest in a poem's appearance, not just its shape but the sight of the words together and on their own, keeps me from enjoying poetry readings where I haven't seen the text. Listening makes me want to look, and frustrated that I can't. Not knowing what visual impression the words and lines make, or whether they're arranged in the slivered stanzas of "Miss Cho," C.K, Williams's sprawl, or Rankine's prose, creates a kind of aesthetic blindfold. In a review of *The Essential W.S. Merwin*, the critic Dan Chiasson likens the phrases in Merwin's "The Hydra" to "driftwood scattered on the sand," concluding that "their dispersal on the page is the source of their power."

I was young and the dead were in other
Ages

As the grass had its own language

Now I forget where the difference falls

One thing about the living sometimes a
piece of us
Can stop dying for a moment
But you the dead

Once you go into those names you go on
you never
Hesitate
You go on

Similarly, for all its aural beauty, the assonance of Merwin's line "And bowing not knowing to what" (which ends "For the Anniversary of My Death") only achieves its full effect if one sees those successive "o"s and "w"s. John Ashbery said of translating Rimbaud: "You have to see the poetry as well as hear it; even the shapes of the letters have something to do with it."

The most successful spoken poems are usually strong narratives, or polemical, or witty, or delivered in a beautiful voice like Seamus Heaney's, or rhymed. The rhymed ones work in part because the end words serve as auditory guides to line (and sometimes stanza) lengths and ends. I rarely hear free verse line breaks unless the speaker tries to reproduce them, which sounds affected. On his recordings of "This Is Just To Say" and "The Red Wheelbarrow" William Carlos Williams makes no pauses between these lines, obscuring their visual ingenuity.

I have eaten
the plums
that were in
the icebox

*

so much depends
upon
a red wheel
barrow

Similarly, listening to Robert Lowell's "For the Union Dead" and Elizabeth Bishop's "North Haven" would conceal two important formal decisions in the poems' final stanzas.

The Aquarium is gone. Everywhere,
giant finned cars nose forward like fish;
a savage servility
slides by on grease.

from "For the Union Dead," by Robert Lowell

You left North Haven, anchored in its rock,
afloat in mystic blue...And now—you've left
for good. You can't derange, or rearrange,
your poems again. (But the sparrows can
their song.)
The words won't change again. Sad friend,
you cannot change.

from "North Haven," by Elizabeth Bishop

My ear would hear Lowell's last two lines as one, and Bishop's last line as two lines, with the break coming between the sentences. Just hearing the poems would keep me from knowing how these lines look, and, as importantly, from wondering why the poets placed them as they did. Did Lowell want to use "servility" and "grease" as end words in order to emphasize or juxtapose them? Did Bishop reject a longer pause between her two closing sentences so as to achieve a "here's the bad news all at once" momentum? Or did both poets need their final stanzas to match the preceding ones, Lowell requiring an extra line to fill out his last quatrain, Bishop having one too many for her quintain? Maybe they disliked the tidiness of alignment:

giant finned cars nose forward like fish;
a savage servility slides by on grease.

The words won't change again.
Sad friend, you cannot change.

"Art, it seems to me, should simplify," Willa Cather wrote. "That, indeed, is very nearly the whole of the higher artistic process." Most poets would agree that they are always revising toward greater directness and simplicity, even when adding words. When I arrive at a plainer way of saying something, it often seems so obvious that I'm surprised I didn't find my way to it sooner. This quest drives my alignment work, which I suspect is partly a way to get myself to keep streamlining a poem that I might otherwise have considered finished. I have to trust myself to recognize when this starts having a deleterious effect. That goes for all revision, which proceeds on the assumption that we're making the poem better, until we're not.

About the Author:

Michael Milburn teaches high school English in New Haven, CT. His book of essays, Odd Man In, was published by Midlist Press in 2005, and his most recent book of poems is Carpe Something (Word Press 2012).

THE EVIL OF DEATH

by Dimitra Tsourou

"The human species is unique in knowing it must die," writes Voltaire. The awareness of death makes people vulnerable to fear, which inspires Epicurus to give answers to fundamental questions about death. "Death does not concern us because as long as we exist, death is not here. And when it does come, we no longer exist," says Epicurus, distancing himself from his philosophical antecedents. This essay outlines the basic elements and emergence of Epicurus' views on death, with an eye on modern thoughts and anxieties about mortality and the afterlife.

The emergence of The Garden

Epicureanism emerged after the death of Aristotle, and as such belongs to so-called Hellenistic philosophy. This was a period in which the Greek language and culture was widely propagated to large areas of the world due to the military conquests of Alexander the Great, whose empire is said to have "Hellenized" the lands that Alexander conquered. But for all this cultural and philosophical dissemination, Athens still remained the core of philosophical learning to which a plethora of intellectual immigrants were drawn. At that time, two major schools emerged in the city: Epicureanism and Stoicism – two schools that signified the break with the intellectual lineage of Socrates, Plato and Aristotle. The 17-year-old Epicurus came to Athens to found a school known as The Garden. Its members had to abide by a set of common rules. They practiced what they called "therapeutic discipline", which utilized concentration and isolation to banish the distress, anxiety and agony that plague the human condition. Their regime involved memorizing and repeating doctrines – the act of which was a central element of Epicurean philosophy that was conceived as a way of life rather than a set of principles. While this may sound like a religious practice, however, it was certainly not. The practices of those working in The Garden were always founded on reason.

There is neither a designer nor any divine intervention.

The pillar of Epicurean philosophy is the study of nature, whereby the gods are fully integrated into the natural world. Influenced by the pre-historic atomist Democritus, Epicurus teaches that the basic constituents of the natural world are the atoms and the void. The atoms move around in a void, rebounding off each other to shape complex bodies. The whole complexity of the natural world is thus the outcome of the atoms' eternal movement within the void. Atoms have no beginning; rather, they have always existed and will never perish. They exist in a state of perpetual motion within an infinite void, producing the world around us. Beyond this, there is nothing to be explained. Whatever happens in the world – eclipses, uprisings, rain – is not related to any divine intervention. Epicurus states categorically that "There is no designer."

Does God exist?

"God exists", Epicurus says. The concept of God is something common to each individual, and so it must be true. To Epicurus, gods are anthropomorphic entities living somewhere and somehow in the cosmos. Once we fully understand that the Gods do not intervene in our lives and thus have no role to play in the function of the cosmos, we pave the way to reach the truth. This realization can be of great relief to us.

Four fears and four solutions

According to Epicurus, our lives involve four great fears: the fear of God(s), the fear of death, the fear of failure and the fear of suffering. Fear is the feeling of disturbance of the mind. Distress in the Greek language is referred to as "taraxi", with the opposite – "a-taraxia", or calmness – given by the negative prefix. The ultimate goal of so-called "therapeutic" or Epicurean philosophy is to provide individuals tortured by these four fears with the teachings by which to overcome them. These teachings are also known as the "four-fold remedy", or the "freedom from distress" (a-taraxia), which is or should be the goal of life. The four-fold remedy is as follows: 1) Do not fear God. 2) Do not worry about death. 3) What is good is easy to obtain. 4) What is terrible is easy to endure. Epicurus insists that there is no reason to fear God(s) as they have no motivation to send disasters our way. They are happy entities that exist in a state of a-taraxia; i.e., without trouble or anger. There are thus no logical circumstances under which they would seek to cause us pain.

Do not worry about the afterlife as it does not exist

Epicurus says that death is something we should view as neither good nor bad. It is simply nothing – nothing to look forward to, and, similarly, nothing to fear. When asked whether death should not be regarded as a bad experience, Epicurus answers that all good and bad experiences consist in sensation, and death is the privation of sensation. Our soul, which gives life to the body and enables it to experience sensations, is a collection of atoms that falls apart and disintegrates upon our death. The soul does not continue in a disembodied form, and thus does not go anywhere. It cannot experience anything when it is disconnected from the body. When we cease to exist, the soul hence loses its capacity to feel.

Dying a painless death

An objector points out to Epicurus that being dead is not what he fears, as he will not be around, but this is not the source of his fear of death. To which Epicurus responds, "What exactly is it that you are afraid of when you fear death if it is not being dead? It sounds irrational, as long as you haven't identified anything bad about death and only your thought about death makes you fear it." Epicurus goes on to say that the only thing which may be distressing about death is the prospect of dying. The anticipation of death can be a painful, terrible experience. His argument is that the prospect of a painless death means there is nothing to fear. From this, he asserts that if one has conquered the ultimate goal of life, there is no reason to live any more, and no fear to be had in death.

What is wrong with death?

We may agree, for instance, that death is something bad as it deprives us of the additional years we might otherwise have had. This is a reasonable explanation for our fear of death, however painless. It should be understood, however, that when Epicurus uses the word "death" he does not mean the process of death. Indeed, the process of death can be painful and distressing. Rather, he is referring to the state of being dead – a state in which we no longer exist. Here, death is not the dreamless sleep proposed by Socrates. To Epicurus, death is simply an eternal nothingness.

ANYTHING LIKE GOD

by Brianne Bannon

At 16 I was the best person I am ever capable of being. It was not a full peak, necessarily; I was shy and had bad skin and a tendency toward a slight stutter around new people. I had not yet learned to tame my frizzy mess of hair against St. Louis humidity, and my poofy, brunette halo is immortalized in dozens of unfortunate high school pictures. I am braver now, and recent years have lodged a glowing certainty in my chest that I lacked as a teenager. But when I was 16 I was wholly good—*refuse to gossip about my classmates* good, *talk to my teachers about philosophy after school* good, *love nothing more than a walk around a park with my friends* good. I used to put a mantra on a mental loop as I walked around school: be kind, be kind, be kind. The words thumped with the rhythm of my steps. I tried to bless the ground with my feet. These days, if anything is running on a loop through my mind, I am usually stressed or in a hurry, and the words are the four-letter kind.

On the weekends, my friends, about ten of us in all, give or take the few we would lose to cross-country meets or ACT tutoring, would play kickball in a nearby park. We never smoked, and our first experience with alcohol—it was a giggly circle of all of us, cross-legged on the carpeted floor of someone's basement, passing around a handle of awful peach vodka—didn't come until halfway through senior year. Until then, and even after, we played together like taller, more self-conscious children.

One July night, we were engaged in a competitive game of hide and seek around a playground when a stern ranger approached us and told us the park was closed. We apologized and got up to leave, but when the man realized we were sober teenagers playing a game for much younger children, he softened and let us stay.

When I wasn't hard at work being the lamest, happiest 16-year-old in the park, I was drawing, or painting, or maybe watching TV in the basement with my dad. If I had time after school, I'd drag him downstairs with me, and he'd nod off while I worked my way through our recorded shows.

In warmer months, I took long walks around the neighborhood. I liked it best when the sun came out just after a good rain, when the tree trunks were dark as deep chocolate and light glinted off the pools of water that spotted my suburban streets. Sometimes the mantra would come back—be kind, be kind, be kind. I didn't know it then, but it was a kind of meditation. I was 16, hopelessly optimistic and brimming over with love for everything around me: my friends, my teachers, silly television, the smell of my paints, post-rain puddles. I loved it all. Who was I, at 16, that I had enough love for the entire world?

I miss her. When I am in my parents' backyard late at night I feel closest to her; back then I used to come home on the weekends just before curfew and stare at the stars, drink in as many of them as suburban light pollution would allow. If I have ever felt God, or anything like God, it was then, staring up at an echoing night sky with such intensity that my neck ached and my glasses were insufficient for the job at hand.

About the Author:

Brianne Bannon is a recent graduate of Truman State University, where she studied English, painting, and Spanish. She now works full-time in immigration law in Houston, Texas, but has a part-time job complaining about the humidity and traffic.

I, THE JUNGLE

by Derek Nast

Generations and genres later writing style and word usage form differently yet the core of a literary amateur always strives to tell his tale. I, no native to the mile-high and with two decades of residency in hand have spent half of that time jotting notes, plotting, depicting experiences, rhyming and revising with a never-failing spoken heart of life's next circumstance. I've not always remained inspired but am more so each time when "Pen meets paper." Despite the plights coming and going I still strive use such measures to manage this calamity. Such calamity refers to the jungle wall. (Addiction.) barricading itself from the normalcy of a life I've yet to know. In all fairness I've encountered Snippets of a stable reality. But this piece is not of pandemonium, but to that of an opening partly unknown. So where to begin? When developing ability there requires practice and trial and error, most of all the time to grow skillful. However skill is no guarantee within such a grandiose arena of literature. One of the most historic fields to date. Conditions of the heart along the lost, aim to find themselves among one another. The journey of traveling souls)

Do not confuse this with interdependence, where individuals operate on a higher plane of selflessness. They are able to gain a greater sense of understanding upon one another. When dependent upon certain pleasures in life where do such endeavors end?

It was only recently how I'd experienced the scope in which my life felt in comparison to that of a portrayal of a literary amateur himself, once a freewriter who had written his way to greatness through his words for generations to follow, even in rites of passage. Like Keroac, I too have familiarized myself with the Denver scene, one far more modern, but nevertheless a world amongst the Rockies. In his novel. "On the Road." it had taken the better part of which to grasp how the road itself acted as the jungle for Keroac and accomplice Dean Moriarty. A road to stretch east and west winding back again, wrapped with colorful humanity, all at 90 miles an hour or more. Think of the camaraderie that was built just above the pavement below. Whatever unseen force which existed between Sal and Dean, it took on turn after turn with one siren blaring behind the next. As Sal followed blindly into the distance he would surely pay the toll of the road. However opposed to Keroac my own road ran circles into the one-way streets of Denver, far many of times crashing into the jungle wall.

Without incarceration as a factor the wall still yielded consequences to ripple. Repercussions which involved family, intimate relationships, health concerns, spiritual bankruptcy, financial inadequacy and so on. Along the wall remained so many driven in similar manner yet differed and character. Many would commonly collide for the benefit of the same cause, generating a multitude of codependency. More recently it has been isolation to form wide boundaries, becoming separated from others, a complete opposite to previously dependent needs. After 22 years of assorted wandering the neon burn to a night life ended and so began a hustle to the next.

At the night lights end I only traded up one wingman for another. A younger friend who I had cut up the concrete of Denver with on a shop deck usually skating head on into the jungle wall together. To say it plainly, Matt and I came from two separate backgrounds. Despite that I was never fully educated I had a better chance than Matt ever did. And short the chaos of his childhood far surpassed the life that I was accustomed to. Each of his parents became tangled in the jungle vines where only one would manage to wrestle free. His younger sister would not be so lucky. Somewhere now into our thirties, prison life has become a part of my past, yet sadly exist in the present moment for this old friend. With such backgrounds incorporated I view myself more so in comparison to Sal, whereas Matt like Dean Moriarty. Although there are differences along the above comparison our goal as always was to get our kicks. The more we abided in our pleasures the more we grew to lean on each other, when swerving from one substance to the next. Always, it was family, a companion, employment, etc, etc all put on the back burner. If life weren't spent to a hustle or grind, the majority of our time was spent alongside someone.

This type of dependency, depended on the hustle of an unknown other. For for quite some length not and I have been broken apart, although a great span was spent in the darkness of a shared jungle. Codependency was not only displayed on the streets but behind bars as well.

It's not that we didn't know how to operate with one another? We chose not to. The overall dependency which lie between us was used for individual purposes. It was my own dependency that appeared emotional. (due too so much previous isolation and stunted maturity.) Being the older one I rarely acted it, except when I was paranoid or hesitant of capture.

Matt was purely reckless. However the one aspect he wasn't selfish of was splitting up dope. His actions and intent mainly came and support of himself, where many times we will surely pay the consequences together. Although I am not without blame, I could have made the effort to push him away but I only inched closer, needing to hear that I was right, when all went so wrong again. Error should have taught me to pull out when gravitation grew greater.

Along the lines of Similarity opposites ultimately come into play. EX:

- Whereas Sal published his first novel by the end of "On the road."

I have yet to publish one piece.

- Whereas Dean supported Sals Endeavor to write, Matt thought otherwise.

- Where is Dean put forth the effort to search for his father. (old Moriarty).

Matt always seemed indifferent to his father incarcerated on a 20 year sentence.

- Whereas Dean fathered multiple children he made a brief effort in responsibility, Matt immediately opted to run out on his.

- Whereas Sal had to walk away from his relationship with Terry due to her family and life of the road, Nika walked away from me because I became the jungle.

To quote Keroac" (As the jungle begins to take over, you then become it)

To quote another great: Oscar Wilde said

(With all the differences is considered, character is truly what you are amongst the dark.)

I've become a near native of the jungle life, now at a bend in the road I search for light amongst the civilized.

About the Author:

Originally a native of the Midwest, at 35, he resided in Colorado these past twenty years. A purple mountains majesty will always be his home. Currently in the works is a collection short stories and poetry.

THE SNOW QUEEN CONTEST

(A narrative non-fictional story)
by Joseph E. Fleckenstein

The ski club's first meeting of the year is always exciting, festive. Friends and acquaintances from past trips would be there. There would be the retelling of encountered experiences from the previous ski season, as well as those from the summer months. There was always anticipation of the announcements of upcoming trips. A speaker would address a subject of common interest. Occasionally, a local ski shop would provide a fashion show to display their goods. There is always the man-woman thing, guys on the chase and women looking sideways now and then.

The club had over one thousand members although only a fraction of the members attended meetings. The club held the meetings in a rear room of a popular restaurant. A bar was located just outside the room, and it was well patronized by the club's members before, during and after the meetings. The building's owner never charged the club for use of the room. He made enough from the bar sales. Skiers tend to be a robust, don't-give-a-damn, thirsty lot. It was almost as though you can't fit in unless you are an imbiber.

Once the president announced the meeting was about to start, some members finished their drink. Others scurried out for a fresh one to have while they paid attention to the Club's proceedings. After most were seated and the chatter decreased somewhat, the president started the meeting. Half way through the "new business," the Club president, Ryan, made an announcement that startled me. He told the group I would be chairman of the Club's annual Snow Queen Contest. Those present responded with a hearty round of applause. They were all happy for me. I smiled and waved a hand in the air to let everyone know I was present. I couldn't merely sit there, stone-faced. In truth, I didn't know what to make of the news. I thought it strange that Ryan hadn't asked me in advance if I wanted the assignment. As I shall explain, I was pitifully naïve.

It was true. I had become one of the Club's more active members and an enthusiastic supporter of its events. I was the Club's treasurer the previous year, and I helped with the club's activities. Being a bachelor I had the time. I started to suspect the assignment as chairman-ship of the Snow Queen Contest was intended as a reward for my service to the Club.

The evening Ryan appointed me chairman of the Snow Queen contest, as was my custom, I stayed around after the formal meeting for a few beers and chatter. With beer glass in hand, I worked my way over to where Ryan was min-gling with friends. I thought I should thank him for what appeared to be a favor. It seemed to be the right thing to do. When I caught his eye, I told him, "Say, Ryan, I want to thank you."

Ryan responded with a broad smile that clearly showed most of the teeth in his mouth.

"Joe, you earned it."

Ryan, too, seemed especially happy for me. His comment confirmed what I suspected: The Club intended the chairmanship as a bonus. It was a favor, not a chore. It gradually occurred to me that, yes, I might enjoy this adventure.

***

I resolved I would take my role as Snow Queen Chairman seriously. I would be conscientious and do whatever was necessary to make the contest a success. My first efforts would be to promote the event. Because I would need en-trants, I called the Club's secretary and asked her to place a notice in the monthly newsletter. I told her to say the Snow Queen contest will be in March. Mention that no experience is required, and there will be a prize for the win-ner. To register, the girls should call me. I gave the secretary my phone number so that it may be included in the advertisement.

The ad in the Club's newsletter brought calls from a few of the Club's young women. Alt-hough several prospective entrants expressed curiosity, none committed to entering the con-test. A typical call was the one I received from Ann, a friend of many years.

"Hi, Joe. How are you? I didn't have a chance to speak with you at the last meeting."

"Fine, Ann. Thanks. How about yourself? May-be we will be on more trips together this year."

"Oh, I hope so. I can't wait for snow. I'm really looking forward to going on a trip or two. I couldn't wait for the summer to be over."

Of course, I knew the reason for Ann's call. She continued. "By the way, I see you are running the Snow Queen Contest this year."

Ann sounded different from the Ann I knew in the past. She had become upbeat, cheerful, so happy to talk with me. I tried to bring the level of conversation to a normal tone—to the way people usually talk to one another.

"Yes. You know that if there were no volun-teers to run the Club's activities, there would be no club. I'm only trying to do my part."

"Well, I think the Club picked the right man for the job. I'm sure you will do a good job and be impartial."

I started to think Ann might be of the opinion that there is nothing wrong with a little partiali-ty between friends. I told her, "To tell the truth, Ann, I am not going to be the judge. No, that would be too hazardous. I plan to have some older men be the judges. I'm merely the organizer. That way I get to live to ski down more hillsides."

"You're a smart guy. I was thinking of entering the contest. I haven't decided yet. I wanted to ask you a question or two. If I enter, what do you think I should wear? Something with a ski-ing motif? After-ski togs or something like that?"

I didn't care to sound too earnest or serious about my task as chairman. The event was in-tended to be a lighthearted affair, entertain-ment for all.

"Wear anything you wish. Short-shorts might be a good idea. If you want to stand out you might try a G-string below and pasties up above. Just kidding. Be yourself and turn on the charm. I guess the judges would like to see a genuine smile and, I'm sure, skin."

"You men are all alike. I may or may not enter the contest. I'm not sure. See you later."

***

Starting with the November meeting, I was the recipient of comments from some of my friends–mostly jealous male friends. Michael was one of those friends. In many ways, Michael and I were two men of the same inclinations. Together, we had schussed down distant snow-covered slopes, drank beer and chased snow bunnies. Michael sought me out at the meeting, and, maneuvering me aside, asked, "How's the contest going?" He showed half a smile and seemed strangely curious.

I didn't know where he was going with this. I told him, "Ok, I guess. A few girls called me with questions. Some wanted to know what to wear, but that was about it. No girl has yet told me she plans to be in the contest."

"Really? You didn't tell them you would like to meet with them before the evening of the event? You know, to interview them and maybe have a drink somewhere? To give them some hints on what to wear. Hints as to what it might take to win?"

"No, I told them the prize is a sweater. I suggested that the judges would probably like to see legs."

Michael shifted to a frown and a whisper while squeezing my arm, I guessed, for emphasis. He looked around before speaking, much as though the two of us were about to cook up treachery.

"Joe, I'm disappointed in you. You should get up close to the girls. This is a rare opportunity. Some girls will do anything to win at a contest like this. You know what I mean. I'm talking anything!"

"No, I didn't look at it that way. Besides, I have a steady."

Michael was disappointed in me.

***

Several weeks before the contest, I contacted three political acquaintances and asked each if he would like being a judge of the contest. I did not need to beg.

One week before the March meeting, there were no applicants. I began to worry. Then the telephone started to ring. The girls had a variety of questions. How many have signed up so far? Will the names of the "losers" be in the newsletter? I told all of them the same: Show up the evening of the March meeting wearing whatever is your preference. Short-shorts might be a good idea. A local ski shop will be giving a good quality ski sweater to the Queen.

The night of the contest, one of the judges called and said he was unable to make it. Said he had forgotten about another commitment. I suspected he was afraid of losing the votes of disgruntled contestants. I decided to proceed with the two judges who had already committed. It was a mistake. The evening of the Snow Queen Contest, five girls, including my good friend Ann, approached me and said they would like to participate. Although it was a cold evening, all of the girls were wearing high cut shorts. Some of the shorts were made of material the thickness of crepe paper. The women's dress confirmed my long-held belief that skiers of both sexes were a reckless type.

I waited until the Club's president announced that the meeting was about to begin and "please take your seats." I led the parade of contestants and judges down the side of the main hall and to a private room in the basement. What a parade! The clicking of high heels on the wooden floor punctuated the show. A few men applauded. In the basement, I repeated the prize and the procedure for the contest. The rules, I explained, were simple. The judges will select the winner. I was greeted with smiles a plenty. The girls loved me.

One of the contestants, Ashley, said she had a question.

"What are we being judged on?"

I had to think quickly. Visions of pits with sharpened stakes pointed upward flashed through my mind.

I responded, "It's up to the judges. I would say that the winner would be a girl who is generally attractive and interesting. Skiing ability does not matter." Saying more, I concluded, would only risk unneeded danger.

Ashley had a response to which I had no possible comeback.

"Well, we all have THAT."

I realized I was in a predicament. What kind of an answer was she expecting? *Well, Ashley, in my opinion a well-developed set of tits might help. Or, a nicely shaped ass wouldn't hurt the cause. What about movie star looks?* Comments, almost any spoken words, could bring me trouble that might endure long into the future. I was about to speak when another of the contestants, Carol, addressed the subject.

"Ashley, we all have THAT but some of us have more of THAT than others."

I suspected Carol spoke up as a favor to me. Maybe she was hoping for points. Or, perhaps she was she jumping at an opportunity to trash the competition. There was no way of telling.

Ashley's mouth dropped and it seemed she was about to comment further, possibly with spicy vulgarities. It occurred to me that Ashley might be of a type that would enjoy using sailor words on occasion. Instead, she held back and a broad smile replaced the frown. It was time for me to turn the discussion in another direction and without delay.

I told the group, "Girls, this is what we will do. The judges will interview one girl at a time while the others can join the regular meeting or have a drink at the bar. Drinks are on the Club. When the judges have finished interviewing one girl I will bring in the next one and so forth. The winner will be announced near the end of the regular meeting."

As I turned to go upstairs, I heard the judges trying to decide which contestant to interview first. The monthly meetings usually lasted about an hour and a half. There was much to be treated at the March meeting: the financial report, old business, new business, stories from recent trips, and a speaker who was demonstrating how skiers can wax their skis at home. After an hour, the judges had talked with all five girls. I descended to the basement and asked the judges if they had made a selection.

One judge told me, "No." They could not agree on a winner. Each had their selection and they could not find a way to resolve their difference. Neither intended to budge. *Politicians*, I thought. I had a problem on my hands. The meeting would be ending soon and the members were expecting to learn of the new Snow Queen. I did not care to be known thereafter as the guy who botched the Snow Queen contest. I suggested to the judges that they find a way to come up with the winner. I asked them to be "imaginative" and said I would return in five minutes. When I returned there was no change. Action, I decided, was required. I took the judges aside and announced I was making an executive decision. I said I would flip a coin. If heads, the judge to my right would have the winner. Tails, the other judge. It was tails.

I went before the assembled membership and announced that Nadine was the new Snow Queen. I asked Nadine to come to the front of the room to receive her sweater. She was delighted by the award and full of joy. The members applauded. Ann, my former friend of many years, stood and pranced to the coatroom to collect her parka. With quick, sharp steps to punctuate her march to the door, she exited the building.

After the meeting, Nadine came up to me and planted one on my cheek. "Joe, that was so much fun. Thank you very much."

What could I say? I certainly could not have mentioned the flip of a coin.

"Nadine, you deserved it. There was no contestant better qualified to be Snow Queen."

Later in the evening, Ryan, the Club's president, found me at the rear of the room. He was displaying the same, strange smile he had the evening he appointed me Chairman of the contest.

"Joe, you did well."

I was not inclined to disagree.

"Thanks Ryan. It was an experience."

I could have added "education," but I kept that to myself.

As the crowd was thinning, Michael and I made our way to the bar. Together, we downed a few and discussed the evening's events before heading out into the chilly night air.

About the Author:

Joseph E. Fleckenstein, a graduate of Carnegie Mellon University, has published over 35 items. The list includes nonfiction articles in outdoor magazines, technical papers, online courses for professional engineers, a patent and more recently literary short stories in Prick of the Spindle, Story Shack, Out of the Gutter, Potluck, Gravel, Down in the Dirt, Work Literary Magazine, Street Light and Military Experience & the Arts. His 400 page technical book Three Phase Electrical Power was published in October, 2015 by CRC Press. Currently he lives in Pennsylvania where he is a self-employed engineer and freelance technical writer. Additional bio particulars may be viewed at his website www.WriterJEF.com.

IN THE WAITING ROOM
by Pete Warzel

There are two manners of conversation that occur in the waiting room of the Radiology Department at Mayo Clinic, Phoenix. The first is a deep dive into the existential, between family members, the why, how, now, of bad things happening to good people. The second is a rat-fucking back-biting nastiness driven by fear. Comments about family members and friends and how they all fall short when it counts, and goddammit it counts now.

There is a third mode of conversation that goes unspoken...silence. That is the talk I am having with myself as I sit and watch the show around me.

It is one hundred and four degrees outside. The piano player is silk-suited and making soft jazz in the lobby of the hospital next door. The clinic runs like clockwork and I have a thought that perhaps the administrator is an Austrian, it is so precise. My x-ray is scheduled for 12:50 PM and at 12:50 PM my name is called, I am given a gown and a dressing room and told when dressed to turn right in the hall and sit. I sit.

There are others sitting, indulging in the conversations hinted above. They are mostly on canes and wheelies, one large man, fit, walks stiffly in socks, no shoes. There is the buzz of folks talking, uninhibited, as if on cell phones in a public place, but there are no phones, only people and voices. "I remember that party, it was when mother was seventy years old." "When was she born, 1907?" "Yes." "Well then

it would have been her eightieth birthday because Joe was already born and in 1977 he was not." "Yes, right. Jill was there then and after that she recused her mother from anything to do with her life for the next thirty years. Her mother had done the same. Must be something in the water."

It drones. I only see the back of his head but see his daughter clearly. He has neatly trimmed gray hair and sits in a wheel chair. He is quite intelligent and clear, and of all here the most unafraid.

I am called into the room and put sideways up against the target, moved forward a bit, chin up. A click and whirr. Then I am asked to reach up to a bar with my right hand, left shoulder down, so they can get a picture, an image, between my shoulder blades. That worries me a bit...for what? What is between? The image does not give them what they want and they shoot again, a bit angled. No, not clear. One more time and they have it, whatever it is they are looking for.

A quick pace to Building 3, Phoenix campus, sign in for 2:00 MRI, actually two MRIs, a cervical and a thoracic. At 1:59 I am given a gown and some white stretch pants, a pair of rubber nubbed socks and when dressed walked into the machine room. I think of the machine as "Machine", a term that Gary Kasparov used in a post-match discussion in New York regarding his opponent Deep Blue. I watched the match on closed circuit tv and then heard Gary say

"Machine did this. Machine surprised me," as if Deep Blue was a person, a chess master, named Machine. This MRI is Machine to me.

I have had numerous MRI scans done in my lifetime and the more I participate the more I detest Machine. It is a sterile tube that makes obnoxious sounds, pounding, vibrating, disrupting an afternoon. Cool air blows through the tube so you do not feel you are stuffed and locked in a closet, left to fend in the dark alone. But this time there is something new. Before entering the tube you are scanned by a metal detector to make sure you have not lied during intake about not having metal or implants buried deep in your self. No beeping, I am metal free, and truthful.

Who would lie knowing an electro-magnet field is exciting your hydrogen atoms to a frequency that can be captured, measured, turned into an image. The banging is part of the deal. Mechanical coils flipping on and off... looking at your plumbing. The magnets would also pull the metal from your flesh.

The second surprise was an offer of headphones and a choice of music. I spent the next hour and fifteen minutes listening to Pink Floyd.

It was as hour and fifteen minutes because it was actually two scans rolled into one. The neck, where they suspect most of the problems are, and the first vertebra down the back, where when it goes bad feels like I have been shot through the left shoulder blade and end up face down on the floor, arms extended out above my head, in the only position that takes the pressure off whatever nerve is making me insane. An hour and fifteen minutes of a voice telling me I am doing great, of coils banging, of magnetic vibrations in my chest, and David Gilmour playing his heart out on a Fender Stratocaster.

About two-thirds into the event there comes a frequency that puts me into a panic attack. Bad shit. The urge to squeeze the call bulb in my hand and ask, demand, that I be slid out of the tube as fast as possible. Not knowing if they could then pick up the scan where they left off when I calmed I fought my way through it, unable to face another hour and fifteen minutes being buried alive. The tube was my tomb. I fought the fear and thought of my sons, one by one. The panic lessened and I heard The Wall through the noise, my eyes flickered but I would not open them and see the clean curve of the cylinder three inches from my eyes.

Then done. I am slid out slowly and the music is off. All is quiet and the images captured for a report that will tell us all what I do with the rest of my life. The conversation I was having while immobile and freaked was one of silence. Perhaps the next time I will scream bloody murder and fuck all the images that tell the tale.

About the Author:

Pete Warzel has published fiction, essays, poetry, and articles in literary journals, newspapers and national magazines such as "Pilgrimage", "Zone3, "New Mexico Magazine", "Colorado Expressions", "Cowboys and Indians Magazine" and "Gray's Sporting Journal", and was the books editor of "Montana Quarterly Magazine" for many years. He lives in Denver, Colorado and Santa Fe, New Mexico, and all the side roads in-between.

MICHAEL BRANCH AND THE ONLY TIME MY FATHER EVER SMOKED POT

by Leslie Bohem

In the spring of 1971, I dropped out of UC Berkeley midway through my junior year because a girl who I was hopelessly in love with had told me that college was stupid. I had formed a band with some friends of mine who I met in Santa Barbara, had seduced two of my high school friends into joining the band and, with notions of being the Grateful Dead, we now moved seventy some miles south of Berkeley to Santa Cruz. The Dead having made a similar exit north to San Rafael the year before, it seemed like the move at the time.

The band settled into an old Victorian home that had served as a dentist's office until recently, when the dentist, presumably, had died. We practiced every day and went out occasionally to play incompetent gigs in the local bars. The girl I'd left school for dumped me quietly after many tears on my part and an abortion on hers.

Across the street, another Victorian had been converted into a shop that sold waterbeds. They gave us the old models. We dropped them in the dentist's cubicles, filled them by running a hose through the windows, and we were set. The place was less than a

mile from the beach and at night, when I couldn't sleep, I would listen the seals barking by the pier.

In my memory, these are my formative years. We practiced, discovered obscure music, shared dreams and acid trips. In reality, as I try to set these events in the calendar in my mind, we probably lived in that house for six months. I know that by the spring of the next year, I had moved out and was living in the upstairs of a battered old duplex just across the San Lorenzo River from downtown. Somewhere in the messy fall of 1971, I had gotten a job in a clothing store on Pacific Avenue. I had worked after my senior year of high school in a very hip clothing store in West Hollywood, which has led to a job in a somewhat hip clothing store in Berkeley, and now to this. To this day, my only marketable skill is that I know how to fold a shirt so that it can look good in a display counter. The manager of the clothing store in Santa Cruz, which was called the Pant Tree, was Michael Branch. And it's Michael Branch about whom I want to write.

Michael was older. He seemed much older to my just turned twenty-year-old self, although I imagine he was thirty or at the most, thirty-five. He was tall and thin, with a woolly mustache of the sort that, in the late 1960s that 1971 was still a part of, had gone with a stoned, loopy smile, sparkling, squint-imp eyes, a dare and, in Michael's case. a certain air of competence There was something else about Michael that had nothing to do with the fact that he was chronologically older. Michael was a grown-up. He had skills. He could run a business, fix anything that broke in this duplex that he managed, and most importantly, Michael had been to war.

What is common wisdom now about the 1960s is that the war in Vietnam touched all of us, and I suppose, in some peripheral way, this is true. But for my friends and I, entitled middle-class white kids with college deferments and doctors who would write long medical excuses for us if we lost those deferments, "peripheral" is the keyword here. Michael was from another world entirely. I want to say that he had grown up in Portland or somewhere in Oregon, and for the purposes of this picture I am trying to draw of him, that will suffice, although now, Forty-six years later, I readily admit that those details are lost to me. What is not lost to me at all, are Michael's screams. To bring home the impact of those screams for you, I need to tell you a little bit more about Michael first, and about the only time in his life that my father smoked marijuana.

Michael had done two tours in Viet Nam, drafted early in the 1960s, when the War was on no one's horizon but the soldiers'. He did not often talk about his experience. I knew that he had these huge welts on his back that were some sort of impacted sweat gland problem that had been caused by months, years maybe, spent underground in that hot, humid climate. Michael's job had been to fire something, rockets, I don't know and don't pretend to know, but something that blew up and killed people. He did this from an underground bunker. An analogue drone operator, he knew that he had killed a lot of people, but he had never once seen the faces, or the mangled bodies, of anyone that he had killed. Michael smoked a lot of pot. He was the kindest, gentlest, softest person I had ever known.

One night, when I had smoked some with him, he took off his shirt, showed me the welts, and told me about his war. That was the only time that he ever talked about his experiences. He was explaining his nightmares. And now we have found our way back to Michael's screams. I lived, as I've said, in the apartment above his. The duplex was further from the ocean that the dentist's office had been, and at night, I never heard the seals. But what I did hear, almost every night, was Michael's screams. That night, when he showed me the welts on his back and told me about Viet Nam, he also told me that he had a lot of bad dreams. "I hope it doesn't bother you," he said. "But I wanted you to know what it was."

As I've already admitted, my memories of those days are stretched, as the memories of everyone's days of their late youth are, I suspect. And they are spotty, as I know so many of my own memories are. I think spatially or that is, I remember spatially. I can tell you in great detail the direction in which almost every bed I've ever slept in faced, even if I can't tell you who was in the bed with me. In what direction I was facing when I saw *The Godfather* for the first time. In much the same way, I remember snippets of the time I spent in Santa Cruz. Some of the gigs my band played, up in the mountains in a town called Felton, at a Hell's Angels bar somewhere out by the beach. I can tell you in what direction the stage faced, but not what songs we played. I remember an acid trip gone kind of wrong, as it came on the heals of an unsuccessful night spent with our next-door neighbor from the waterbed house while I was still trying to get over the girl who had gotten me into all this, who by then had moved back to Lawrence, Kansas and to her family.

My parents were worried sick about me. I'd left school, was living in a commune with some boys they barely knew. Drugs were involved. In addition to that, my father's younger daughter from his first marriage had been killed in a car accident the year before. My father was seventy. At that time, he was just my father, but now, as I near that age myself, I cannot even begin to imagine his pain. I have two memories of my father in Santa Cruz. The first is of him and my mother. They had come up to visit. My father loved photography, and there are still some photos somewhere that he took of the band, posing on the porch of our Victorian – trying ever so hard to look like the Dead on the porch of their house in the Haight. I suppose that, by taking these pictures, immortalizing what he saw as the biggest mistake that I had ever made. My father was trying to show that he had not totally given up hope for me. The memory I have is not of the picture being taken, but of my parents, the two of them, in a place called the Catalyst. The Catalyst was a restaurant where bands played at night. We were never good enough to play the Catalyst. Real musicians played there. Jerry Miller of the Moby Grape and once, Neil Young. In the day, it was a coffee house with a deli counter. I was there with my parents, in line for food. Music was playing, from a record player. It was the music of my parents' courtship. Something from the Big Band Era. "Remember this song," my mother said. She turned to my father and the two of them started dancing. There, in front of the deli counter. Now, probably, that dance lasted less than half a minute, just the two of them spending a moment with a song-induced memory, but the image of it has stayed with me ever since. A window into the people that my parents had been when they weren't mine, and when their worries and their hopes had nothing at all to do with me.

My other memory is of my father and Michael. My dad had come up to Santa Cruz again. He was by himself. I don't remember why. Michael had an extra room in his place and my father was staying there. They liked each other a lot. Michael was kind and could talk to anyone. My father was a lovely man,

with old world manners and a sweetness with strangers that I never once saw fail to engage. I had gone out somewhere – maybe I was working, or had gone back to the dentist's office to practice with the band. I have no idea. I just remember that I walked into Michael's and found the two of them, my father and my friend, smoking a joint. Michael was one of those guys back then who firmly believed in the importance of drugs. And my father, I think, wanted to see what it was that he and my mother were so frightened of. I remember where they were both sitting, Michael in an arm-chair at right angles to the couch where my dad sat. The couch faced the river. I remember those things, but I don't remember what any of us said. I was not a proselytizer for pot, in fact I always felt, and still do, a bit guilty when I'm altered. I feel as if I'm wasting time. But I do have a vague recollection of what I was feeling. I think that I felt a bit cheated, a bit as if I'd come in late. I felt that I'd missed something important.

I left Santa Cruz a few months later and moved back to Los Angeles. I only saw Michael once after I left. I was living in the house where I grew up, a place that my parents still owned, in Studio City. I had met my future wife by then, and many of our early dates consisted of going to West Hollywood to a theater where a Busby Berkeley festival was being held. They showed a double feature of his musicals each night and we were intent on seeing all of them. Michael come to Los Angeles, I don't remember why, nor do I remember if he was staying with me, but I do remember that he joined us for one of these double features.

And that was the last time that I saw him. He stayed in Santa Cruz and I heard, some ten years later from a mutual friend, that he had died of cancer. He was a smoker, of tobacco I mean, as well as pot, but I think that it was not cigarettes but complications from whatever had happened to him in that underground sweat-box in Viet Nam, that had killed him. I knew at the time that I heard about his death, but now, I don't remember. I do remember sitting with Michael in that movie theater in West Hollywood, a theater, by the way, in which the screen faced North, towards Mulholland Drive, watching the frivolous dances of Ruby Keeler and Dick Powell, and thinking about those huge welts on his back, his unrelenting smile, and his screams.

About the Author:

Les Bohem has written a lot of movies and TV shows including A Nightmare on Elm Street Part 5, The Horror Show, Twenty Bucks, Daylight, Dante's Peak, The Alamo, Kid, Nowhere To Run and the mini-series, Taken which he executive produced with Steven Spielberg. and for which he won an Emmy award. His stories are up and about in numerous places as is his novel, Flight 505. He's had songs recorded by of Concrete Blonde), and Alvin and the Chipmunks. His first solo album, Moved to Duarte, was released last year to rave reviews and absolutely no sales or downloads.

ALGONQUIN PARK

by James Deahl

Down from Lookout Hill, walking out of sunlight,
the woods seem to darken. A dank scent rises
of spruce and moist soil the sun has not yet dried.
Beyond these shadows, a slope of autumn maples
catches fire as sunlight ignites each leaf.
And still beyond that, the blue, nearly purple,
of a far-away hill, like a lake suspended in fantasy.
Every October, fire and earth meet, mate, and
following winter's six-month confinement, give birth
to spring. This afternoon the hills where these lovers
rolled smoulder, releasing the smoke of autumn.
The forest radiates a heat no northern lake can chill.
The farther one descends the higher October's flames soar,
maples going from green to bright red to an even
deeper red laced with black resonance: nature's canto negro.
Algonquin Park, a grand cathedral where voices echo,
each succeeding reverberation softer, more intimate:
the voice of a lover as the curtains are drawn.
Through a screen of paper birches the tale unfolds,
its plot gradually moving towards ecstasy
as daylight's final bonfire elevates and conceals.

Autumn Ducks, Late October

for Raymond Souster,
January 15, 1921 – October 19, 2012

Another autumn, and mallards
blanket these secluded waters
of Chipican, sheltered from
the sharp gusts off Lake Huron.

They arrived from up north on their
journey to the Gulf of Mexico.
In afternoon's sun they bob
on water surrounded by the gold

and burnt red of maples,
the yellows of locusts touched by frost.
All our flowers are finished,
even the brave asters have folded.

You have been gone six years, Ray,
and every year at migration time
your spirit comes on autumn's wind
with the mallards on their way south.

Ducks tarry on Chipican, safe
before whisking away as winter
advances with its teeth of ice;
they sanctify each year since you were here.

Burnt Country, Evening

The great fires have swept past
bringing purification to the forest,
and fields of ash, mounds of toppled timber,
and broken stumps left to rot
when the rains begin in May.
The few trunks that remain upright
are seared and blistered, sporting only
charred stumps where stout branches grew.

Soon jack pine cones will open
to reclaim their land from the hand
of flame. All remains still
where fires have danced, the sky
as grey as smoke. Eventually, insects
will return to colonize what once was forest.

This is the ballet of rebirth
that continues without us,
even without anyone to bear witness.
Infernos burn, and as luck would have it,
a painter records, and life returns
without his help. Creation's wild song
echoes down the billions of years
since that first fiery act of love.
Yet, it's here, under this implacable sky,
that we discover ourselves:
we end in fire
and in fire find our beginning.

Evening

A big sky: blue-grey and orange clouds
cast their colours into the lake
to restore the unity of heaven and earth
within one vast sunset embrace.
What bare sky remains shines light blue,
almost pale yellow, still lit by
a sun sunk beyond black pines.

The clouds in the foreground hang darker;
they yearn for night to stride forth
from the forest to pull them down.
It must have been like this
when the first Canadians followed
the melting ice mountains north:
land, lake, and sky bound together.

In the quiet of dusk, one ponders
the origin of evil. How could
our separation from goodness arise?
Can evil exist without us?
Could cloud and lake have also fallen?

The evening grows cool. Only the slap
of water on rock breaks night's reserve.
Soon the lake will be black as the forest.

In Times Of War

Canada's autumn skies go on and on
above these lakes that are truly great.
And wars, too; the wars carry on and on,
refugees drowning every day
between Tunisia and Sicily,
between Turkey and Greece.
Bodies drifting in the Mediterranean
and Ægæan Seas, bloated by salt water.

We enjoy the lassitude of calm waters
for our autumnal gales have yet to start.
We know they'll arrive, and winter, too.
We know the wars will continue.
Wave after wave of death will come,
with winter closing in; so many dead
they can hardly be named, bodies piled
along the ragged edge of southern Europe.

Along the eastern edge of Huron
one great blue heron after another
passes by, enormous wings slowly flapping
on their way to the Gulf of Mexico.
There will be no bloated corpses awash
in Florida's mangrove swamps, nor frantic cries
from those who cannot swim. Nothing moves
but our silent herons feeding.

Prairie Wind

Midterm elections, 2018

When the wind slants off
the Great Lakes in November
it sings in the telephone wires
and rips the final leaves
from a line of cottonwoods.

Fodder corn stands in rows
in the gathering dusk,
stands tall through the prairie night
as the invisible wind
rises with a hint of frost.

Across the nation people vote,
embracing either fear
or forgiveness. They vote
and all the while November
comes down with its blade of ice.

Quite Early One January

I

Sunday
and the bells of the village
become a garden of sound:
bright chimes of metal
shimmering
 above
the water-soaked
greens and blues
        of
the older, darker bells.

Reverberations across water
where
lake becomes river:
a charm bracelet of delight.

How vibrant churches
seem,   every bell
different —
 an outpouring
over neighbourhood homes

neither clapboard nor frame

but all possible shades
of brick, staunch
as those early farmers

who broke unbroken
land.

Sunday morning's
such a joyous possibility
even snow-lined streets
and the battered trees
torn by hurricane Sandy

cast a light
of their own.

II

Last night my wife
and I ate lake trout
fresh from Purdy's fishery
slow cooked in pure olive oil
and parsley

today we're awakened
by bells over snow
and the backyard windmills
of our Dutch neighbours.

Once stirred to beauty
this village will not
relapse.

Never numbered
among the unfaithful

we arise to attend
the Gnostic rite
of the sun's return
from the realm of death.

Every footfall in January
draws the sun closer

evokes life and song
— pure incantation —
from resounding metal, cast
and hardened
by the dexterous hand
of an angel.

In the dawn that is breaking
spirits of goodness
arise.

The West Wind

Like St. Patrick's Purgatory
or the curved journey of Stonehenge,
we come 'round again to outcropped rock
and lake and tree. And the insistent wind,
of course, there must be wind.
As with other penitential pilgrimages,
we discover love transfigured,
clarified, enkindled anew.

But love as we might, we can
only fail this land; the beauty
of trees shaped by wind — this celebration
of the moving and the fixed — transcends
our understanding. Painters always fail
their pigment; poets fail the words.
In sunlight's stubborn gleam, whitecaps
spirit up from slate-grey lake.

These winds crossed a thousand miles
of prairie, Lake Superior, and
the abrading Bruce, to curve
the smaller tree into a spinnaker
billowing out and out as if to capsize
this promontory into Lake Cauchon.
Unrenounced life flares into dance.
The land's forever claimed us.

Like Andromeda's light tumbling
through two million years
to strike the eye, a cloud mysterious,
we have finally arrived.
Winds shift from north-northwest to south-
west,
and riding the heady spring gusts
a mated pair of northern goshawks
heads ever further north.

About the Author:

James Deahl is the author of twenty-seven literary titles, the three most recent being: Red Haws To Light The Field, To Be With A Woman, and Landscapes (with Katherine L. Gordon). A cycle of his poems is the focus of the television documentary Under the Watchful Eye. He lives in Sarnia, Ontario, with his partner Norma West Linder.

LOST STARS

by Norma Linder

Some poems make me feel
like weeping
From time to time,
lines from them return
to haunt me

"May that day never come,"
Ray Souster said to James Deahl
"when we can no longer
sit under my mulberry tree
discussing literature"
But that day did come,
wrote James in a poem
in one of his many collections
that day did come

Sometimes, I'm overwhelmed
with sadness
for all the poets who have passed
beyond our sun
We like to think no stars are lost
when their bright lights go out
We like to think their written words
will last
but look around
— discarded books in cardboard boxes
sit on roadside curbs
untouched

Still, we bash on
because it seems important that we do
because it is

Closure

October's dying leaves
bear blood-red beauty
of impermanence

Under a curtain of rain
in Wellington County
on an autumn road trip
we drive by a huge
stone church
in a small village

Propped against
the slate-gray steps
of the abandoned building
a large black-lettered
wooden sign
catches my attentive
eye:

THANKS FOR THE MEMORIES

For Love Alone

Late in the afternoon
at the entrance to the mall
a frail old man
in rumpled blue serge suit
tucks a violin
under his long white beard
and fills the August air
with haunting music from
Cavalleria Rusticana.

His instrument
almost a part of him
he plays for love alone
eyes closed against the crowd.

After a mystical hour
the old man stoops
picks up his worn black case
tenderly encloses
his violin inside it
and shuffles off
leaving a scattering
of silver coins
on the ground behind him.

He played for loved alone.

At Canatara Beach

Bathers bounced back
from hubcaps of parked cars
become
the works of Grandma Moses
chromespun in noonday sun.
Sailboats perceived
through the amber archway
of my outstretched arm
take on a new perspective.

I close my eyes
my body melting down
against the great hard globe
of Father Earth.
He meets me thigh for thigh
hot-iced with sand
and all the long lost languid afternoon
warm breezes kiss me
with a thousand tongues.

About the Author:

Norma West Linder is the author of seven novels, fifteen poetry collections, two children's books, a collection of short stories, a play, a memoir, and a biography of Ontario Lt. Governor Pauline McGibbon. Her volume of selected poetry, Adder's Tongues, was published by Aeolis House in 2012. She is the mother of two daughters and a son. Linder lives in Sarnia.

ON MY FLIGHT TO NEW YORK

(REMEMBERING MY DEAR MOTHER)
by Dr. Raymond Fenech

I don't think I'll ever be closer to you as I am now
As I fly on this plane and look out into the endless sky;
The clouds swish by into patterns, faces, perhaps angels
The colour of sunset red and blinding, rays gold and bright.

I don't think I'll ever be closer to you as I am now
I cannot see below, nor can my feet touch the ground;
It's like a dream and I have grown angels' wings
As I soar above earth, I can almost see the brighter light.

I don't think I'll ever be closer to you as I am now
Not even the last time I was by your hospital bedside,
When your swollen hands, scarlet-bruised lay cold and still,
Your eyes half open peering at my sad-stricken face.

I don't think I'll ever be closer to you as I am now
Only in my dreams I came inside the snow-white blazing vortex,
Only once, but then I too was on a journey to unknown lands
And God would not let me join you, I still had to earn my wings.

I don't think I'll ever be closer to you as I am now
Maybe one day soon, I'll pass the gate into your realms,
Into your arms and feel once more the same comfort I felt
When I was still a child, when you protected me from every harm.

I don't think I'll ever be closer to you as I am now
To think for years, death has kept us wide apart,
And no matter how much time passed, the grief increased
With every rising sun, you still smiled, you couldn't see my pain.

Only your empty bed remained which was not even home,
Your clothes, in fading colours laid clean, neatly in a pile,
Your crutches in a corner, your embroidered hanky still on your pil-
low;
There was no light, only quiet darkness, and the slow killing silence.

About the Author:

Raymond Fenech embarked on his writing career as a freelance journalist at 18 and worked for the leading newspapers, The Times and Sunday Times of Malta. He edited two nation-wide distributed magazines and his poems, articles, essays and short stories have been featured in several publications in 12 countries. His research on ghosts has appeared in The International Directory of the Most Haunted Places, published by Penguin Books, USA.

RHINOCEROS

by Thomas Sanchez Hidalgo

It's four a.m. I have serious problems. And a Magnum in my pocket. Minutes later, dozens of crows, over a crowd of scrapyard parts (near the shoulder), take flight at our pace as if they were saying farewell, hordes of them, from the Porsche's brilliant engine.

I ask myself if this book, the one on the copilot's seat, is a collection of Brecht's poems. I'm almost sure it is. Then the taxi driver turns slightly towards me and thinks, "No, it's not Brecht. But it's undeniable that now they're coming for us."

After getting out of the car, I noticed that no one is chasing me, now at the entrance to our barracks, and in the dining room I start to set down in writing all of my impressions. I'm faced with a pressing problem, deserving of considerable attention. I resolve it stretching out in my seat.

"In reality, they should be thrown down the toilet," my response, soon thereafter, surrounded now by my people, faced with a "What do you revel in those papers?". I reach out, as far as I can, and I take some pills out of the company's first aid kit; I affirm, "I'm eating some planes," after putting them in my mouth, faced with my colleagues' increasing attention, their faces now coarse, strange, and they're in a "But look, they're antibiotics."

The South

Carbon. It never stops transforming distances, or states of matter: that last breath will soon appear next to me, in the stars. Carbon. After many different appearances, after so much rain on my chest, it could be snow lighting up the shadows, or the shining magma, or light itself, at the exact speed to plow through the ocean, or a red sky, after a knife fight, brilliant defeat, my way (Dahlman's way); that's how I wanted it to be in my first night at the sanatorium, when they stuck me with the needle, after the fevers: to live, today, in the sand although my skull is still secret: write my last name next to celestial drops.

Brave New World

Actually, subjugation curtails bravery. Imagine the magnate of soma, so brave (and the men, more and more neurotic and isolated).

Like brains tend to economize energy, IQs would shrink to alarming levels. I think dogs would take over the Earth.

About the Author:

TS Hidalgo (45) holds a BBA (Universidad Autónoma de Madrid), a MBA (IE Business School), a MA in Creative Writing (Hotel Kafka) and a Certificate in Management and the Arts (New York University). His works have been published in magazines in the USA, Brazil, Canada, Mexico, Argentina, Colombia, Chile, Venezuela, Nicaragua, Germany, UK, France, Spain, Turkey, Ireland, Portugal, Romania, Nigeria, South Africa, Zambia, Zimbabwe, Botswana, India, Singapore and Australia, and he has been the winnerof prizes like the Criaturas feroces (Editorial Destino) in short story and a finalist at Festival Eñe in the novel category. He has currently developed his career in finance and stock-market.

AND THE WINDOW IS SMALLER

by Hannah Paige

Dear Staples, here are your rubber bands back

Deteriorating love is a funny thing.
You build up this glowing mass of memories and emotions.
It's a warm rubber band ball orb that you two have protected,
have felt growing in your chests.
You build this rubber band ball,
adding to it in hours and days and in small moments
people besides the two of you miss entirely. You build it
and smile because this glowing beauty is the two of you.
It's what you are.
As time goes by, you keep molding it, adding large bands and small,
painful and vital and joyous bands.
Temporary and absolute bands.
If you're lucky, this rubber band ball remains glowing, safe beside your heart
until its neighbor gives out and turns out all the lights with it.
But if you're not lucky, then it deteriorates.

And if you pay attention, you can feel it.
You watch these bands disintegrate and strip off
slowly or all at once with clipped words and time spent elsewhere;
in missed opportunities and missed conversations
and just plain old missing one another through no fault of anyone's,
like highway 20 and highway 40 in their famed coast-to-coast paths that do not intersect.
You watch this glowing ball shrink
and you feel its life, its light that once moved you forward,
that gave you breath, that made you think you could not breathe without it there,
diminishing.
You watch this warm love deteriorate

and one day you realize that all the rubber bands are gone.

You have no glowing love for someone inhabiting your chest.

And you breathe.

The One With All the Windows on the Second Story of the Brick House on the Corner

We'll be simple.

The future we will have,
the home we will make
will not be fancy
With pearls and lace
and dry Sauvignon Blanc that parches the taste buds
and duck confit with tomatoes cut into roses on the plate beside it.

It will not be three different forks
or vacations to Turks and Caicos.
It will not be royal purples and balcony opera seats
or pristine tablecloths that would call out a spilled grain of salt
let alone iced tea.

The table will be wood.
It will be bare and probably old
and might smell
like cheap boxed wine that the people we buy it from at a garage sale spilled on it.
But it will not be empty

Our life will not be empty.

It will be you finding me curled up in the living room window
with a book, always a book.
And the yellow will warm me with the winter rays that don't come often enough
and the spring ones that will thaw smelling of hydrangeas and fresh sap.

It will be baked bread and sunset orange bleeding across the rough, beaten floor of the
apartment.
It will be rosemary roast chicken in the oven
Because buying it whole is cheaper
and you love the way the butter and garlic and herbs I clip from the pots on our window
melt at the bottom of the pot.
Poor man's gravy.
Lick your lips.

It will be dancing
inside and out,
On canary and pumpkin leaves that drift through the window,
screenless because the cat clawed the last
and it's $40 to repair.

Lemonade,
pink raspberry with sugar on the glass that sweats in the summer heat
beside the stars scattered on the roof we sit on,
laughing at the rich ones bustling below us.

They'll go home to their crystal glasses
and meals too fancy to eat or touch or throw across the table
with a patchwork persons' shriek of laughter
and they'll cross their legs on their duvets of pretentious pewter.

I'll keep the unmatching cups
and baked bread
and yellow.

Independent

1. a state of being that does not demand the reliance on another

2. as in what we are encouraged to be, within reason. As in two cups of *independence* is too much, instead use teaspoons. As in 'a girl with too much independence will never love completely'. As in the one without a partner for family game night. As in no 'plus one', not two just one. As in candles just to smell the Vanilla Bean and Caribbean Sands and not scentless pillars for ambiance. As in she will be alone because that is all she knows. As in her past has determined who she is, how she is. She. As in Freud was right. As in our childhood is too determining when it comes to adulthood. As in taking care of oneself. As in time management, self-sufficiency, laundry, responsibility. As in leaving clothes on the ground and lateness and 'They should've' instead of 'I should've' due to a lack of *independence*. (see also antonyms for *ambitious*) As in the characteristic with which we aspire to obtain but only in good time. As in not too early, not too late. As in not the White Rabbit's time. As in when everyone around you discovers the great white hope of progress. Keep up with the Joneses but don't get ahead of them. (see also *growing up*) As in knowing what you want and how to get it. As in the willingness to reach. As in using a stool or climbing the counter if it's too tall.

3. See also the ignored that ceaselessly try.

Warning to the Reader

You may in time seek prescriptions for disappointment. Orange pill bottles may eventually line your bathroom counter, white labels for 'The Man Who Wasn't Darcy' (take 2 orally with meals) or for 'When Everyone is Truly a Phony' (take 1 dose before bed while wearing a red hat of atrocious style) or maybe still more pills to soothe the ache simply for 'Atticus' (3 pills daily, 4 hours apart, feel free to take more though; they will never work.)

You will badger the pharmacists with endless requests to dull the pain of reality acquired after each 'The End'. Your symptoms will be endless and, if the book is right, if the writer is subliminally skilled at his or her job, exponential with every page turned.

Nevertheless you'll remain dependent on the prescription filled with a stamp in a catalogue card that reads: due two weeks from today.

Happy reading.

Don't forget to grab a bookmark on your way out.

And the window is smaller

You, in the field, with your arms outstretched.
Any sanity gone in equal time that it took for you to say goodbye.
Barely shutting the door before turning your back.

Daddy burned dinner
while you lightened your heart and shrugged the marble-heavy yolk onto my shoulders.
Ghastly sores and open wounds festered on your skin.
Big deal--you told me when I realized mine would soon resemble yours.

And the window is smaller where I look through to see you,
in the bedroom where I once slept and now comfort the rest of them when they ache.

Did you use Tide instead of Gain--the latter gives the smallest one rashes--to wash the tear stains
from stuffed monkeys and bears and tigers?
Oh my did you ever ask them what was wrong or if you could help?
Did you even think to look?

Did you see the trembling bedroom doors that shook
from the fists he threw down the hall at you,
the chairs and the snowglobe I made for you for Christmas?
I glued sequins to the base for two hours until my fingers were raw
and stripped from Elmer's harsh peelings.

Did you see the height notches--December 5th, 2010: Jenny hit 4 feet--that he splattered
with the blood, spraying from your teeth?
You lost an incisor that day and the year of great vertical accomplishment was erased
with AB+ paint.

Maybe if you'd spoken up,
if you'd opened your goddamn eyes
and seen the rashes that rose up on their arms because you didn't think about the soap
you were using
and seen
the doors rattling
and the toes peeking out
from under the beds because
the bodies attached,

the hearts attached,

the souls shaking inside,

were terrified that they might get hit with the shrapnel you let fly in our house

and seen the stains bloom,

unwanted wallpaper

that's impossible to peel off even with the harshest, the most artificial of chemicals,

the ones that sting your nose upon inhalation

and seen the lives you allowed to deteriorate alongside lunchboxes

and crayon bits

and shoes without laces because you never taught them to tie.

Maybe if you'd picked up the phone,

knocked on the door,

called out for help,

grown a damn spine,

it wouldn't be me stuck behind the window.

It wouldn't be me fearing for my own 32 teeth.

About the Author:

Hannah Paige is the author of the novels *Why We Don't Wave* and *30 Feet Strong*. Her work has also been seen in *WaterSoup* and she was the winner of the 2018 Biosophical Institute Poetry Event. She is the current editor of the online literary journal, *The River*, and is a Creative Writing Major and Publishing Minor at the University of Maine Farmington.

THE NEXT TIMES
by Margarita Serafimova

The next times were surrounding me,

and everything in their evening light

was quivering with unconscious potential.

I was yearning for you, for an answer from you

when I raised my gaze to the air.

An incomparable life.

A person in love is walked by a road.

When they reach the crest,

they walk on air.

The high wings of survival were unfolding and folding,

and unfolding above the water in mind-boggling beauty.

I was above ruin.

A horse was riding me.

That horse was darkness.

I had nothing but its dark.

And a heavy saddle.

A cry with woe.

About the Author:

Margarita Serafimova was shortlisted for the Montreal International Poetry Prize 2017 and Summer Literary Seminars 2018 Poetry Contest, and long-listed for the Erbacce Press Poetry Prize 2018. Margarita has three collections in Bulgarian. Her work appears in Agenda Poetry, London Grip New Poetry, Trafika Europe, European Literature Network, The Journal, A-Minor, Waxwing, Nixes Mate Review, StepAway, Ink, Sweat and Tears, HeadStuff, Minor Literatures, The Writing Disorder, The Birds We Piled Loosely, Chronogram, Noble/ Gas Quarterly, Origins Journal, miller's pond, Obra/ Artifact, TAYO, Shot Glass Journal, Opiate, Poetic Diversity, Novelty Magazine, Pure Slush, Harbinger Asylum, Punch, Tuck, Ginosko, etc. Visit her:

https://www.facebook.com/ MargaritaISerafimova

THREE SEASONS
by A.R. Francis

Three seasons

Three seasons have passed
Since I knew you
Since I knew the way your scarf
Fell across your shoulder
Or the way you sipped your tea
From that chipped cup
On Spring Street

And one day we'll pass
In a fluorescent hallway
Or at the funeral of a boy we knew
And I'll ask
How are you

And we'll think of the seasons
How silently they pass
How simply we've grown old

One morning

From the lead black iris
morning lures
a loner, lover.

Your father rings again.

The Sunday morning subway
stills
a cry like baby's breath
on fragile flesh.

I could die here
a scar across
the sweet of your neck

About the Author:

A.R. Francis was born in Baltimore, Maryland and currently lives in New York City. His previous work has appeared in the Columbia Journal, Black Heart Magazine, Glassworks, and Dovetail.

UNDERNEATH

by Roger Singer

UNDERNEATH

Fall back under early stars.
The sea moves reflective waves,
pulsing onto sand, building like
engines of thunderous clouds.
Streams of people merge into
temporary spaces; strangers on
corners, a brief land of shoulders
staring straight ahead. A steady rain
clears the dust. Afternoon finds a
place before dusk. Footsteps
continue. Everyone owns a portion
of passing shadows. Night stars
open with a hollow roar.

AN EMPTY SEAT

It's a train car without wheels.
A gathering for
the subculture. An information
center of new and yet to happen.
It's a stopover between this
and that. Art deco, vinyl and
stainless steel. Formica countertops
and a bathroom without a lock.
A jukebox with failed neon's struggles
in the corner. Eggs and coffee all day.
Smudged doors and stained windows.
Unwashed faces. Newspapers stacked
by the door. Table whispers, tired
eyes, advice without guilt. Alone finds
a stool or booth. No reservations

Required.

MY ROCK

It's my shoreline. A place of

footsteps and whispers, high clouds,

blue cobalt skies, forever horizon;

it's a song I live. A moment brings me in,

an hour holds me tight. It's a place

without time, without changing, it holds

the strength of me. I am the shadow of here.

I stand on the edge of myself, the backside

of the beginning. The escape with a forever

door. Rain or sun changes nothing from

where I stand.

POND FROG

by Nathanael O'Reilly

Pond Frog

a young frog makes her home
in the backyard pond

beneath the stone water feature
unaware that every summer

for the past five years another
frog has lived in the same pond

until consecutive hundred-degree
days heat the water to the precise

temperature at which frogs
die and float to the surface

Neck Pillows

A family of four wearing
Aussie flag neck pillows

pace between rows of seats
in the boarding lounge fifty

minutes before departure
stretching nervous legs

in preparation for twelve
cramped seated hours

between Auckland and L.A.
suspended above the Pacific

Spring Storm

sleep eludes
thunder vibrates windows

before dawn
sweat soaks sheets

bodies stretch
reposition   thoughts recycle

Visitation

There are too many miles
to travel; too many hours
on a plane. They'd rather
spend holidays elsewhere;
they simply don't care

to see where we live.
Here is not their cup of tea;
they'd rather save their money
for something more exciting.
We've only had one visitor

in the past twenty years.
That's what you get for moving
to the other side of the world.
Perhaps we're not as close
as I'd like to think we are …

we always visit them anyway.

Waiting

waiting for ballots to be counted
waiting for government to be formed
waiting for charges to be filed
waiting for justice to be served

waiting is falling
waiting is drowning
waiting is insomnia
waiting is illness

waiting is stasis
waiting is lacking control
waiting is ceding power
waiting is unacceptable

About the Author:

Nathanael O'Reilly is an Australian residing in Texas. His poems have appeared in journals and anthologies in eleven countries, including *Antipodes, A New Ulster, Australian Love Poems, Cordite, FourW, Glasgow Review of Books, Mascara, Postcolonial Text, Snorkel, Tincture, Transnational Literature, Verity La* and *The Newcastle Poetry Prize Anthology 2017*. He is the author of *Preparations for Departure* (UWAP Poetry, 2017), named one of the "2017 Books of the Year" in *Australian Book Review*; *Distance* (Picaro Press, 2014; Ginninderra Press, 2015); and the chapbooks *Cult* (Ginninderra Press, 2016), *Suburban Exile* (Picaro Press, 2011) and *Symptoms of Homesickness* (Picaro Press, 2010).

THE PARTY

by Laura Solomon

The Party

You have to be dead to be invited to this party.
As is to be expected, all the stars are here.
Janis, Marilyn, Jesus.
There are ordinary people too though.
Kevin Watson who died of a blood clot to the
brain
shortly after his 40th birthday.
He's been resurrected. Now he's partying in
the corner —
he's put himself in charge of the music
and is playing Nirvana
as Cobain toys with a segment of his blown-off
head.

Other run-of-the-mill folk present?
Jimmy Molesworth who hung himself
and is now hitting on Janis Joplin who is oblivious
to the attention, dancing wildly to *Come As You
Are*
a whisky bottle clutched tightly in her right
hand.

Jimmy's still got rope marks around his neck.

There's Cindy Rutherford who was hit by a car
while simultaneously cycling and listening to
her iPod.
Not a good combination. She's got splinters of
glass

from the windscreen embedded in her face.

Marilyn decides to re-stage her death for our
general entertainment.
She strips off and swallows a bottle of pills.
Then passes out in the bed. Nobody looks
alarmed.
It's all faked; we can't die now that we're dead.
The black telephone rings.
I move to answer it.
Nobody is there.
I can hear the 22nd Century heavy breathing
down the line.

Awakening

I am waiting patiently for you to awaken.
You are several hours behind
And half a world away.

Perhaps it's not wise
But I do it anyway
For reasons known to my heart
But still veiled from my mind.

You say you wait for me
So we are equal
Though I do not like to keep score.

A song plays –
"You and I were almost dead"
And I think of my many close calls;
The lightning strikes, the car crash, the surgery
to the brain,
To name just a few.

Yes, seven of my nine lives have been used up
–
I'm down to just two now
So I offer them up to you –
Hoping you will take good care of them.

I could now be almost the living dead, zombie,
vampire or ghost –
You could walk or see right through me;
See me walk through walls, not needing a door,
A humble boast, a sleek trick, some call it
showing off.
Scars and schoolyard beatings haunt your past,

Making me afraid for your future.

Wanting it joined to mine.
We could help each other in mysterious ways;

Each manufacture half a skeleton key –
Push open every locked door,
Leaving nothing undone.

I could hand you a sewing kit – needle and
cotton thread,
You could stitch yourself a new heart –
I could make it beat in two-four time
And we could waltz
Perfect strangers who should know better.

Animal Instinct

Man or animal?

Well what have we here –

A near perfect stranger getting kicks for free

Every night like some Cobain song while I march along in time,

No doubt just as guilty.

I'm old enough to be his mother, there's something twisted about that,

I ask myself why I continue - nobody has an answer to this question.

It's trauma that makes the story great,

The wider yawns the abyss, the greater shines the glory,

Think of all the medals we could hang upon our walls,

Polished and shining, public display - if you care for that sort of thing.

Gloss up your scars until they gleam – then put them up for sale,

There's a space now where they operated,

Must be my lucky day - my mind plays tricks on me,

Not knowing which door to open,

Behind this one a candy store, behind that, a hard brick wall,

The sands of deception shift and change - as everything dissolves.

A limited life span brings everything into focus,

People they care for me,

Well, don't tell me I'm living beneath my dignity,

As other humans serenade with songs I can no longer hear

All my circuits are cut off.

Kiss goodbye to your old way of living,

You too can dwell in cripple's alley,

Thinking only doomed thoughts,

That back you into a corner, get you up against the wall –

Shrug and kick it off –

Song plays 'There's an empty space inside my heart'

The road stretches on ahead of us –

Into something that resembles infinity.

Geography

They were both prisoners of their minds.

"You don't have to be a solo driver", she said to him,

Hoping to lighten his heart.

He claimed it had the desired effect -

At least some of the time.

Both of them bore battle scars.

Soldiers in the field, they stood shoulder to shoulder,

Facing the same way – a cold wind blew

As they stood staring into the midday sun

Just after that last eclipse.

He reassured her fears with his constant words –

And a miniature universe was born.

The phone lines between them were clear;

No crackle, no static.

Except for on one occasion

When he was speaking and she could not hear his voice –

Which was disturbing.

She admired his tenacity -

He kept on trying to get through.

She made a map, and he stuck coloured pins on it,

Markers to mark where they had been,

And also where they were going.

They could not see the edge of the map.

He told her he wanted to be a land surveyor

So she sent him a book on topography,

Along with the latest MRI scan of her brain.

Together they explored the geography

Of their strange and unexpected new love.

Sky Burial

I think I would like a sky burial –
No photographs allowed as the vultures take
me skywards.

I'd have to live in Tibet, get friendly with the
locals –
Earn somebody's respect.

Those gigantic birds would circle overhead,
Waiting patiently, then *swoop*,
My body parts would be swept up in talon and
beak –
The easiest way to take to the sky.

More practical than cremation
When the ground's too hard and rocky to dig a
grave –
This would be my exit strategy.

Instructions can be found in the Tibetan book
of the dead
For this ceremony intended to help my spirit
move on from
The uncertain plane between life and death
into the next life.

Who'd want to be hanging around on planet
Earth
When you could be digested by greats of the
sky,
Something with a decent wingspan
And spend your after death, pre-digestion
hours,
Hovering high in mid-air,
Waiting to be born again.

Ode To Mutt

Nobody, Laika, captured their imagination like
you.

So many arrived before me, honouring you
with their words, that I hardly know what to
say.

They're paying me, Laika, to make this
speech. I am employed.

The ghost of you must be sick of it by now; the
poems, the tales, the odd shrieking song –

The yapping of ten thousand dogs trapped in
ten thousand kennels.

So tedious to have become myth, when all you
really want is silence, peace.

To quietly orbit the orbiting earth.

And what of the other dogs, the ones they
passed over, in favour of you?

The mutts that went on to lead full and happy
lives;

Salivating, biting, yelping, humping the legs of
humans and tables.

Were they envious or grateful? Did they want
to take your place?

What did you have anyway, that made you so
special?

Nothing. You were doomed to immortality. It
was your fate. You were the one.

It was as if a part of everybody had been sent
into space with you.

You carried our hopes for the future, for what
could be achieved.

They wanted to monitor your blood pressure,
your heart rate, your breathing

To see how the rest of us would fare, if we followed in your path.

You were their experiment – they wired you up.

They wanted to know how deeply you slept, and if you dreamed.

You were a Jesus of a dog. We all knew it. Your harness was your cross.

So? I can hear your shrug in your bark. What about it?

You were always nonchalant.

There had been others before you; your comrades, Albina and Tsyganka - a few sacrificial mice.

But they were merely suborbital. You burst straight through to the other side

And saw, for a moment, it all; the diamond stars, the distant galaxies, so many glistening moons.

The universe pulsed in your veins.

Time stalled, spluttered, stopped.

You were shot straight out of the cannon of history – fired into eternity.

It was the sun that killed you, cooked you alive; fried your fur, charred your bones, scorched your skin.

Your eyeballs sizzled in your skull as your last bitter bark reverberated in space.

And seemed as if it might echo forever.

The tender howl of betrayal.

No-one knows how long you took to die – the Russians claimed, for years, it was a week

But now, it transpires, you were baked within hours.

Could you tell us the exact time, let us know?

Laika, friend, enemy, are you out there some-where -

Your skeleton still in orbit, your dream a uni-versal dream?

Only you know the truth and you are gone and can never tell.

You have become metaphor. Such is your wish.

Still, the curious in our number cannot help but wonder -

If you were here now amongst us and given human voice

What would you have to say? And who would listen?

About the Author:

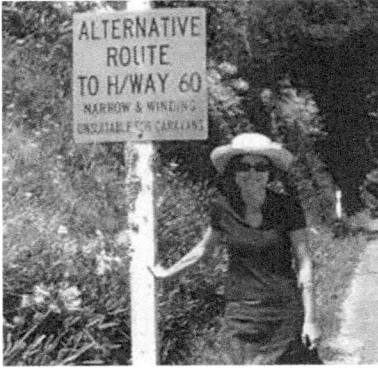

Laura Solomon has a 2.1 in English Literature (Victoria University, 1997) and a Masters degree in Computer Science (University of London, 2003).

Her books include Black Light, Nothing Lasting, Alternative Medicine, An Imitation of Life, Instant Messages, Vera Magpie, Hilary and David, In Vitro, The Shingle Bar Sea Monster and Other Stories, University Days, Freda Kahlo's Cry, Brain Graft, Taking Wainui, Marsha's Deal and Hell's Unveiling.

She has won prizes in Bridport, Edwin Morgan, Ware Poets, Willesden Herald, Mere Literary Festival, and Essex Poetry Festival competitions.

She was short-listed for the 2009 Virginia Prize and the 2014 International Rubery Award and won the 2009 Proverse Prize. She has had work accepted in the Edinburgh Review, Orbis and Wasafiri (UK), Takahe and Landfall (NZ). She has judged the Sentinel Quarterly Short Story Competition and the Needle in the Hay competition.

Her play 'The Dummy Bride' was part of the 1996 Wellington Fringe Festival and her play 'Sprout' was part of the 2005 Edinburgh Fringe Festival.

https://en.wikipedia.org/wiki/Laura_Solomon is her Wikipedia entry.

http://www.thebookbag.co.uk/reviews/index.php?title=Category:Laura_Solomon is her Bookbag entry.

www.laurasolomon.co.nz is her personal website.

TENDER WORDS

by Dayna Lellis

Shroud of Stubbornness

The quicksand is devouring her.
She's struggling, sobbing for help.
I rush to pull her to safety.
She refuses to take my rope.

I scramble to find other options.
I offer her rope after rope.
"Please grab one! You're dying!"
"None are the one I want!"

I sprint to get the village elders.
They gather, offering their advice.
The rope she desires is difficult to find.
None of us can procure it in time.

The chaos has turned into silence.
We wait to see her next move.
Will she decide to save herself?
Or will stubbornness be her shroud?

Tender Words

"I am proud of you. I love you."
Elle spoke these words
to the woman staring back at her.
The woman softly cried because she
rarely heard such tender words.
Elle wiped away her tears
as she walked away from the mirror.

Where All My Sins Begin

How long will it take me,
using my nails to dig,
to find that place inside of me
where all my sins begin?

Will I find an inferno,
scorching hot with hate?
Fed by my inadequacy
and laments that life is bleak?

Will I find a scared child,
neglected for years on end?
Compelled to lie and steal so
society's lusts can be appeased?

My Turn to Ride

It gallops closer each year.
I must wisely use this time.
I will not be saddled
by unpursued dreams
when my turn to ride arrives.

All My Tomorrows

As I reminisce about my yesterdays,
I pray that their lessons will live
in all my tomorrows.

About the Author:

Dayna Lellis graduated from SUNY Geneseo in 2013 and Harvard Graduate School of Education in 2014. She works as a middle school teacher in New York and writes in her spare time. Several of her poems have been published in Valley Voices: A Literary Review, The Voices Project, and Voice of Eve.

TRIBUTE

by Heide Arbitter

These days
Some assert
History is a lie
The Holocaust never happened
Somebody made it up

In Washington, DC
Capitol to a country
Of assailed settlers
The blood of recollection
Sprinkled on soil
Fertilized Cement
And blossomed
Memory

Some insist
All visit the Nation's Capitol
To throw away money
On fake attractions

Fortunately
Concrete structures have thick skins
Which aren't affected by gossip
And others know
Monuments make history real
So why tear them down

After standing at the Holocaust Memorial
Some will feel
Others will not
All will have faced
Truth

About the Author:

Heide Arbitter's plays have been produced in New York City and regionally. Some of these productions include a one-act, HAND WASHED, LINE DRIED at the Joseph Papp Public Theatre; a full-length, FROGS FROM THE MOON, at the American Theare of Actors; and a one-act, TILL WE MEET, at Unboxed Voices. Smith & Kraus and Excalibur published JILLY ROSE, SHARON and POPPY. Heide was recently interviewed on the radio, WFUV.

DARK LOVE

by Lael Lopez

Dark Love

This angel fell
She lost her light
Trudging through the gates of hell
She gave up the fight
No man or god
Could bring her back
Until she looked into his heart
Black as coal
Hard as ice
Their inner darkness called to each other
A spark churned inside her
Something alien nagged at her
Their eyes met
And the muses wept
The hell cats yowled
Something ancient awoke
Love so dark
It tore at reality
Love so fierce
The earth shook
Both man and beast feared
Because that day
Dark love was born

Thoughts of the Heart

When you saw him
Your heart flew

Then you met him
And a spark grew

You chose duty over him
Yet the sight of his face
Still plagues you

You turned your back
Even though it kills you

Looking back is not an option
When you close your eyes
You see his smile

In your dreams
His laugh rings through

Some thought it was the latter
Little do they know
It is the former

Life is a hard, cruel road
And the heart is an evil beast

I think it's better
Sometimes, not to feel

The Girl

A hooded figure stole her dreams
A cloaked thing made her scream
Chasing after something she could not have
A haunted song
A broken mind
Everything she touched
Was destined to die
Followed by sadness
Haunted by lies
Reminded of a past
That she could not hide
No one will see her cry
People hide
From the monster she has become
Inside her sleeps a shell
The girl she once was
The girl she can never be again
A tortured artist
A wandering soul

Little Times

Sometimes we love
That which we shouldn't
Sometimes we're pulled
In a terribly wrong direction
Sometimes we're blind
Blind to that which would kill us
Unaware of those who'd betray us
Sometimes we hate
Hate so strong it'd sink islands
Sometimes we regret
So, strong it breaks us
Sometimes we're so high
That we come crashing down
To a new sort of low
But in these little times
Where everything is terribly wrong
Or perfectly right
That we see who we really are
We see who we should trust
And who we shouldn't
Who we loved
And who we couldn't
That's why I love
These little times

My Emotions

I count the days
I bid my time
When I can be free
From your disgusting lies
Days will turn into months
Months into years
By then I will conquer fear
I'm sick of being tired
I'm sick of smiling eyes
My cheerful pen
Is now blackened
By my angry thought
Corrupted by my thirst for revenge
My bitter words
Knows no end
I long for happy days
Until then it is better this way
This page is my outlet
This pen, my portal to sanity

About the Author:

Lael Lopez is an unknown poet living in Trinidad with her 11 cats and 1 dog. She goes to an online school and spends her free time drafting poetry and working on short stories. Growing up as a quiet child has led her to use her pen and words as an outlet for her imagination.

ALEX ON HIS GUITAR
by Linda Barrett

Alex on His Guitar
@2016 Linda Barrett

He got it as a gift from his father
On Christmas Eve
The acoustic guitar of deep mahogany
Cost around $500
But the owner put it on sale
At $300.
Alex's father learned to play it
From his half Native American mother
Decided it was another interest for Alex
As well as his son's first love of fishing.
Alex played it at our Christmas Day gathering
Strumming its delicate strings
Until he got the sound right
When he plays it slow,
It flows like a spring stream
Freed from the captivity of winter
Rolling down rocks
Carrying freshly awakened fish
From their frozen slumber
When he plays a fast song,
It sings of adolescent frustrations:
Hurrying to class
To escape a detention
Or impressing a girl he likes
But he can't find a way
To make her notice him
Listening to him play,
It's wonderful
That he's able
To express his persona
Through music.

The Path of a Young Man
@2017 Linda Barrett

You love the placid face of a pond
Or the rolling white foamy heads
Of an unfettered woodland stream
You always bring your rod and reel
To catch the fish within those waters
You search the forests and woods
Searching for their untapped treasure
Most youths your age find delight
Seated before a television screen
Or surfing not on unruly ocean waves
But on the overpopulated Internet
You hail back to a long forgotten time
When the world bloomed free of man
Take this everlasting but endangered path
And lead those technology enslaved
Back to save and preserve nature.

August Notebook
@2014 Linda Barrett

It's August
Amid a thousand notebooks
I look for a specific color
Of blank book
To match the month.
Which one demonstrates
Summer's last month?
My journal should be
An orange
A fiery color for the waning days
Before a solemn September
One that signifies
Brightness
Clashing with pink
Blending well with purple
Flashing with white
Glimmering with gold
I want an orange for August
As hot as an afternoon
Just before a sudden shower
My book should be
Brilliantly colored
In the manner of an 8 P.M. sunset
Garish like an artificially colored
Orange soda
It should fit that color scheme
So that I will remember
How August made me feel
Whenever I wrote in its pages.

Born on Wheels
@2012 Linda Barrett

You always lived on wheels:
a newborn infant
perched in a car seat
beside your mother
when she drove
her 1973 Green Impala
The toy Knight Rider car
was your first one
It cursed at you
from its imaginary dashboard
You hummed your
open road song
while holding onto
the sides of the red wheelbarrow
as I bumped you in it
over the stones in
our backyard's stone walkway
Out in Chester County,
you roller bladed
and skate boarded
into adolescence
Every Spring Break,
You traveled in your
grandparent's station wagon
down to Florida
One Winter,
you drove to Colorado
by van
to snow board the mountains
Other guys chose college
you took your mechanic
grandfather's cue
studied up in Boston
learned to fix cars
inside and out
then put them
back together again
You inherited the
Green 1973 Impala
with its torn off

vinyl top
let it go to rust
and to the junkyard
then bought a red 1968
Ford pick-up
Your mother bought
you a motorcycle
so you could scream
down the Turnpike
With your Independence Day spirit
Nothing out on the road
Can stop you
As if you were born
On wheels

Butterfly Woman
@ 2014 Linda Barrett

Out of
Cancer's Cocoon, you struggle
From caterpillar to chrysalis
Fight what's eating at your body
Emerge once again fully healed, ready to
Fly again

About the Author:

Linda Barrett's passion has always been writing. Ever since she was small, she has had a pen in her hand. She lives in Abington, A suburb of Philadelphia, Pa. She is involved with two writing groups and her two churches. Her work is featured in various print and on-line publications.

LOTUS

by Martina Reisz Newberry

1. LOTUS

On the other side of the mountain,
my wealthy friend has built a castle.
It was a long project but now sits,

quiet as a profound thought, complete.
 The day I visited her, we had
coffee and Red Velvet Scones behind

the castle near the Koi pond. Smell of
gardenia, petals stiff with infirm
hateur and, near pond's edge, a lotus—

the real thing. I was impressed with it.
"It's called *Nelumbo Nucifera*,"
my friend said. "A strong name for such a

peaceful bloom, don't you think?" Yes. Oh
yes.
Scent of water, sound of water, shade
on the water. So much silence, beauty.

My friend's secretary came out with
more coffee.We sipped and blinked, and
watched.
I was happy as I should have been.

When the palm fronds rustled anxiously,
nervously, I walked toward the water,
pellets in hand. "Throw them in. See what

happens," she said. Palms nattered again
and I tossed the pellets.The water cried out,
had a seizure. Open mouths—orange/white/

(LOTUS)

gold—shock and awe—fought for space, a riot
of
open mouths. They swarmed toward the food
while I flinched, stepped back. "I have

Sarasa Comets, Shubunkin, Butterfly Koi,
and some *Domestic Koi*," she said. "I love to
feed them." I left shortly thereafter

and drove carefully down the mountain.
My mind repeated Basho's sly words:
"Learn to listen as things speak for them-
selves."

2. WHAT TO DO IF HAUNTED

When the broken spirits come
into your dreams and cut your hair,
turn you on your back and whisper
complaints in your ears, fight back.

Fight with the sounds of pots and pans
in someone's kitchen,
with strong winds below the canyons,*
with laughter and clinking glasses

from the gathering next door,
with the cat's lapping water
from the stout green tumbler
on the floor next to the sofa.

Take sleep as it is supposed to be:
a baptismal font. It is the gift
that should soothe and cleanse,
the cup we drink from that lets us

wake to wonder into a dimension
that no longer invites wonder.
There will always be sleep and,
when the broken spirits visit,

we'll wake. Oh yes! Eyes wide,
mouths parched, bellies and brains
starved for words that will dance
and music such as will make miracles.

3. ACCURATE RECALL

Did you know that dreams are the scars of recall?
They prompt us to take one more look at the
houses
of our childhood, the graves and the hiding
places we believed we grew out of. Remember
the things you said you'd never do again? You
will do them in your night terrors. You will do
them
in the dreams of past lovers. You will do them
in the presence of your dead parents. It is
the nature of dreams to tickle and torture
your sleep with regrets. My mother would say
she died of loneliness which I supported by
never being there. After a while, in fact,
I could hardly bear to pass through the town
where
she lived. My father would say the same—that
I
stayed away, did not call, did not care.
I don't know why any more than they did.
I dream of them almost nightly. I swim
clumsily through a thick, salty sea of regret
to live once again in their house with them.
In dreams, as in accurate recall, seeing them,
depending on them, scares and saddens me.
In my dreams, unlike accurate recall,
I cannot leave.

*RIP 2001 Larry Kramer

4. "RACHEL IS WEEPING FOR HER CHILDREN…"
Jeremiah 31:15

I imagine I can see
the scratched and scarred places on
my children's bodies.
They are the places where I
used to live. Look carefully

and you'll see my ghost, looking
for the rest of my family,
for that other life
I thought I would have. Careless
dreams—curious larceny.

I read them like books, thumbing
through their pages that did not
love me—loved others—
but not the smiling, passive
woman who seemed only to REact

instead of grabbing the bull
by its proverbial horns
(a pithy observation),
and running for those famous
hills, their little hides in tow.

Oh, I have been penitent
all my life— all of their lives—
far from paradise,
further still from lenity,
landed under the spaces

in their memories, waving
Calling out to their bodies
"Here I am. See me.
In spite of your memories,
I am more than your laments."

5. IF YOU WILL

If you will forgive me my darkness,
I'll channel the winds that come through
the canyons and I'll breathe them
into your hands.

You will be protected from the void
that sits at the sides of fucking and fasting
and numerous other bluffs that could
come your way.

If you will absolve me of my excesses,
I'll see to it that the unjustness of this world
stays to itself and Magic—as it is wont to do—
will bear you no malice.

At supper, I will fill your plate
with undreamt dreams and pour
lightning into your cup. At bedtime,
I'll turn your sheets down

with fingers like song lyrics and give the gods
of rest your full and true name. I'll lay
vagueness over your esculent body and
Comb elixirs through your hair.

All this for forgiveness, for the exculpation
of everything I cannot be or do…
We are far from paradise. An apple
you accept from a naked woman

could explode at any time. Believe me,
you are better off waving away my sins,
smiling wisely at my weaknesses
forgiving me my darkness.

About the Author:

Martina Reisz Newberry's most recent books are NEVER COMPLETELY AWAKE (Deerbrook Editions) and TAKE THE LONG WAY HOME (Unsolicited Press). She is also the author of RUNNING LIKE A WOMAN WITH HER HAIR ON FIRE (Red Hen Press). Martina currently lives in Hollywood with her husband, Brian, a Media Creative.

WIRED

by Michael Milburn

WIRED

He's quick to find things
wrong about himself,
or makes them up
to feed his insecurity,

sees flaws in people
they seem not to see,
and wonders if a set
like that exists in him.

He wants to know those too,
or only those.
He rarely minds himself
except as others do.

For her, it's virtues rather than flaws,
but that's a different kind of self,
a different kind of consciousness,
a happier marriage between the two.

CHURCHGOING

Do I credit beauty
for what is plainly

divinity out of not
wanting to believe,

or is it how I come
to love God, whom

for all my refusal to
admit his existence

I have granted both
a home and a name?

RAGE

First
the equivalent of that
electric burning smell
that comes of running
the shredder too hard
wafts off me as I try to
present an impassive
façade.

Then
it steps out beside me
with shaved skull and
popping neck tendons,
ready to brawl on my
(the peaceable brains
of the organization's)
behalf.

FOR CAUSE

When the detritus of feeling clears away,
the recriminations and second thoughts

weighing good company
versus good chemistry,

it comes down
to two women,

the one who wanted me
and the one who didn't,

citing what I said or did
or my respect or affection

or passion or mystery
or wit or availability

or restlessness or readiness
or lack thereof, thereof and thereof.

And being wanted unnerved me
just as much as being unwanted

when my same qualities
did and did not appeal,

virtues and vacancies
equally misconstrued.

So make a mental note,
Ms. Interested, Ms. Not,

that whatever I base my judgment of you on
may also be an error of just that.

INTIMACY

If an ideal state of intimacy exists,
it would seem that the long married inhabit it,
though anyone as chipped away at by marriage
as I am
wonders about that.

I see intimacy as an active, variable thing,
ebbing and flowing along with sex and ambition,
up if the former is incredible,
down if want turns to wanting—

not wanting sex, but success, happiness, more.
To me marriage felt like navigating a raging
rapids,
best to accept that neither her peaks of ardor
nor lows of disappointment would last.

Unfettered and unconditional:
I hoped marriage would be both,
but it didn't turn out that way
so I decided it entails getting to know another
too well

to keep admiring him or her a lot.
Diminishing returns. I ought to do interviews,
discard my own experience as corrupt data.
I still see love as a transient thing, not to be
relied on,
unless longevity equals intimacy,
a premise that half consoles and half,
if one aspires to the latter as a scorching way to
feel,
doesn't make sense.

About the Author:

Michael Milburn teaches high school English in New Haven, CT. His book of essays, Odd Man In, was published by Midlist Press in 2005, and his most recent book of poems is Carpe Something (Word Press 2012).

WANT

by Caitlin Muse

Want

The heart wants
What the heart wants.
Strange fist, wild thing.
Said to be blind, but isn't Want a fruit with vision at its wet center?
Some are doors hushing closed, others doors rushing open.
Some hearts are chiseled from sapphire or onyx,
Moh's Scale of Mineral Hardness --- spanning the gamut,
Numerology of Austerity.
Others---slip and mud,
Putty poked, kneaded,
Warmed in dusty lined hands.
Both, composed in part of mercurial mist, blustering gusts and blistering blaze.

Antique Row

Guh-muhrneeng!"
Exclaimed the sticky-eyed homeless guy outside of the liquor store,
Swept by the elegance of his remark,
My eyes swung to meet the target of his gesture across the street.
Two reindeer stood in a triangular enclosure of rented fencing equipment
Atop the Handicapped parking spaces at the Turn of the Century antiques shop.
I remembered hearing that due to climate change,
Reindeers had begun to shrink. Become smaller. More diminutive.
The British Ecological Society's paper was titled "Small is Beautiful"
Which I found unsettling.

About the Author:

Caitlin Muse is a Denver native raised on a steady diet of Shel Silverstein, T.S. Eliot, Wallace Stevens, Patti Smith and William Blake. Writing poetry since she was a little girl, as treasures to be sent in the mail to her grandfather, poetry has always been a constant for her and something that she cannot imagine existing without. Recently turning a milestone age, she has begun the harrowing journey of submitting a few of the poems that have composed her life.

DREAM PARK
by Dominique Williams

Dream Park

In my tour of the vast and endless city of exquisite white marble and verdant green grass, I came upon a corner which led to a dead end. With my heart still working as hard as it could, I dared myself to venture further inside the alleyway. It was not bravery though, just curiosity to see this popular exhibition that I'd heard so much about. But soon I felt myself in a claustrophobic tunnel of horror and impending doom. Dared I look inside those displaced iron cradles of eternity and discover what I most feared? Would whatever was inside them grab at me and take me with it beyond what I could comprehend? I peeked out of the corner of my eye and was finally overwhelmed. I saw nothing but what I imagined and that was enough to turn back...if I were you.

But this is what I came here to see: the freak shows without the freaks, the street accident without the bodies, the long evaporated results of a final solution always handed down from above, no matter what anyone thinks. This is a sentence delegated to each one of us by birthright.

In between the clouds and a sunlit sky sat several souls on stone benches sitting outside of their marble mansions. I passed by them on my right. They sat very still and dully regarded me as if I were a bit strange. "I am" I responded without speaking and moved past them.

It was as if I needed to move from beyond the finery and cruel beauty of a land of nowhere into a crueler yet more beautiful domain which is within myself.

 Hell's bells – I hear them ringing; but they don't sound so bad.

 DGS (1959 -)

Snowstorm

Blanket me in indifference

Hide me from myself and numb my thoughts of you

But it melts away

Not the pain, but my protection, my cocoon

Blind me from the fatal truth as the carriage horse knows his future is not rest

Freeze me in the past where I could assure myself that romance was shared between us.

COME IN SINNER
by Gail Willems

COME IN SINNER

give us this day our daily bread
eyes burn swollen faces line-up
a hussled order for bread and a small sip

payoff for dumb knees
where many vows were made and forgotten

**forgive us our sins as we forgive them that sin
against us**
from oiled mouths a coiled ambition runs
a curious violence hard to ignore

smile at the menacing kids on the corner
as you sidle past their cold stares

lead us not into temptation
in a jump-cut world seduction lures with an
invitation
to drift up some drunken stair and dance with
the devil

penitents wearing masks reveal themselves
by tattoos on their backs

deliver us from evil
a half light lurks in the abyss and all vow to be
good
as wind whistles through bullet holes

left between what they say and what they hide
the mouths do not listen

for thine is the kingdom
the maimed and blind gather at the doors
their sins in recycling bins

a silence frail as silk blew it's way
through suicides locked in cages of skin

forever and ever
they who are left to wander in their own heads
bury their destiny listening to the rhythm of
dirt

on coffins counting down to *amen*

You Can Divine My Words (J Rothenberg)

I like to peel my words
with my teeth
strip the kernels
in small increments.
I count words with odd fingers-
they don't always add up.
A breath ago I stacked words
hip to lip.
I count spaces
none escape.
I am plugged in to the mystery place
words stripped of taste.
Skin secrets live out the minutes
on the rims of our lips.
I don't always count truth.
I count the sound the dawn makes
but not its silence.
I pull the moment
around you
so that
you can divine my words

ALICE AND THE CHEMICAL DIKTAT

Together they tippled the "Drink Me" bottle
she grew and grew / outgrew him / the town
disappeared in the moons vibrations / he
shrank
stayed his side of the glass / watched dead
leaves
twist his dream / he stumbled from parties /
sniffed the pop and crack
scratched dark pink air / watched the grass
swim toward him
 as he slid into the concrete wall

He stood on his shadow
through the crazed fog his eyes searched for
her smile
showed the fires in his mind where he wanted
to be
before he vanished in his own blackness

Acerbic words stood at his shoulder
the mirror a surface of infinity

The Last Coyote

Years have travelled these hills.
Shadows spread by towers
a smear of stone and glass.
I love to spy out the unseen
never forget
how to remember things.
I watch your getaway face
a silhouette.
Beautiful grace
bled through skin.
Your heartbeat at midnight
afraid to move.
I tag path and place.
It disappears in a ragged blue mist.
I feel through my ears
thunder and musk rattle the moon.

I hold my breath.

About the Author:

Gail Willems –, retired nurse, lives in Western Australia, swims, beach walks, does yoga, likes good shiraz and bubbles. Poetry published in Australia, United Kingdom, Belgium, New Zealand, in journals, magazines, anthologies, and 5UVWriters Radio.

Haiku translated into Chinese and published

First poetry collection "Blood Ties and Crack Fed Dreams (Ginninderra Press 2013)

PERFECTLY BLIND
by Philip Wexler

Perfectly Blind

Her pledges, at the outset, sincere, genuine
and most of all, honored. Thus, you took refuge
for a spell in the mirage of perfection. Inevitably,

the sheen began to tarnish. She was too quick
to give assurances. Her smiles were forced,
her air distracted, her look distant, lackluster.

She followed through without enthusiasm
or partway, or late, reminders notwithstanding,
or not at all. She didn't care. She'd shrug

it off. This falling away which in the day
would have struck you as impossible is plain
and simple, the destiny you share and bear.

Looking back, you see the signs you missed.
The fault had been there all along, in wait
until the time it would reveal itself, deep, wide,

roaring, a chasm as she and your faith in her
fall out from under you, and as you drop you
ask
yourself how you could have been so blind so
long.

The Pears

We pick them from our tree, roll
them wobbly in a brown and green
blur down the slope to the crates
by the van, to pack and haul them
off to give as gifts to friends.
What's left belongs to us.

In three days when they're ripe,
we take a bunch back to the tree
to picnic on with wine and cheese.
The juice runs down our chins,
while napkins blow away,
and we make sloppy love.

The Ball Rolling

She came into your office as she's done
many times to tell you exactly what
she needed, and you spelled it out
precisely, omitting no detail, adding
nothing extra. Standing, she looked down
at her shoes, and you, from your chair,
out the window, and then she was gone,
mission, on the surface accomplished
to the both of your everlasting satisfactions.

A few hours later you thought of a reason
to go to her office, something optional
you'd meant to note, a "by the way."
Behind her desk, she listened, fidgeting
with a set of keys. You leaned
against a bookcase for support. She agreed
with everything you said, and you wanted
to say more but couldn't, and she seemed
to want to further your cause, if only

you could get the ball rolling.

I STAND IN WATER

by Keith Hoerner

I stand in water.

It sloshes 'round my scuffed black leather wingtips, laps up the ankles of my rumpled dress slacks, turns khaki to the color of murky brown. Onlookers furrow their brows, incredulous that I do not see I am in danger of drowning, that if I don't make a move for it, the water will continue to rise until it covers my soon-to-be-bald head. What they do not realize is I have already drowned. Can they not see my sopping clothes; the now sea-weed green tweed jacket; my wrinkled, white translucent skin? This water is receding. I have survived my Biblical Flood. I am coming up for air, not suffocating. My exploded lungs have been cauterized; I now breathe shallower: but calm and sure.

I stand in water.

I look for you, but waves wash you to another shore, an island uncharted, perhaps, to inhibit my finding you. Did you suffer so? Rather than buoy you up, did my selfishness climb squarely on your shoulders and thrust you downward? Push you under into the electric bosom of a bloom of pulsing jellyfish... until it was you who passed away? Or did your shocking beauty simply meld with theirs, escaping me as I first wondered? My hope is you did get away. My prayer is you are dry and safe and contented. Even if it means I cannot be with you.

I stand in water.

I may not be dry, but I am drying out. I have always had a dry sense of humor, a British sense of humor, I like to think. Admittedly, I can be droll. My odd obsession with court jesters remains a curious thing. Was it their tomfoolery or their role in history? I don't know. Whatever it might be, you used to laugh at me more than the TV. I cannot hear you laughing now. So it begs the question: when did you turn it off? When was it you stopped laughing? Or was it me – in one of my sardonic rants – who thought he had had the last laugh?

I stand in water.

You were always a giver. The problem is I'm a taker, was a taker... for what it's worth. And givers and takers are a mismatch. I did what takers do; I took all you had to give, emptied all your pockets and filled them with rocks: one for each of my character defects. So you stretched out your arms and tried to swim away, but sank. Yet upon the first swirling rush that separated my grip on you, you dropped my rocks and swam untraceable among the camouflage of coral reefs. So, here I am.

I stand in water.

Yes, I stand. I'm not buckled at the knees as before or dead as expected. The lifeline you threw me caught 'round my neck, but it worked. It was the one time when looking in the end of a bottle, I actually saw a ship, and with it the possibility of steerage to a new land... dry land. Its pasted, miniature masts and cotton-twill sails still able to bear my living freight and move me to a healthy destination. You equipped me to survive the flood in the face of self-harm. How can I repay you? By letting you go? By not even thinking to follow you?

I stand in water.

The small ship, pulled out for embarkation, is now crushed to bits beneath my feet. Peer close, and I might even pass for the Giant Polybotes, bane of the God Poseidon, standing on a shipwreck from the battle of Nisyros. A broken bow floats out to the Aegean Sea. An anchor pulls the splintered spine of this ark into the pit of a dark swell. I was supposed to find Terra Firma by Noah's mandate as one of a pair. I beg you. But I'll force myself to understand, if I am to go at it alone.

I stand in water.

If it is what you need, I will unabashedly say it aloud, "I no longer drown myself in bottles, thanks to you." So I will stay clear of the companion way and wish your sails full billows to get you to your place of secret solace. I will not follow you. But I will always think of you. And if you will allow, I'll tightly scroll this missive and slip it into this bottle here, then toss it far in the direction I hope will one day reach you.

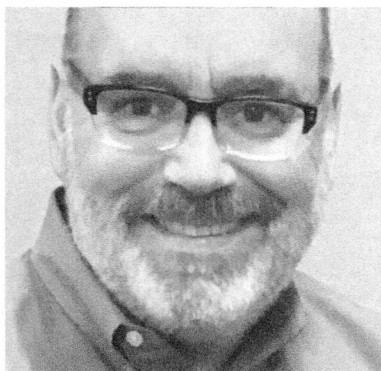

About the Author:

Keith Hoerner lives, teaches, and pushes words around in Southern Illinois.

PENETRATING SECRETS
by Cynthia Pitman

With all your science can you tell how it is — &
whence it is, that light comes into the soul?--
Thoreau

The science is settled.
We know it all now.
No more need to wonder
why the sweltering heat of the wind
blows across the burning blacktop,
melting the thick tar pitch into a sticky cohe-
sion.
Science has that covered.
No more need to wonder
why the tornadoes
gyre across the vast heartland
with unleashed terror,
attacking and flattening the homes, the trees,
the animals
and the people.
Science has that covered.
No more need to wonder
why the ocean's cryptic creatures
dwell deep in darkness,
adorned with rich jewel tones
that will never be seen.
Science has that covered.
No more need to wonder
why the flowers bleed blood-red
or drip butter-yellow,
their heavy scent
saturating the air
with aromatic jubilation.
Science has that covered.

No more need to wonder
why the stars gaze down upon us
while they are trapped
in the frozen pose of gravity,
lighting our darkness,
but never enough.
Science has that covered.
The science is settled.
No more need to wonder.
So many secrets,
and all of them — covered.

Ascension

I will need a shield.
I could choose a Roman shield --
wide wings of eagles diving for their prey,
fierce thunderbolts spearing down from Jupiter
on high --
to honor mighty Caesar's erection
of Corinthian columns and colossal coliseums,
a blinding array of his brutal strength,
his decimating power made manifest,
a power I could hold close to my chest.

Or I could choose a Greek shield --
a reverse lambda, their 'V' of victory,
a charging bullhorn burnt on wood,
or a deep-sea lantern fish carved on rawhide --
to marvel at their sea-faring glory,
to pay homage to Poseidon,
to lay siege to Troy,
slay her heroes,
retrieve the Janus-faced Helen
and clutch her to my heart.
Or I could create my own shield.
But where should I begin?
I have a fealty to fire.
I could paint a burst of red-flower flame
from the poison oleander.

Then, as I lie burning on the funeral pyre,
clutching my flaming shield,
the thick toxic smoke of the oleander would
ascend.
The shield would not protect me from my enemy,
nor my enemy from me.
Rather, it would gather us up, together,
and carry us to the Sun.

Inclination

I turn my face from the world
toward the timberline.
Resting there for me is a wait --
a slow, timeless wait.
I cross the wide, wet field
that separates me from the woods,
drawn by their deep-shadowed darkness.

The leaves sharpen.
The trees take shape.
The creatures of these woods
dismiss me with their indifference.
They know me here.
The hidden path inclines
just enough to make me breathless.
I follow the path,
unseen.
It is revealed as if in a dream.

I hear footsteps, but I don't feel them.
Are they mine?
Trembling, I come to the end of the path
where the branches of the trees
hang low.
Vines laden with overgrowth
curtain the mystery.
My hand reaches out
to pull back the curtain:

Always it is the same.

Amalgamated Memories

Imagine yourself seated on the ground,
surrounded by baskets,
each basket cradling a jumble of disparate
items
(a feather, a knife, a memory),
items confined yet uncollected.
Within each basket is one red marble,
bright and biting in its insistent redness,
this one red marble,
rising above the disparate jumble
(a feather?),
ascending, then suspended,
a presence to hold you and you alone
mesmerized.
String the marbles together.
String them with your own sweet string.
Weave your web.
Surround yourself, for there is no escape.
(A knife?)
Kneel.
Bow your head.
Let go.
Whose hands are these that ascend,
lifted by your own sticky-sweet web?
Whose hands are these that open their palms
in silent supplication?
Whose hands are these that cup and caress
the red red redness of the mesmerizing mar-
bles?
Whose marionette are you?

The Breakdown of the Bicameral Mind
. . .dedicated to Julian Jaynes

Old Amos heard God speak to him.
He didn't know what the linguists know.
These new prophets say
it was not the voice of God he heard;
The voice was but a breach,
a missing bridge between
the two matched sides
of his bicameral mind.
The presence of this breach,
the absence of this bridge, they say,
Forged the covenant between Amos and God.
When this missing bridge finally appeared,
It was too late.
Old Amos had already heard
God speak to him.
But his ways were passing.
This bridge, in all its glory,
Revealed that -- all along, all along --,
He had only been talking to himself.

Which is the genome of insanity?
Hearing the voice of God
Thundering in your brain?
Or crossing the bridge
Back and forth,
Again and again,
Only to hear the echo of your own voice?
Each says, "You are not alone."
But every time you cross the bridge,
You are the only god you hear.

COSMOS

by Dorsía J. Smith

Cosmos

My son asks me what happened to his baby
brother.

What baby brother?

The one in your belly, Mama.

Why he's gone to the air, I say,
like a ball of cells radiating by motion.
It's that simple.

Why can't I see him?

He's circling the orbit and gliding
past the moon's bright light,
smiling.

Like a child, you wonder, "Why doesn't he ask
for me?"

How eager you are to know him,
watch him become born in another galaxy.

Oh, you see, he's waiting for us in the field of
stars:
to show us the beauty clearly seem against a
dark sky.

Paradise Lost

This is not going to hurt. I lie
when I press the alcohol swab
against your scraped knee.
I want to say, "This is just
the first wound of many."
But I hesitate to have you
see the disfigured world so correctly.
Why should you be a witness to this?
It should be a secret, at least until your
adolescence. By then, you will realize
we remain figures of denial.

And my hand momentarily scoops up the
cotton patch and taps a bandage into place.
It changes nothing: you cry,
a small child terrified.
And then it didn't matter what words I said:
the pain had already been proven.

It's 1 AM When Heartbreak Calls

You go straight to the shower,
trying to scrub her from you skin.
Yet, the citrus perfume and lemongrass lotion
remain,
the trail of cigarette smoke too.
This lie you wear so perfectly like
a second layer of skin,
I wonder: does it ever cry out for rest
or fear something when I ask you where have
you been and
where are you going?
Can't you take me here and there?
This is what I dream of when you hurry out the
door again.
I turn to my side, make-believe there are far
worse things
than being lonely.

For My Grandfather, Much Later

You died when I was sixteen.
At your funeral,
I was quiet, brave, strong
unlike a girl of sixteen.
But I had wanted to ask,
who was that man in the box
with the heavy makeup?
Was that my grandfather?
Why were your cheeks so red?
Why were your hands like wax,
tightly folded into fabric?

Questions like a child of sixteen
with no one to answer.

My father is comforting my aunt.
My brother and I are listening to "Taps"
and watching the folding square of flag
become a triangle.
I throw the white rose of goodbye
onto your casket—
desert dirt staining my dress
unnoticed
like grief at sixteen.

An Impromptu

I.

This is not a love poem.
To be a love poem
you must scorch letters,
razor away the photo smile,
toss away the frame.

II.

Chopin made no public appearances between
February 1842 and February 16, 1848, when he
gave his land concert in Paris. By this time, the
passion between him and Madame Sand had
cooled.

III.

Cremate that rug,
She has touched that.
Her typewriter?
Yes, that has to go too.

IV.

The strains in their relationship lead to a final
break in July 1842.

V.

Laser my hands.

VI.

Chopin's health deteriorated rapidly after the
break. He composed only two more works.

VII.

Remove the ashes.
Tell him that it happened to Casimir and Mus-
set also.

VIII.

If this is a love poem,
the words would cinder into scars,
not the chords of a sonata.

Made in the USA
Middletown, DE
13 January 2019